THE NEW EVANGELICALS

THE NEW EVANGELICALS

Expanding the Vision of the Common Good

Marcia Pally

WILLIAM B. EERDMANS PUBLISHING COMPANY
GRAND RAPIDS, MICHIGAN / CAMBRIDGE, U.K.

2\12

Published 2011 by
Wm. B. Eerdmans Publishing Co.
2140 Oak Industrial Drive N.E., Grand Rapids, Michigan 49505 /
P.O. Box 163, Cambridge CB3 9PU U.K.

Printed in the United States of America

17 16 15 14 13 12 11   7 6 5 4 3 2 1

Library of Congress Cataloging-in-Publication Data

Pally, Marcia.
   The new evangelicals: expanding the vision of the common good /
Marcia Pally.
        p.   cm.
Includes bibliographical references (p.   ).
ISBN 978-0-8028-6640-0 (pbk.: alk. paper)
   1. Evangelicalism — United States.   2. Church and state — United States.
3. Liberalism — Religious aspects — Protestant churches.
4. Democracy — Religious aspects — Protestant churches.
I. Title.

BR1642.U5P35   2011
277.3′082 — dc23

                                                       2011020583

www.eerdmans.com

Contents

Foreword

As I write, the recent atrocity in Norway and the recent attempts by a Tea Party-influenced Republican Party to block measures needed to save the United States from bankruptcy are tending to consolidate in the public mind an association of evangelical Christianity with extreme right-wing politics. Yet the insane fantasies of one lunatic, almost accidentally articulated in terms of exaggerated fear of Islam, and the disproportionate political grip of a small minority are no guides at all to the reality of evangelical approaches to the political. As Marcia Pally shows in this excellently documented and lucidly written book, it is a yet smaller minority of Americans who are both conservative evangelicals and Tea Partiers, while the tendency of American evangelicals as a whole (including those who are theologically conservative) lies currently in a more leftward direction.

Moreover, the adherence of evangelicals between roughly 1973 and 2004 to the "religious right," as Pally also shows, is historically an aberration. For evangelical Christians have traditionally supported — indeed helped to shape — a strong separation between church and state, have upheld individual liberty in all fields, and have shown a consistent concern for poor relief and social justice which has sometimes led them to support state welfarism and even socialist programs. The latter support was no aberrance of the "social gospel," but was sometimes sustained by evangelicals who considered — like Karl Barth in Europe — that the social gospel movement had forgotten the primacy of the transcendent and the eschatological.

However, it is a great merit of Pally's treatment — and all the more commendable coming from the pen of a New Yorker who has taken the unusual decision actually to *visit* Middle America! — that she does not simply excoriate the epoch of the Religious Right, but tries to comprehend it, and sometimes with more sympathy than the left-leaning "new evangelicals" themselves. Thus she notes that evangelicals were understandably dismayed by the failure of the Democrats in this period to withstand the forces of big business and emerging globalization which bore down heavily upon the "little guy." At the same time, they feared that a left-liberal support for individual liberty was losing the traditional American sense that such support assumed an exercise of self-discipline and moral conscience toward others, in favor of a wholly novel narcissistic self-indulgence. (And here many recent European Marxist voices retrospectively concur with their judgment.) Without doubt, it was a lack of both intuition and analysis which led evangelicals in consequence to embrace the unfettered "free market," but this was encouraged by a sense that the United States was proving militarily and culturally ineffective in the face of both communism and a resurgent Islam.

Given these considerations, Pally is able to propose, with considerable plausibility, that there is an underlying consistency in American evangelical theology, outlook, and practice, which has assumed different — and sometimes seemingly opposite — political expressions in response to changing exigencies and changing hierarchies of anxiety. The consistency resides above all in a stress upon the primacy of individual salvation and concomitant freedom of conscience and of religion, combined with a powerful stress upon the performance of good works as a sign and fulfillment of redemption. In the nineteenth century this generally lined evangelicalism up with both liberalism and activist social concern. And this alignment was continued in the twentieth century in the support for state intervention seen not as collectivism but rather as an attempt to give all individuals a fair chance.

Yet already at the beginning of the twentieth century a countertendency was apparent: horror at urbanization and mass warfare gave rise (again as with German neo-orthodoxy) to a mood of apocalyptic pessimism that often combined with a new suspicion of secular reason as tending to cast doubt upon the veracity of both divine creation and the truths of the Bible. Only at this point did any inconsistency between evangelicalism and "modernity" in American terms become apparent. And indeed, as Pally crisply recounts, a Protestant dissenting concern for the free and authentic exercise of religion was the initial driving force in North America behind both liberty of conscience and the separation of church from state. (To a degree this is true also in Britain, but in that case there were also certain Anglican and Jacobite — High Church and Catholic — pressures in this direction.)

How, then, does she explain the recent pronounced beginnings of a "reversion to type" with the new evangelicals? Importantly — in the face of so much secular prejudice — she lets these people speak for themselves, and they uniformly come across as thoughtful, engaged, generous, well read, well informed, and multifaceted individuals. Their varied voices also exhibit, besides a "family resemblance," a crucial spectrum which Pally classifies and seeks to explain. Her analysis shows that the differences betray certain inevitable and continuing tensions of which the spokespersons are well aware and which they struggle valiantly to resolve. These tensions concern above all the need to sustain a separation of church and state and yet not simply to repeat the — often nearly deranged and quasi-anarchistic — suspicion of the state on the part of the Religious Right. This same theme emerges with respect to issues of school prayer, school vouchers, religious symbols in public, cooperation with state welfare programs, and the question of preferential recruitment of coreligionists to faith programs partly funded by the state.

With respect to these tensions, Pally is careful to explain that they cannot simply be characterized in terms of secular right or left. For here one discovers some "new" evangelicals who sustain the dislike of the Religious Right for high taxation and bureaucratic, impersonal state charity, while nevertheless believing that church voluntary work, far from being "remedial" in character, should be so radical and so far-reaching as to sustain everywhere a just economy and local practices of neighborly reciprocity that would ideally preclude the need for a "welfare state" altogether. And here it should also be mentioned, as Pally at times hints, that there is no very perfect correlation between evangelical thought and practice: the very same "right-wing" evangelicals who apparently adulate the market may in practice actively run all sorts of social enterprises which every American "liberal" could surely only applaud.

Indeed, in this phenomenon resides one reason for a shift in attitude: the more evangelicals have sought to help those whom they nonetheless deem to be sinners (women who have had abortions, AIDS victims, etc.), the less they have found it possible to be judgmental about them, and the more they have reminded themselves that there are many other sins from which they themselves are not immune and that there are, for example, social and economic factors causing a high rate of abortion that really no one favors (another reality of which the evangelicals have gradually become more aware).

But more crucial than this, according to Pally, is that evangelicals have slowly realized the irony that by explicitly supporting the supposedly "antistate" Republican Party, they have themselves got more and more embroiled in a state apparatus that has led to their collusion in unjust wars, governmental lies, and torture. So no mere reversion to the "social gospel," but rather a recall of eschatological impartiality and Augustinian suspicion of the political as such, has led to a new distancing from party politics and a new tendency to take issues one by one. In practice this means that many evangelicals find themselves closer to the Democrats than the Republicans, because they now recall that, as biblical and traditionalist Christians, they believe in stewardship of nature, helping the poor, and suspicion of the state's power to kill just as much as they believe in the sanctity of very young and very old human life.

But there is no mere conversion to a liberal statism necessarily involved here. Some evangelicals have, indeed, reverted to a Rooseveltian or a Johnsonian position, but others, as the interviews record, wish to increase the role of the civil society sector to qualify the impersonalism of both state and market. Moreover, amongst this group there is a further division as to whether or not churches should rightly expect to be able to show preference to coreligionists as employees or to promulgate religiously based positions, if they are receiving state assistance. This implies, then, two different accounts of the role of the state with respect to both religion and civil society even amongst those evangelicals who embrace an "associationist" and "social market" rather than "social democratic" political stance.

It is with respect to this tension that Pally offers perhaps her most searching insight in the book (p. 93). This is the point that all liberal democracies assume a "religious exceptionalism" as one of the very conditions of their existence. What this means is that, in principle, a state can adopt any ideology it chooses, *except* a religious one. Historically this must be seen as a reserve that derives in part from the need to safeguard religious pluralism, beside religious independence and integrity, besides an admitted enlightenment desire to exclude the churches from political influence. However — as Pally notes — the American mode of reservation is more extreme than those countries (today Norway, Finland, Denmark, Scotland, and England, for example) which have established churches, but still tolerate other religions and sustain a distinction between secular and sacred realms. And given this extremity, as she further notes, measures designed in part to protect religion also in practice tend to inhibit it. For in reality religious bodies always do depend on some measure of state support (tax relief, for example), but this will generally come at the price of yielding to governmental assumptions and acting with secular neutrality when carrying through aspects of the state's business.

In this way, the rigorous separation of state from church turns out to be more in the end to the benefit of the former. And could one not suggest that "the religious exception" is the concealed face of Carl Schmitt's "political exception" upon which modern sovereignty is founded? For it is *this* exception which enables the state to take Schmittian decisions to establish and maintain itself, as though any enforceable solution to the problematic of the state of exception — whereby the law is established by a power necessarily beyond the law — is equally as good as any other. In other words, the political refusal of taking any religious stance can be construed as a mask for legitimating a nihilistic voluntarism — a founding of the legal upon *any* decision whatsoever — at the heart of the modern polity.

Thus Pally and some of her interviewees validly ask just why it is considered all right for the state to fund psychotherapeutic practices founded upon diverse and controverted theories — Freudian, Gestalt, Cognitivist, etc. — and not social practices linked to religious outlooks which can in consequence only be carried through by adherents of those outlooks (just as only a Freudian can proffer a Freudian therapy). And surely the implicit answer assumed here by secular reason is that these admittedly somewhat conjectural theories can be held to be subordinate to an instrumentalist end — namely, the "normal" functioning of a citizen which is in the interest of the state. Hence the "emptiness" of its purposes is not here challenged, as it would be by any sort of religious or metaphysical commitment. In this way Pally's "religious exception" is crucial in order to underwrite a political exemption from "everyday" morality or from any avowed pursuit of virtue, any specific teleology of human flourishing.

Such a conclusion would appear to be at something of an angle to Pally's primary thesis, which is that evangelical religion is a support of, not a hindrance to, "liberal democracy" (taking "liberal" here in the broadest sense of meaning constitutional government plus the guaranteeing of the reasonable liberty and just treatment of the individual person). For it suggests that there is an inherent instability in the specific mode of American liberal democracy that has to do precisely with church-state separation.

It is consistently stressed by Pally, after Tocqueville, that the United States works at all only because the churches constitute a powerful civil society which counterbalances the separation of church from state. Otherwise, as Tocqueville intimated, one would lack a check either upon a mass-legitimated government or upon individual economic greed. However, the fact that this counterbalancing is by no means clearly *intended* by the American Constitution, nor by the *Federalist Papers* (which, to the contrary, see size and centralization as the preconditions for balance), is often too readily glossed over. Certainly, as Pally describes in her chapter 3, they automatically assumed the role of religion as a mechanism of ethical and social control, but they did not explicitly see it as qualification of political and economic power, or as supplying the older role of an aristocracy in the manner described by Tocqueville.

One consequence of this nonintentionality is that there is an inherent and unresolved tension in American religious civil society as to whether it is indeed a "civil society" of the sort envisaged by Adam Ferguson that covertly serves the state's purposes of control (a government by stealth, as deciphered by Foucault) or is rather the heir to a more nineteenth-century adumbration of a "social" sphere in excess of the merely political and in continuity with the surplus of the *ecclesia* over the coercive state. Tocqueville himself thought that most of the time American religion, with its blandness of content and excessive civility of behavior, merely serves an essentially secular, civil religion. This is surely borne out by the staggering secularity of American public space and time (compared with Europe) which ensures a drastically interiorizing and indeed "gnostic" bent in American spirituality.

But clearly there is also present in the United States a sincere counterthrust to these tendencies.

From whence does this derive? From the Puritan legacy? Perhaps not, since that legacy was divided between an initial theocracy which tended to substitute political community for the church and a later compromise with secular Republicanism and "commonsense" ethicism which stressed the sovereignty of the private conscience. Here indeed the common thread, as Pally stresses, would be a fundamental individualism, self-preoccupation, and "do-it-for-yourself" approach to social action.

Yet in that case, is it merely individualized altruism that helps to engender such a powerful religiously based civil society with sometimes a strong sense of mutuality and reciprocalist practice? The individualism may well take either neoliberal or welfarist forms in the present day, but does it entirely account for the more associationist strand in evangelical politics — the strand which also most tends to surpass a "left-liberal pietism" of unexceptionable concern for the poor, the marginalized, and the environment, etc., etc., in the direction of a real critique of the ravages wrought upon our humanity by scientism, economism, and consumerism?

My suspicion is that it does not. As Pally notes, the overwhelmingly largest Protestant denomination in nineteenth-century America was *Methodism*. And Methodism, not directly Puritanism, nor the Radical Reformation currents which were the ancestors of the Baptists, is the real source of "evangelicalism." What is more, it was a relatively late import into the United States, distinctly marked by a British legacy that had arisen after the departure of the Pilgrim Fathers and not in any real continuity with their outlook. This may be one crucial thing which even Tocqueville failed adequately to think about. For as Mark A. Noll (whom Pally cites with frequency) notes, American Methodism to begin with in the late eighteenth and early nineteenth centuries was *not*, like the evolved Puritan legacy, prorepublican or favorable to Scottish commonsense philosophy.[1] To the contrary, it was suspected of crypto-monarchism and crypto-Anglicanism, which is wholly unsurprising, given its high-church and high-tory English origins. (One suspects that, ever since the 1950s, American commentators have tended wildly to exaggerate American independence before 1939 from the wider culture of the Anglo-Saxon world.)

Unlike the now bifurcated Puritan legacy (between traditional predestinarianism and a new Arminian stress upon freedom and rea-

---

1. Mark A. Noll, *America's God: From Jonathan Edwards to Abraham Lincoln* (New York: Oxford University Press, 2002), pp. 330-45.

son), Methodism newly combined a strong belief in freedom and the universal offer of salvation with a powerful emphasis that nothing good could be achieved without grace. At the same time, it saw salvation as inseparable from the practice of "holiness" or sanctification. Given that there must be a free response to grace, the offer of grace is now far more seen (in a "Romantic" era) in terms of a divine downreach of love, that must be mediated through the true human community which is the church. (From the outset Methodists held "love feasts" which later gave rise to the mass conviviality and ecstasy of revivalist meetings.) Thus for all its insufficiencies of ecclesiology, Methodism (even though it later somewhat itself succumbed to rationalist republicanism and commonsensism) sustained a more "Catholic" sense of the vitality of association for salvation and the idea that good works are the furthering and extending of a grace-filled community.

A great deal of the extraordinary social activism of the American churches in the nineteenth century would seem to spring from this Methodist and Romantic revivalist root. So if the French historian Elie Halévy famously claimed that Methodism saved Britain from revolution, is it not legitimate to ask whether Methodism was needed to make the American Revolution workable by providing it with mediating institutions that were otherwise unprovided for? This is of course but a specification of Tocqueville's general thesis — but attention to the crucial role of Methodism underlines the fact that the "extraconstitutional" religious element that has made the United States work and helped to make it peculiarly American derives from a bizarre eighteenth-century *British* movement which popularized certain originally patrician enthusiasms. Perhaps this point clarifies just *why* American churches were able to operate as the equivalent of an "aristocracy."

For this reason one might want to pose the question of whether, thanks specifically to this Methodist inheritance, a more "relational" and "communitarian" strand remains one component in the evangelical legacy. And in terms of the best logic of this strand — as some of the interviewees in this book implicitly realize — an outright separation of church and state on the U.S. model becomes problematic. For if the ultimate purpose of human life is association for a common purpose and not mere individual freedom or well-being, then, even if this associating is achieved in the realm of civil society, the state cannot be regarded as ever wholly neutral in its stance from a theological point of view. It must rather be judged in the end by whether it hinders or promotes what is taken theologically to be a good mode of association. (It is obvious, for example, that appeal to state neutrality cannot really resolve arguments over abortion — though it might help to calm the culture wars if we recalled here that historically some atheists have opposed it, while not a few evangelical Christians have supported it, as Pally mentions.)

The same consideration would suggest that the evangelical political legacy in the United States at its best tends toward the personalism and subsidiarism of the Catholic "third way." But just this approximation poses questions about evangelical ecclesiology. Surely church division — "Antichrist" according to one of the finest of American nineteenth-century Reformed theologians[2] — is wholly inimical to the good delivery of church-based civil society, simply at the most pragmatic level? Indeed, it was denominational fragmentation of effort which in part led to a state takeover of welfare in twentieth-century Britain. Moreover, no social goals can be consistently pursued with sufficient radical consistency without an organized tradition of reflection and transmission such as the episcopally based churches provide.

I raise these questions about the limits to both American and evangelical politics from a deliberately askance British and Anglo-Catholic perspective. However, it is a consequence of the probing honesty and objective fairness of Marcia Pally's work that they seem naturally to emerge from the *aporias* exposed by her text itself.

JOHN MILBANK

---

2. John Williamson Nevin, "AntiChrist," in *The Anxious Bench/AntiChrist/Christian Unity*, ed. Augustine Thompson, O.P. (Eugene, Oreg.: Wipf and Stock, 2002), pp. 1-71.

Acknowledgments

My first thanks go to the thinkers of the early modern era who imagined not only an end to religious persecution but a political system that upholds religious freedom. Faiths — including those not favored by the monarch or state church — would have robust life within their communities and outside them, in the public sphere. Over time, this vision worked its way into political practice, where government is permitted to hobble no religion, and where laws are constitutionally constrained to treat the nation's many-faithed citizens equally. This made possible several linchpins of liberal democracy: that religious and secular groups flourish, their ideas debated seriously in the public arena, and that citizens are free to criticize government from a broad range of perspectives, both religious and secular.

In the present century, I would like to thank all those who sat down and spoke with me as I researched this book — the office workers, political consultants, firemen, ministers, students, and academics. They gave generously of their time and their hearts. I learned much and am humbled. A few deserve special mention (alphabetically): Robert Andrescik, Greg Boyd, Richard Cizik, Shane Claiborne, David Gushee, Joel Hunter, Joe Ingrao, and Dan and Barbara Lacich, Nan, Tim McFarlane, and Tri Robinson.

I am indebted to my publisher, Bill Eerdmans, for his support and for his unique feel for ideas and books, and to all the people at Eerdmans Publishing for their help in bringing this manuscript to the public: my editor Tom Raabe, Willem Mineur (cover design), Linda Bieze,

Anita Eerdmans, Victoria Fanning, and Rachel Bomberger, among others. Special gratitude goes to John Milbank, for his insightful foreword; his writing always brings me to new vistas. Warm thanks go to Rolf Schieder; our transatlantic research has enriched my thinking and this book. Much gratitude also to Allison M. E. Gill, Ross Bennett Harrison, Thomas A. Luckini, Rachel Newman, and Joan V. O'Hara for their careful review of the legal issues raised in this book. They greatly sharpened my thinking. For her support throughout the many stages of research and writing, I thank Parker, who has vetted so many ideas and given me such good cheer over the years.

I would like to thank my earliest teachers at the Solomon Schechter School, who taught me the value of freedom of conscience, economic justice, religious community, and critical, independent thought. It was a great gift from my parents, Nettie Rose Pally and Sidney Pally, to send me there.

Prologue

ROBERT ANDRESCIK, FLORIDA

Robert Andrescik is a gregarious, affectionate guy in his thirties whose bumper sticker reads "Peace, Love and Twins." His were three and a half at the time of our first talk in May 2009; we talked again a year later. After majoring in journalism at "a little Christian liberal arts college in Minnesota that no one's ever heard of," he became the editor of *New Man,* a Christian men's magazine with offices in Florida. However, Andrescik "did not want to be hammering home the Christian Right agenda all the time." Already a member of Northland Church in Longwood, Florida, he was asked to direct the church's public relations department, which he now does.

    Andrescik picked me up at the airport and fixed my laptop. He has two state-of-the-art computers on his desk, one with a screensaver of Captain Kirk from the original *Star Trek* TV series. ("I'm a big fan," he said. "Have you seen the new Star Trek movie? Awesome.") I did not see a cross on his office wall, though his bookshelf is lined with Bibles and books by C. S. Lewis. Hanging on his wall are several framed covers of vintage comic books and a portrait of Barack Obama. Andrescik's wife is a triathlon competitor.

MP She is?

RA Yeah. She just competed yesterday. I don't know how she does it, but women are amazing. They're just faster, in many ways. They have millions more connections between the right and left hemispheres in

the brain through the corpus callosum. You know this thing about
God creating Adam first? Some people argue that he was superior, but
Eve was second, and anything you create after the first is 2.0. Adam was
1.0. In women, the processor is faster.

MP Was your family like that?

RA My family's from the Pentecostal, word-faith tradition. The Arminian tradition is strong in that branch of Pentecostalism, where the individual is responsible for what happens in his life and God's sovereignty isn't really emphasized. Of course, man does not do it all himself
— God's hand is involved. Anyway, when I started college, it was very
conservative. We couldn't use VCRs, watch movies, dance, or even wear
jeans with holes in them. But the teachers were excellent. So for the
first time, I really studied theology and Scripture, moving from
Arminianism to a more Calvinist Reformed tradition, where you can
see much more of God's involvement in the world. Look at nature; look
at science. So I started reexamining everything I had believed.

The church I grew up in taught that you could not be "in relationship" with anyone without trying to evangelize them. That's not what
Jesus did. He hung out with sinners. The church I attended growing up
was full of sincere, well-meaning believers . . . but the theology was
suborthodox at best. One night in college I came back to my dorm and
said, "God, I know you are moving me away from everything I used to
believe, but please do it slowly, because it's really hard to realize that everything I've believed is off base."

I saw that we weren't going to bring justice to the world by getting
the "right people" into office — that meant Republicans. My family
voted for Pat Robertson when he ran for president in 1988. We thought
we'd "won" when we elected George W. Bush. Anyway, when I started
reading Joel [Hunter], I thought he was right about bringing social justice back into Christianity.

Like with abortion. Screaming and vilifying the other side — is
that Christian? No, it isn't. We can do more to reduce and even elimi-
nate abortion if we work together — helping women financially, with
medical care and issues like that. Joel Hunter is good friends with Rachel [Laser, who at the time of the interview was working at the Third
Way, a progressive think tank]. They hug when they see each other.
Now think about it: a pro-life evangelical minister and a feminist, pro-

choice attorney working together because they both want to reduce abortions. That's an example of what we should be doing — finding common ground for the common good.

*   *   *

The church Robert works for is "a church distributed": it meets in several locations in mid-Florida to serve a widely dispersed community. This requires several pastors to work together, among them the soft-spoken Amerindian Vernon Rainwater, who, after time in the military, got a degree in social work, then was ordained, and came to Northland in 1990.

The main church "is not in the best part of town," Andrescik explained. "But that means when we work with the homeless, hundreds of people show up." The church was originally built in an old roller-skating rink, "real grunge," according to Andrescik. The growth of the congregation has allowed it to build a larger building next door, with airy hallways, offices, classrooms, conference rooms, a café, a book-store, and a sanctuary that seats 3,100. Roughly 2,500 attend each of the three services on Sunday, and thousands "attend" online. Several screens throughout the church project the pastor as he preaches, and they scroll the words to the songs that have replaced more traditional Protestant hymns — which creates something of a church karaoke. A twelve-voice choir and eight-piece band accompany. Additional services are offered on Saturday night and Monday evening, with about 1,000 attending each.

The Sunday after September 11, 2001, Northland held a joint on-line service with a church in Egypt as a protest against polarization be-tween Americans and Arabs. The church also provided volunteers to protect Muslim women from anti-Muslim attacks as they went around town.

In 2009, Becky Hunter, Senior Pastor Joel Hunter's wife, stepped down from the presidency of Global Pastors' Wives Network, which ad-dressed a wide range of needs: "everything from training women as public speakers to Muslim women who converted to Christianity and need to know what they should study — quickly." About Northland she says, "No one is obliged to have any particular confession to pray or be-come a member at Northland — no denominational version — but agreement to historic creeds of the church are required. But if you do join, you are committing to have a ministry aspect, a service aspect, in your life. There's no 'pew gum' here."

Northland has ministries in marriage counseling, divorce, grieving, substance abuse, cancer care, applying scriptural values to business, orphans, foster children, the homeless, free food and clothing distribution, the elderly, the deaf, and "people struggling with homosexuality." Its prison ministry ranges from running prayer services to helping prisoners develop plans for their lives after release. The church has an employment network, several men's groups, groups for both men and women postabortion, "without judgment," and discussion groups on faith and science. One Heart, a Northland partner, works with city and county agencies to repair the homes of the area's poor. The church also has a bowling club, soccer games, a motorcycle group, and classes for children, including a course in Mandarin.

Overseas, the church works with national and international organizations in Egypt, South Africa, Brazil, Sri Lanka, Argentina, China, and the Ukraine. For Catholic or Orthodox Ukrainians, the appeal of evangelicalism stems, according to Northland copastor Dan Lacich, from evangelical hope and optimism. "The Ukrainians I've met view the Orthodox Church as defeatist; it just hung on during the Soviet years — 'we're going to circle the wagons' rather than 'we're going to make a difference.'"

In South Africa, Northland partners with the Vredlust Dutch Reformed Church to build a school and do community development in a small town in Swaziland. The project is run, as Lacich put it, "by people who instead of taking a vacation at the beach volunteer for Swaziland. What started out as two campfires and a kettle is now several classroom buildings, a medical clinic, and we're doing microloans for business start-ups." The funding comes in large part from a young Vredlust couple who earmark their yearly living expenses and donate everything else they earn to a trust for ministry. Northland contributed an additional $30,000 to $40,000 in 2009, and overall spends roughly $1.5 million a year on social justice projects, about 20 percent of church income.

"We do not tell a community," Vernon Rainwater notes, "that we know what their problems are and how to fix them. We try to find out what the perspective of the community is, and we often learn more than they do." Compassion International, another Northland partner, began in 1952 to bring food, clothing, and education to children orphaned in the Korean War; today it serves children throughout the developing world. Another partner, With This Ring, uses funds from the sale of jewelry (and other products) to dig clean wells in Africa. It estimates that it cost "one hundred and eighty thousand dollars to save the lives of thirty thousand people in Yendi. That's six dollars a life — the cost of a latte and a cookie."

NAN, IOWA

Nan describes herself as an administrator; she is married and the mother of grown children. The ministry with which she's most involved in the Evangelical Lutheran Church in America is immigration reform, which works toward legislation that would allow America's thirteen million undocumented immigrants to work toward citizenship and that would deal more compassionately with those struggling to get into the country.

NAN I grew up in what you'd think of as a traditional evangelical, Baptist home. There were lots of prohibitions, no dancing, that sort of thing. But religion was all about your personal salvation. But that's not what Christianity is. It's giving to others, serving others, seeing what you can do.

I was not very connected to the church for a long time. About ten years ago, I was at a particularly low point; my teenage daughter was driving me crazy, and there were other things. I finally threw up my hands and said, "God, if you exist, I need you now. You made me. If you're there, you come find me." Then out of nowhere, I got a call from someone in the church asking if I would do something — and three years later I was president of a large church. I guess what happened is that I stopped trying to do it all myself. I trusted God. I felt like I was asleep and then I woke up to life.

I went on a church trip to Mexico and saw the poverty and the desperation to get to the U.S. Of course I knew this before, but firsthand is different. I came home and thought, what am I supposed to do with that experience in white, white Iowa?

Then AMOS[1] came along. God has such a plan. So I became ac-

---

1. AMOS (A Mid-Iowa Organization Strategy) takes its mandate from Amos 5:24: Come, build a land "where justice shall roll down like water, and peace like an ever-

tive in immigration reform. We have many immigrants in Iowa working in the meat-packing industry. *And* we have a lot of nativist prejudices. White people are afraid, and maybe that's natural. They're afraid of losing what they know, that life around them will change. They have this idea that America is a "white country." Talk to the Native Americans about that! When people are afraid, they feel more secure in groupthink: "I must be right because everyone thinks like I do and I think like everyone." That's why there's such a fuss about gay marriage. But groupthink doesn't explain or solve any problem. Most Americans are completely unaware of the effects of U.S. trade policy on Mexico and the poverty it creates. We enforce a trade policy that benefits us; they have to buy from us.

MP Do you think you hold a minority view in Iowa?

NAN I think the nativists, those who fear, are the loudest. But there are many who don't agree with them, who are silent. Maybe I'm deluding myself, but Iowa was the first place to vote for Obama [in the Democratic caucus for the 2008 election]. We were shocked when so many people came out for him. Something had really changed from four or eight years earlier.

MP What?

NAN Where did this crazy Religious Right — the Jerry Falwells — come from? All of a sudden they were speaking for all Christians! The Moral "Majority" — I resent that. They got on the bandwagon before we did — that's all. The Religious Right took the "abortion" and "gay marriage" banner, so people feel if they don't support them, it means they want to kill babies. I was hung up on that too. When I came back from Mexico, I thought, I can't be a *Democrat* because I oppose abortion. After September 11, there was an important feeling of standing together. I thought that since Bush is a man of faith, he must be sincere in what he is saying. But he lied. He wasn't practicing his faith at all. Someone in my church — the guy who leads the church's relationship with a dio-

flowing stream." In 1996, the United Methodist, Episcopal, Catholic, Evangelical Lutheran Church in America, and Disciples of Christ churches joined with local synagogues to develop social service projects for the mid-Iowa region.

cese in Tanzania — explained to me that there are a lot of issues in the world; abortion isn't the only one.

MP Tanzania?

NAN Like a sister church. We have a lot going on there. Anyway, he opened my eyes. My brother thinks I'm bound for hell because I'm a Democrat. I told him, "I'm a pro-life Democrat. A lot of people are being killed every day, living children, women, men. So abortion isn't the only issue of murder. That's why I'm a Democrat."

The other day one of my neighbors had the audacity to say, "When do we quit referring back to when the Europeans took over the country and marginalized the indigenous people?" He didn't use these words; his were more vulgar. I said, "Never! We have marginalized them and their whole culture. We're trying now to do that to the people who come up from the south [Latin America] who are trying to survive. Never." Those familiar words: "From those to whom much has been given, much is expected." We've been given so much! Now are we going to turn our backs and say, "Enough time has passed; we don't owe anything"?

MP Should we give reparations to indigenous peoples and minorities, or is leveling the playing field today sufficient — giving more job and educational opportunities?

NAN The Indians are in disagreement among themselves. Some of the indigenous people of South Dakota on principle refused court-ordered reparations for the takeover of their spiritual and burial grounds. But now some are saying, "We've been screwed over enough; we'll take the money."

There's charity and there's justice. There's no way to make reparations for what we've done. We've lived here, populated this country, and changed it entirely. Respect, opportunity, recognition, that's what we owe. At least we now have that beautiful Smithsonian museum in tribute to indigenous peoples.

One of saddest things in our immigration policy is kids who are born south of the border, brought here as babies, and don't know anything about Mexico, Honduras, Guatemala, or wherever. But they are not U.S. citizens. They graduate from high school and maybe from college but they can't get a job because they are undocumented. The

Dream Act — it's one of my main concerns — is to help them earn permanent residency if they complete two years in the military or college.

It's the same as with the African Americans: they're not Africans but they've never been embraced here. How do you make that right? We are a country of displaced people and colored people who were brought here against their will. We are not a white country. We are Irish-potato-famine people. Where does anybody get off about this nativist crap?!

MP Is your church multi-ethnic or multicultural?

NAN On a national level, the Evangelical Lutheran Church in America is very social-justice oriented. In membership, we are not terribly multicultural. Historically, Lutherans came from Scandinavia, so they're white. The joke is that we are just our staid, stoic, emotionless Scandinavian selves. We certainly wouldn't want to boogie with a hymn. But that's not very appealing to young people — or a lot of people. But our theology is good.

MP Earlier, you criticized the Religious Right. Did you mean their positions, their tactics?

NAN It's interesting: We go to our legislators and say, "As people of faith, our values, our convictions are such that we need to take care of the poor of this world." How is that different from saying, "As people of faith, we don't support abortion"? Hmmmm.

I view faith as my *context*. I can't separate my faith from everything else that I am. God created us to love each other. That's my purpose. That is why I care to live. So when I go to a legislator, to not mention my faith would be leaving out who I am.

MP So far, what you've said is easy — not that it's easy to live a life of faith. But you're asking government to act justly to all . . .

NAN Yeah . . . so . . . ?

MP . . . the concern about the Religious Right is that they want to impose their views, which is not fair to others . . .

NAN I've been thinking about this. I've been troubled about missionaries, those who say, "If you don't believe in Jesus Christ, you're doomed to hell." That cuts out an awful lot of people. Jewish people, Chinese people. But the God of love created us with minds, intelligence, and diversity — are we supposed to just cross out a whole chunk of the planet? I don't think so. If I were a missionary, sharing my faith would be through loving. If you get to know what makes me tick, my faith, and if you choose to join, that's fine. If you don't, I don't presume to judge.

That's why I'm okay with the whole homosexuality thing. I'm not God. But I do know that God has instructed me to love and care for all people. I know gay and lesbian people who are super-duper people. I can't believe God is going to cross them off. Jesus seemed to have a real problem with the organized church, with all the rules and corruption. He talked about the poor and about money. He didn't talk about gay stuff. I was quite proud of our church when we had this wonderful music director — awesome guy, good with the kids, good with everyone. He left because his partner got a job somewhere else. In his parting comments in our newsletter, he mentioned his orientation. There are some people in our church who would have a problem with it. The Evangelical Lutheran Church in America is divided over this issue. But to think that someone could presume to judge our music director and think he was less worthy — come on!

I never embraced my parents' prejudices. Isn't that strange that a small child recognized her parents' bigotry? They weren't hateful but they were bigots. They had little innuendos, asides, and I cringed even as a child. I always thought God created everybody: Why would he create some people to be treated less? A lot of the troubles in this world are because people shut others out and marginalize others. When I was little, I remember hearing about the *Zapatistas;* they were "bad." Then I learned more about the history, and I could see why they rebelled. So now when the media tells us, "These are the good guys and these are bad," I question. Why would the "bad guys" rise up and be bad guys unless they're lacking something? Yes, there is evil in this world. I believe the Taliban is evil. But if everyone was fed, housed, and educated, I bet there would be a lot less conflict.

When I was first learning about social justice issues, I read a book by George S. Johnson, *Beyond Guilt.* It's a simple little book. You know that old saying, "If you give a person a fish, he'll eat for a day. If you teach him how to fish, he'll eat for his whole life"? But what if they don't have rights to use the stream, and what if the stream is polluted? You can't separate these things: we have to deal with pollution, sustainability, poverty, education, and information together. There is no "they" and "us"; there is just "we." That's why we can't all of a sudden say, "We're drawing the line" against immigrants. Some politician on our side of the border was recently asked, "Do you support undocumented immigrants?" His answer was, "I guess I do. I stay at hotels; I eat at restaurants." If they threw all those people out, America would come to a freakin' standstill.

You and I have such power. We have the freedom to travel, stay at hotels, eat when we want to, to voice our thoughts and not be arrested. We don't even realize how privileged we are. We can't realize. We are in the top, top percentage of income-earners in the world. We don't have a clue. So we whine that [since the 2008 economic downturn] we can't eat out as often. The stuff I throw out of my refrigerator would feed families for weeks. Have you read *The Kite Runner* and *A Thousand Splendid Suns* [by Khaled Hosseini]. Some of what has happened in Afghanistan makes me sick. But those books were enlightening. There is so much I don't know about this world.

CHURCH AND STATE

What Are the Questions? What's at Stake?

Let it be known unequivocally that we are committed to religious liberty for people of all faiths. . . . We are firmly opposed to the imposition of theocracy on our pluralistic society. . . . Thus every right we assert for ourselves is at once a right we defend for others. A right for a Christian is a right for a Jew, and a right for a secularist, and a right for a Mormon, and right for a Muslim, and a right for a Scientologist, and right for all the believers in all the faiths across this wide land.

Evangelical Manifesto, May 7, 2008, signed by over seventy leaders of American evangelical institutions, including the president of the National Association of Evangelicals, Leith Anderson, and Mark Bailey, president of Dallas Theological Seminary

chapter 1

Benighted, Befuddled, Fundamentalist, and Fascist?

An Introduction to the Book

The Resurrection of the Repressed

This book describes a group of devout believers, a portion of America's evangelicals, whose faith leads them not to dream of theocracy but to support liberal democracy,[1] indeed to contribute to it. They are, so to speak, part of the solution — at least for those who find citizen participation in self-rule and the classic liberal rights (freedom of speech, religion, press, etc.) preferable to their alternatives.

But if these evangelicals are part of the solution, what was the problem?

In part, it is that evangelicalism over the past forty years has been associated with prototheocratic yearnings — with using the offices of government to impose evangelical interpretations of Scripture on a pluralistic nation, on government, and on law. Paradoxical to this

---

1. This is a term with a long line of definitions and takes different forms from country to country. Here, I use it to mean government where the actions of elected representatives are defined by constitutional (e.g., the United States) or common law (e.g., the United Kingdom) and where state power is constrained by checks and balances among the branches of government, by an independent judiciary and media, and by legal protections for the civil rights of all citizens (freedom of speech, press, petition, assembly, association, movement, conscience; the right to vote and hold office; the rights to due process, privacy, property, etc.). Liberal democracy in this book aims at safeguarding both negative liberty (impositions by government or groups on other citizens) and positive liberty (the ability to participate in self-rule).

heavy use of the state, evangelical activism has been associated also with neoliberal economics, in which "small government" is the best government because it leaves individuals free to grab the opportunities of the open market and solve whatever problems ail the land. In short, evangelicalism has looked like a natural predator both of liberal democracy (in imposing sectarian views on the body politic) and of regulating the market for the sake of the common good (in championing neoliberal market deregulation).

Another part of the problem is that not only evangelicalism but religion overall has become associated with fundamentalism, fascism, and terrorism — be it the Catholic Church in Poland or Islam in the Mideast. This critique in fact reaches back through modern history, which it sees as a thriller: nefarious religion tries to kidnap the Infanta Democracy only to be foiled by the Knight of Secularization, who in turn ensures democracy and our modern way of life. In a bit more detail and less bathos, the historical critique runs like this: Liberal democracy is a system that relies on human reason. As it considers the world, it asks, "How can citizens think through problems and rationally develop the principles that are to govern?" This makes liberal democracy unlike other forms of government — dictatorships, monarchies, and so on. And this means that political forms are something that evolve. Religion, by contrast, relies on the mysteries of faith, and asks not how mankind can reason through challenges but "what does God want from us?" It does not evolve but holds fast to old beliefs and practices. Since democracy is a form that evolves while religion is not, religion must be a fossilized form of something undemocratic. Unless carefully restrained, it will break out and devour modern life in a resurrection of the repressed. Since September 11 and the rise of various religious right wings throughout the world, this polarized view of illiberal church versus liberal democracy has been reinforced.

On this view, the role of religion — especially devout forms like evangelicalism — should be none or very small in any society that hopes to be liberal and democratic. To base government on reason, liberal democracies would have either a strict de jure separation of church and state, yielding a secular government like that in France, Kemalist Turkey, or the United States. Or they would have a delimited cooperation between church and state where the terms of the cooperation are set by the constitution or common law, not the church. This is the case in several European countries, England, Norway, Denmark, Germany, and the Netherlands, among them. Some quarters also hold that democratic government flourishes best in societies that are secular as well — that not only government but also civil society promotes the most democracy when it is most secular. Still others, embracing secularization theory, have claimed that religion would in any case fade as countries modernized and rationalized.[2] The French *laique* tradition, with its emphasis on "privatizing" religion, follows along these lines.

The benefits of strict-separation and delimited-cooperation would be threefold: a neutral government that treats all citizens with procedural fairness (political and legal); a government that is protected from religion's doctrinal imponderables; and pluralistic freedom of conscience for all, including the rights of citizens to criticize the state.

Yet the idea that liberal democracy and national conduct improve with secularization has not entirely held up. As both secular and religious thinkers have noted,[3] secular governments — those that do not base their authority in the divine — have not guaranteed liberal democracy (the Soviet Union and Maoist China are examples). Moreover, modernization has not guaranteed the secularization of society (United States, South Korea, United Arab Emirates). Renouncing the transcendent divine for man's reason has not necessarily led to more just economies or peaceful societies. Some argue that it has led instead to runaway neoliberalism with only greed as motive for our actions. Given man's tendency to validate self-interest with reason — to rationalize war, extortion, and oppression — one might ask why we assume reason is our best guide. Perhaps man's reason is precisely what should be checked by a (transcendent) ethical system that man cannot manipulate to suit himself. Finally, religion has not been an enemy to progress, change, or reason. It would be trite to note that the list of analyti-

---

2. With roots in the work of Ludwig Feuerbach, Emile Durkheim, and Max Weber, secularization theory gained significant ground in the postwar period in the works of Thomas Luckmann and Niklas Luhmann, among others; for a summary, see J. Casanova, *Public Religions in the Modern World* (Chicago: University of Chicago Press, 1994), chapter 2.

3. P. Berger, ed., *The Desecularization of the World: Resurgent Religion and World Politics* (Washington, D.C.: Ethics and Public Policy Center; Grand Rapids: Eerdmans, 1999); G. Davie, "Europe — the Exception That Proves the Rule," in *The Desecularization of the World*, pp. 65-84; F. W. Graf, *Die Wiederkehr der Goetter: Religionen in der modernen Kultur* (Munich: Beck Verlag, 2004); D. Martin, *A General Theory of Secularization* (Oxford: Blackwell, 1976); among others.

cal and scientific thinkers who have been believers is long, among them Isaac Newton. Moreover, religion, like any human institution, changes over time and place, even as it works with enduring principles. While confessions have core tenets, these are rarely the only determinant of how faiths are practiced. Catholicism in fourteenth-century Ireland is not the same as in twenty-first-century South Korea — or twenty-first-century Ireland for that matter. Islam in an Algerian town is not practiced as it is in Auckland.

The idea that religion is a fixed foe of democracy reifies and deifies a human institution — ironically by those who wish to desacralize and tame it. It turns out that liberal democratic nations with just economies need not require citizens to be only rational, to have no transcendent values. (One might ask if political and economic systems are ever value-less.) Democracies also may not permit all values save religious ones. That discriminates against religion, which liberal democracies are committed to protect. Indeed, historically, religion has grounded many of the principles that liberal democrats endorse (see chapter 2).

Thus, the issue for liberal democracies is not how they can efface religion to create a secular society. The question is rather how religious citizens, like their nonbelieving neighbors, can support, thrive under, and contribute to liberal democracy and economic fairness. Given that there are today 600 million Buddhists, 800 million Hindus, 1.5 billion Muslims, and 2.3 billion Christians — many more believers than nonbelievers — if we cannot find ways toward that end, the prognosis for liberal democracy is bleak.

This returns us to our problem and solution, which we can refine. The problem is not whether devout faith is inherently incompatible with liberal democracy but rather, *what are the religious beliefs and political practices that advance vibrant religious life, liberal democracy, and economic fairness? Are there examples where all are robust?*

These examples might be interesting, not so beliefs and practices are mechanically reproduced — as that is impossible from faith to faith, context to context — but so political practices may be debated, possibly modified, and made useful to people as they consider the kind of society and government they want. Throughout the world, the role of religion is being rethought in light of immigration, demands for democracy and just economies, and fear of fundamentalist usurpation. This holds in the United States, the United Kingdom, France, and Poland, as it does in Turkey, India, and the Maghreb. The present economic crises have sharpened this discussion. On one hand, do religious beliefs lead to violence or the "Balkanization" of nations, especially under economic duress? On the other, how might they facilitate conflict resolution and what (transcendent) standards should be used to guide the open market — might religious traditions have anything to offer? In answering these questions, one thing people do is look around. Reactions to what others are doing are inevitably complex. But the alternative — not knowing what others are doing — is not better.

This book describes one example of beliefs and practices that have advanced religion, liberal democracy, and just economic distribution. That is, the book makes no attempt to develop a theory with predictive value for which faith traditions will be compatible with liberal democracy — an endeavor that in any case would be frustrated by human creativity in the arenas of religion and politics, and by the changes that religious practice undergoes over time. Instead, we look at one current example where faith and liberal democracy are strong. The group studied is what Richard Cizik, former vice president at the National Association of Evangelicals (NAE), calls "new evangelicals" — evangelicals whose priorities have broadened from those associated with the Religious Right — a broadening toward an antimilitarist, anticonsumerist focus on poverty relief, immigration reform, and environmental protection.

Evangelicalism is an approach to Protestantism, applicable to many denominations. Emerging in the eighteenth century from Europe's dissenting and "enthusiast" churches and from the pietistic and Moravian movements in Germany, it sought a renewal of faith toward an inner, personal relationship with Jesus,[4] emphasizing the mission to bring others to that relationship; the cross as a symbol of service, sacrifice, and salvation; individualist Bible reading by ordinary men and women; and the priesthood of all believers independent of ecclesiastical or state authorities. (Chapter 2 offers a brief historical overview.)

"New evangelicals" retain these beliefs but differ from the Religious Right in self-identification and political ends and means. Tony Campolo, former professor of sociology at Eastern University and the

---

4. For a more detailed discussion of evangelicalism in the period, see M. Noll, *America's God: From Jonathan Edwards to Abraham Lincoln* (New York: Oxford University Press, 2002), and M. Noll, *The Rise of Evangelicalism: The Age of Edwards, Whitefield, and the Wesleys* (Downers Grove, Ill.: InterVarsity, 2003).

University of Pennsylvania, a Baptist minister, and founder of the Evangelical Association for the Promotion of Education, writes, "there are millions of us who espouse an evangelical theology, but who reject being classified as part of the religious right."[5] Should "new evangelicals" at some point work less well with the liberal, democratic state, their present writings and practices will nonetheless remain as examples of how the devout may think about pluralism, economic justice, and liberal democracy. In considering "new evangelical" views, religious communities may be interested in this question: *How do "new evangelicals" retain their religious values while embracing constitutional law and liberal democratic government?* Secularists may be interested in the answer to this question: *How do "new evangelicals" embrace pluralism and liberal democratic government if they retain religious values?* Indeed, of eight types of conflicts that have arisen between religious groups and the liberal, democratic state,[6] only two have arisen between the state and "new evangelicals." The principal reason for this relatively light level of discord is the belief that liberal democracy is the sort of government that best protects religious belief and practice for all citizens — those in dominant religions and those not. "The United States is governed by a constitution whose First Amendment guarantees free exercise of religion," David Gushee, professor of Christian ethics at Mercer University, wrote during the controversy over the proposed Muslim center at Ground Zero. "This is one of the very best practices of our country. Millions of people have come here through the centuries because of this constitutional guarantee of the free exercise of religion — including many, many Christians."[7]

Any inflexible demarcation between "new" and other evangelicals is of course artificial, as certain priorities and political approaches remain common to evangelicals across the political and religious spectra. Yet there have been noticeable shifts since 2005. Reflecting these, the NAE, in choosing a new vice president for governmental affairs in 2009, promoted a candidate from its relief and development division. In accepting the job, Galen Carey announced his aim to "protect children

---

5. T. Campolo, *Red Letter Christians: A Citizen's Guide to Faith and Politics* (Ventura, Calif.: Regal, 2008), p. 17.

6. D. Grimm, "Conflicts between General Laws and Religious Norms," *Cardozo Law Review* 30 (2009): 2369-82.

7. D. Gushee, "The Shameful Mosque Controversy," *Huffington Post*, August 11, 2010.

and families, promote religious freedom, peace and human rights, seek sustainable solutions to domestic and global poverty, promote a consistent ethic of life, and responsibly care for God's creation [environmental protection]."[8] In 2010, a new organization was established specifically to bring "new evangelical" ideas to the public. Richard Cizik, along with David Gushee and Steven Martin, pastor and filmmaker, founded the New Evangelical Partnership for the Common Good, with priorities in human rights, democracy, the rule of law, and peacemaking, including peace and respect among the world's religions. It supports economic justice, expanding access to health care, and strong families, and works against environmental degradation. It advances abortion reduction by preventing unintended pregnancies, supporting pregnant women, and improving adoption laws and procedures so that "no woman feels that abortion is her only choice."[9] In 2011, Peter Heltzel, Bruce Benson, and Malinda Berry are inaugurating the Prophetic Christian series of books (Eerdmans) to invesitgate the prophetic and covenantal traditions of Christian theology.

Positions such as these may be of interest not only in themselves but also for the way they are discussed. They are expressed in the discourses of faith, with the believer's assumptions and language, referring not to Locke, Jefferson, Milton Friedman, and Marx but to Matthew, Luke, and Paul. These are not secularized or ecumenical discourses but doctrinal and sectarian ones. Neither do they fall precisely within standard Republican or Democratic parameters, nor within standard left-right dichotomies. Indeed, to date, a feature of "new evangelical" thinking appears to be policy assessment on an issue-by-issue basis — guided not by a framework external to new evangelicals (Republican, Keynesian, etc.) but by their own framework — or frameworks, as "new evangelical" views themselves span a range. To the nonbeliever, this sort of talk may sound prototheocratic. It may be frustrating — perhaps not analytical enough, not empirical, economic, or politically sufficient. And not like the public discourses of the Religious Right, the secular left, or the mainstream media, which at least are familiar.

But as it has been this religious discourse that has led "new evangelicals" to support pluralism, economic justice, and liberal democratic

8. See http://www.nae.net/news/40=news=item=4.
9. See http://www.newevangelicalpartnership.org/?q=node/1.

government, it might be illuminating to see how it gets there. That is, it's not how close "new evangelical" thinking comes to some other set of ideas — those of Sarah Palin, the late Ted Kennedy's, or one's own — but its suggestions for a society where faith and liberal democracy are robust. An anecdote may illustrate what I mean. During the writing of this book, a colleague asked me if "new evangelicals" agreed with a certain economist she admired. Many would, but not necessarily because of the same economic analysis that the economist had used. "New evangelicals" have their approaches to politics and economics, born of their faith and the reasoning that comes of it, and it is this religious grounding for liberal democracy and economic justice that may be productive for a world with so many believers on one hand and so many debates about good government, human rights, and economic development on the other.

Dan Lacich, a Florida pastor, suggests an example of faith leading not to mutual suspicion or discrimination but to respect and cooperation. Describing a Muslim colleague, he notes, "We both hold to the idea that we are made in the image of God. . . . If I honor God, I must honor my Muslim friend as someone made in God's image."[10] This position has gravitas among believers because of its scriptural basis. It leads Lacich's church to work with Muslim groups on poverty-relief programs. And it led "new evangelicals" to defend Muslim Americans when the Dove World Outreach Center in Florida announced plans to burn the Koran on the 2010 anniversary of the September 11 attacks. The NAE and New Evangelical Partnership issued statements strongly condemning the burning and insisting on its cancellation. They joined scores of religious organizations in signing the Statement Adopted by Interfaith Leaders at ISNA Emergency Interfaith Summit condemning anti-Muslim prejudice and violence overall. The NAE's statement called on members "to cultivate relationships of trust and respect with our neighbors of other faiths," as "God created human beings in his image." It reminded Christians of the NAE's 1996 statement condemning religious persecution and pledging the NAE to "address religious persecution carried out by our Christian brothers and sisters wherever it occurs around the world."[11]

10. Interview with the author, May 11, 2009.
11. See http://www.nae.net/news-and-events/469-press-release-nae-urges-cancellation-of-planned-quran-burning.

These views along with embrace of church-state separation are a rallying cry far different from that at the 2004 Republican nominating convention, where placards read "What can evangelicals do in government? Anything we want!" What prompted the change? In part, it is a generational shift, with idealistic young evangelicals rejecting the Religious Right politics and "prosperity gospel" of their parents. But, as Cizik has noted, "the 'younger generation' appears to be anyone under age sixty-nine."[12] A second factor is the cultural changes of the last forty years. Attitudinal shifts — about sex, the environment, and global connectedness — have occurred not at the radical fringe but in Middle America[13] and are affecting evangelical priorities.

A third factor is conscience. The "new evangelical" shift appears to be not a "sour grapes" tactic of a defeated bloc, as it began significantly before the Republican defeat in 2008. It seems rather to be a reconsideration of ethics by people who take ethics seriously. In their emphasis on covenant and the prophetic tradition, love of others — the covenant with others — is of a piece with covenant with God and is what we are to reach for. By contrast, failure to care for others is abomination, as the prophets of the Hebrew Bible understood.[14] Building covenant is, on this view, witnessing Jesus, who served the needy, stranger, and enemy but rejected both the force of government and the force of rebellion against it. Thus the feeling has grown among "new evangelicals" that, in relying on politics, they lost not an election here and there but themselves. Not only did George W. Bush's policies — especially the endorsement of torture — cease to witness Jesus' teachings of love and service, but the view gained ground that being *in* government, by definition faulty and aggressive, cannot be the godly way. In one of the many unintended consequences of history, Bush may have shattered the religious bloc that elected him.

*   *   *

12. Interview with the author, December 6, 2007.

13. National Marriage Project and the Institute for American Values, *When Marriage Disappears: The New Middle America,* Marriage in America: The State of Our Unions, 2010. Institute for American Values, University of Virginia, December 2010.

14. For a discussion of the prophetic tradition in "new evangelical" thought, see Peter Goodwin Heltzel, Bruce Ellis Benson, and Malinda Elizabeth Berry, *Prophetic Evangelicals* (Grand Rapids: Eerdmans, forthcoming).

Distributed across Protestant denominations and the country, "new evangelicals" come to roughly 25 percent of the American population.[15] To find out why and how they came to their politics, I looked at books, sermons, newsletters, blogs, and political and social activism from 2005 to 2011. Guided, open-ended interviews were conducted with scholars, pastors, political advisers, and the laity from 2007 to 2010: men and women from nineteen to seventy-four, from a wide range of Christian denominations (including Roman Catholics attending evangelical churches) living in California, Wisconsin, Idaho, Florida, Pennsylvania, Texas, Georgia, Minnesota, Mississippi, Colorado, Washington, D.C., Iowa, Virginia, New York, and Illinois. They were students, firemen, teachers, construction workers, office workers, nurses, professors, lay church staff, project managers, pastors, real estate agents, parachurch professionals, and political consultants. There is no attempt here at a statistical survey of all evangelicals to determine general trends. Where pertinent to this study, the findings of such general surveys are included in the chapters ahead.

To date, "new evangelicals" embrace constitutional law neutral to religion to ensure fair government and religious freedom for all. They see themselves as civil society actors (neither state institutions nor self-segregated enclaves) who use religious values to guide their activism and to critique government when they believe it has gone awry, much as other values in civil society are used. Each of these points is discussed below.

Embrace of Constitutional Law Neutral to Religion, and the Pluralistic Corrective to Special Pleading

"New evangelicals" expect that laws will be constitutionally (not scripturally) based, aimed at the common good, and neutral toward religion (promoting no specific religion and treating the religious and secular equally). "There are some issues," Rick Warren has explained, "that

15. This 25 percent includes the "religious left" at 9 percent of the U.S. population (the older Evangelical Left, the Catholic left, and new emergent churches); the "red-letter Christians," who red-line biblical passages as a guide to progressive politics, also at 9 percent; and religious centrists (liberal theology, moderate politics) at about 6 percent. See Pew Forum on Religion and Public Life, "Assessing a More Prominent 'Religious Left,'" June 5, 2008.

have to be dealt with, with everybody, on the common good."[16] Warren is pastor at the influential Saddleback Church, with over 100,000 members and thirty daughter Spanish-language churches. He gave the invocation at President Obama's inauguration and is author of *The Purpose Driven Life*, the biggest-selling nonfiction book in American history. Not only Warren but also the NAE takes the position that the programs and policies it advocates must further the good of all, not the good only of evangelicals, and they must be presented in terms nonevangelicals find intelligible.

"New evangelicals" endorse church-state separation and constitutionally based law for at least two reasons. First, doctrinally, government by definition is an institution of force, and so church must be separate from state in order to pursue Christlike aims and to employ gentle, Christlike means. Second, pragmatically, the state whose neutrality toward religion is constitutionally anchored best protects freedom of conscience for all. To be sure, the neutral state is not the only protector of religious freedom. Several European democracies have established churches and nonetheless guarantee religious freedom for all. The Indian constitution allows government to intervene substantially on behalf of persecuted faiths (that is, to be partial). But state neutrality is at least one way to protect religious freedom; it is the way America has followed, and "new evangelicals" support it. Evident in congregations since 2005, this support was underscored in 2010 when Obama's Office of Faith-Based and Neighborhood Partnerships, including several "new evangelicals," issued its final report. It recommended both that government continue to support faith-based agencies and that it clarify agency regulations so that separation of church and state is maintained.

A key feature of church-state separation and state neutrality toward religion is that rights allowed to one faith group must be allowed to others. This is not unfamiliar to evangelicals because this sort of fair play emerged, at least in part, from Protestantism and evangelicalism themselves. The individual's interpretation of sacred text without priestly intervention is a linchpin of Protestant faith (see chapter 2). Yet each person's passion for his own view assumes that the next person is equally sincere about hers. Since no fallen human can be certain of ab-

16. Pew Forum on Religion and Public Life, "The Future of Evangelicals: A Conversation with Pastor Rick Warren," November 13, 2009.

solute truth, the views of others must be respected. In ways perhaps un-anticipated by early Protestants, appreciation of each individual soul led to recognition of the multiplicity of souls. When evangelicals support state neutrality toward religion and pluralistic freedom of conscience, they are agreeing with their own traditions.

This leads "new evangelicals" to consider carefully what they demand. For the same privileges and responsibilities will be allowed to all other groups, and evangelicals must consider the consequences of this broad application. We can think of this as a pluralistic corrective to special pleading. For instance, arguing that a Christian pharmacist may refuse to sell contraceptives to unmarried couples might mean that a Muslim supermarket cashier, on the same religious-freedom grounds, may refuse to sell pork. If one hesitates to allow the second, it's not easy — under fair, neutral government — to allow the first.

The fairness and neutrality of government may be weakened by any who seek a more partial arrangement. Thus, some vigilance is needed to guard against theocratic flirtations. Some organizations with this mandate are long-standing. The nonpartisan, nonsectarian Americans United for the Separation of Church and State was founded in 1947 and today has chapters in thirty-three states, including Texas, Alabama, Kansas, Florida, Georgia, and other notches in the Bible Belt.[17] Its executive director, Barry Lynn, is a United Church of Christ minister. Somewhat newer are the Mainstream Baptists, a nonprofit, grassroots, volunteer group with fourteen state chapters that advocate for church-state separation and oppose what they see as fundamentalistic tendencies in more conservative Baptist groups.[18] Equally important for this vigilance are the many "new evangelicals" who do not professionally monitor fairness and neutrality but assume it to preserve freedom of conscience for themselves and others, as they build churches and social service agencies.

Voluntarist Associationism

"New evangelicals" both see and conduct themselves as civil society groups — voluntarist associations — that advocate for their positions

---

17. See http://www.au.org/.
18. See http://www.mainstreambaptists.org/.

through public education, lobbying, coalition building, and negotiation. They, like other groups, are constrained by law, yet they — like other groups — have values upon which their positions are based. In short, they do seek to influence the direction of the country but in ways that to date are unalarming to liberal democracy. Agreement among political actors is not assumed. Asked whether the NAE took a position on teaching creationism or intelligent design as science in public schools, Carl Esbeck, legal counsel to the Office of Governmental Affairs, NAE, said, "I don't think we could agree on that even within the organization."[19] Yet when conflict with other political actors occurs, significant effort is put into discussion and negotiation. This can be observed both in grassroots groups and by "new evangelicals" who are consultants to government. Interviews with a number of them — Tony Campolo, Richard Cizik, and Joel Hunter — are included in this book.

Like support for state neutrality, the dialogic, negotiation emphasis in "new evangelical" politics emerges from Protestant/evangelical doctrine. Respect for individual belief and recognition of the fallenness of man lead "new evangelicals" to be loath to judge. Given the many views that surround us, certain political or legal battles — the rectitude of gay marriage, for instance — may not at present be resolvable. So it might be productive to set these fights aside and attend to common goals, like poverty relief. This has allowed for "new evangelical" coalitions with non-Christians, secular institutions, and political progressives on such programs as environmental protection, health care, immigration reform, and abortion reduction.

Indeed, "new evangelicals" are engaged substantially in the economic, social, and charitable spheres of American life. Though they often feel like a minority in a consumerist society, they have not withdrawn into homogenous cul-de-sacs but rather present several models of societal engagement. Some run ministries alone; some partner with other, nongovernmental associations; and others partner with government. Programs typically run by churches in this study include food and clothing banks and free medical clinics for the poor, shelters for battered women and the homeless, tutoring services for inner-city youth, prison counseling, substance abuse programs, programs for environmental protection, plus missions overseas to work on reducing AIDS and other diseases, to build and staff orphanages and schools, to

19. Interview with the author, May 5, 2009.

teach marketable skills to adults, and to reduce environmental degradation. These are run almost entirely by volunteers, who do much of the fund-raising as well.

It can be argued that evangelicals are Americans and thus not prone to the in-group or self-protective mechanisms associated with immigrant populations. Yet many "new evangelicals" are indeed immigrants, increasingly so from Latino Catholic communities. Over half of Latino Catholics embrace charismatic religious practices, and 15 percent of Latinos have converted to evangelical faiths. Moreover, long residency in the United States does not preclude an in-group emphasis. The Amish and certain charismatic communities have been American for generations but nonetheless remain separate from what they see as a contaminated world. The "new evangelicals" of this study have not done so. This should take off the table the idea that robust religion of necessity Balkanizes nations into mutually suspicious groups.[20] Neither can we say that they have avoided Balkanization because they are small in number and cannot survive alone, since by 2009 they came to roughly 25 percent of the population (see chapter 6).

In sum, the self-positioning of "new evangelicals" as civil society actors has presented a "third way" of political activism. It is an alternative to the dualism of entirely privatized religion on one hand and theocracies on the other. Privatization is insufficient for religion's flourishing, as religions need communities, institutions, public expression, and resources. Yet religions that run government may be too much for liberal democracy's flourishing. As an alternative, state neutrality and religious associationism in the civil sphere have allowed religious groups to flourish under liberal, democratic government and to contribute to public debate.

Religious Values as a Guide to Activism in the Critique of Government

On the "new evangelical" view, religious values do not undermine liberal democracy and economic justice but buttress them. Since all governments are corruptible and justify self-interest with reason, "new

20. See M. Marty and R. S. Appleby, *Fundamentalisms Observed* (Chicago: University of Chicago Press, 1994).

evangelicals" understand the citizen activism needed to make them function well and the political vigilance needed to keep them honest. The civil rights movement, opposition to torture, and support for immigration reform are examples of what some call the church's "prophetic role" — not to *be* government but to "speak truth to power."

Essential to the prophetic role is party independence, as one cannot easily critique the government if one is dependent on it. David Gushee describes his test for Christian political engagement: "whether we have the capacity to say 'no' to our favorite party or politician."[21] This does not mean that white evangelicals no longer vote for the Republican Party. They have, in significant numbers, for thirty-five years, 78 percent voting for George W. Bush in 2004. They were less Republican in 2009, when 35 percent of evangelicals identified as Democrats, 34 percent as Republicans, and the remaining third as independents. And in the 2010 midterm elections, three-quarters again voted Republican. A shift toward the Democratic Party would be unlikely in any case, because of evangelical opposition to abortion and traditional preferences for self-reliance and small government.

The significant shift in the prophetic role and party independence was to a broadened activism and to more of an issue-by-issue assessment of policy — leaning Democrat on environment, leaning Republican on abortion, independent on economic policy. This is critical in policy development and implementation, and most politics goes on not at elections but between them, when policy is negotiated and set. In the midst of the fractious budget debates especially in 2010-11, the NAE, for instance, did not toe a party line but rather joined a coalition of groups independently calling for a "circle of protection" around the poor. "As Christians," the coalition wrote, "we believe the moral measure of the debate is how the most poor and vulnerable people fare. We look at every budget proposal from the bottom up-how it treats those Jesus called 'the least of these' (Matthew 25:45) . . . we are committed to fiscal responsibility and shared sacrifice. We are also committed to resist budget cuts that undermine the lives, dignity, and rights of poor and vulnerable people. Therefore, we join with others to form a Circle of Protection around programs that meet the essential needs of hungry and poor people at home

21. D. Gushee, *The Future of Faith in American Politics: The Public Witness of the Evangelical Center* (Waco, Tex.: Baylor University Press, 2008), p. 50; see also, this volume, chapter 8.

and abroad."[22] Coalition recommendations included that programs for the needy be made efficient but that funding not be cut. By the time of this antipoverty effort, party independence had been growing among "new evangelicals" for several years. In 2007, Bill Hybels, pastor at the influential Willow Creek Association, asked that conservative Christians work on environmental and social justice issues with secular progressives. That year, against the Bush administration, the NAE issued *An Evangelical Declaration against Torture*,[23] renouncing "the use of torture and cruel, inhuman, and degrading treatment by any branch of our government (or any other government) — even in the current circumstance of a war between the United States and various radical terrorist groups." In 2008, Rick Warren invited both presidential candidates, John McCain and Barack Obama, to his church. The NAE — against many Republicans — supports immigration reform leading to citizenship for America's nearly thirteen million undocumented residents.[24]

If the research presented here suggests anything, it is that we should refine our categories. For forty years, evangelicals have been associated with the Republican Party, opposition to abortion and gay marriage, and at times attempts to use the state to impose religious views on the nation. Since 2005, "new evangelicals" have still been associated with the Republican Party and opposition to abortion but also with poverty relief, immigration reform, and environmental protection rather than with attempts to penetrate government.

Unresolved Church-State Issues

"New evangelical" embrace of liberal, democratic government does not suggest agreement with other political actors on all church-state issues — on the rights of churches and the rights of the state. Arguments continue, for instance, on whether public monies may be used to support religious education and about whether religious symbols may be

22. See http://www.nae.net/budgetcircle.

23. See http://www.esa-online.org/Images/mmDocument/Declarations%20&%20 Letters/An%20Evangelical%20Declaration%20Against%20Torture.pdf.

24. In the spring of 2010, both the NAE and the Southern Baptist Convention issued calls for immigration reform, including a path toward citizenship for America's undocumented residents; see http://www.tennessean.com/article/20100608/NEWS01/ 6080339/2066/news03 and http://www.nae.net/news-and-events/444-immigration-ad.

placed in public places. These issues will be discussed in chapter 4. But in overview, disagreement between "new evangelicals" and government has to date been navigated in political negotiation and in courts, whose standards are constitutional. Requests that secular courts accept the decisions of sectarian ones have not been made, as they have been by Muslim groups in Canada and Great Britain.[25] This cannot be dismissed as an artifact of citizenship, as though *American* evangelicals would of necessity take this road. Some Americans, Catholics and Jews among them, have advocated for sectarian courts and focused far less on negotiation and extracourt solutions.

Reasons for "new evangelical" compatibility with the secular judiciary echo their support for liberal, democratic government. One factor is the upstream embrace of constitutional law as the best protector of freedom of conscience. If one wants to argue that physicians may not be forced to perform abortions, one would hesitate to discard the underlying legal structures that guarantee religious freedom. Second is the pluralistic corrective to special pleading. The broad application to other groups of rights won in court provides a framework for what "new evangelicals" decide to take to court. Finally is the matter of priorities. While "new evangelicals" do have opinions, for instance, on the legality of religious symbols on public grounds, the time and energy given to the needy mitigate against such disputes becoming foci of activism or resources.

"New evangelical" legal advocacy can be illustrated by three "friend of the court" briefs submitted by the NAE. In one, *Colorado Christian University v. Raymond T. Baker,* the NAE argued that "pervasively religious" universities should be able to use government education grants for nonsectarian programs, just as secular universities are. The NAE's argument applied to all religious universities, not to only evangelical ones. The Colorado Appeals Court agreed, ruling to allow state aid to support the secular activities of "pervasively religious" colleges.[26] The

25. In 2003, for example, the Islamic Institute for Civil Justice offered to adjudicate family law for Canada's Muslim population. The proposal was defended by the Christian Legal Fellowship, B'Nai Brith (a Jewish organization), the Salvation Army, Sunni Masjid El Noor, and the Ismali Muslims. Canada rejected the offer.

26. Indeed, in 2000 *(Mitchell v. Helms)* the Supreme Court voided the distinction between sectarian and "pervasively sectarian," ruling that the federal government may fund schools — sectarian, "pervasively sectarian," or nonsectarian. Colorado's law was written before 2000; this case brought the state law into line with the Supreme Court.

second case, *Rasul, Shafiq, et al. v. Myers, Richard, et al.*, was brought by four former Guantanamo Bay detainees against former Secretary of Defense Donald Rumsfeld and the U.S. military for arbitrary detention, physical and psychological torture, and religious abuse. The NAE argued for the religious freedom of the Muslim detainees. The Supreme Court agreed, instructing the lower courts to review whether America's Religious Freedom Restoration Act applies to Guantanamo detainees. In the third case, *Willis v. Indiana Department of Corrections,* Indiana prison authorities refused to serve kosher meals to Jewish inmates on the grounds that it was too costly. Along with Prison Fellowship, the Christian Legal Society, and the Baptist Joint Committee for Religious Liberty, the NAE submitted a "friend of the court" brief in support of the Jewish prison inmates. The brief argued that cost does not create an exception to the Religious Land Use and Incarcerated Persons Act (RLUIPA, 2000), which compels states to accommodate reasonable religious requests from prison inmates.[27]

Some Definitional Comments

Throughout this book, "secular" and "neutral toward religion" are taken to mean neither governments antagonistic to religion nor societies devoid of religion. Rather they refer to institutions whose authority to develop concepts and implement policy is not seen as coming from the divine. The authority of neutral, liberal democratic government, for instance, comes from citizen consent, common law, and constitutions. It is the governmental and legal systems that are secular and neutral, not societies, which may include many believers. The purpose of neutral, liberal democracy is not to be more antagonistic toward believers than toward other citizens but to allow sectarian and nonsectarian ways of life to develop freely.

Strict disestablishment (church-state separation) has not been a requirement of liberal democracy.[28] The democracies of England, Scot-

27. See http://www.nae.net/news/563-nae-insists-on-religious-freedom-for-indiana-prisoners.

28. Casanova, *Public Religions in the Modern World;* see also J. Casanova, "The Problem of Religion and the Anxieties of European Secular Democracy" (paper presented at the 25th Jubilee Conference on Religion and European Democracy, September 1-3, 2007) (Jerusalem: Van Leer Institute, 2007).

land, Denmark, Norway, Iceland, Finland, and, until 2000, Sweden all have state churches. But the neutrality of government toward religion has been associated with liberal democracy. It allows for freedom of conscience, pluralism (freedom of conscience for all), and the freedom for religious groups to contribute ideas to government as well as critique it. This last point is important as it takes off the table arguments against church involvement in politics. Like other civil society actors, they may be so involved. And like other civil groups, if they are to preserve their critical stance, churches must retain their independence from political parties, government, and the judiciary.

In sum, what liberal democracy strives for is fair, unbiased procedures in government and the judiciary, as well as pluralistic freedom of conscience to criticize the state. Those, we can say, are the aims. Strict governmental neutrality and delimited cooperation between state and an established church have been means to these goals.

One recent suggestion for neutral governments is that they require religious groups to translate their ideas into language that all in society can grasp. The lingua franca is presumed to be secular (those writing in a secular idiom would presumably not have to translate). This requirement, however, is at odds with historical and political realities. The first modern arguments for toleration and church-state separation were made by the religious dissenters of the sixteenth and seventeenth centuries and relied on their religious discourse. Moreover, secular political claims, in places like Pol Pot's Cambodia or Stalin's Soviet Union, did not lead to peace or greater justice. And there are rarely clear divisions between secular and religious formulations of a policy, as all contain premises and values. In some cases, principles that are currently seen as secular have substantial religious roots. Pragmatically speaking, in many societies, including developed ones like that of the United States, more citizens would be familiar with religious lines of thinking than with secular political theory. A secular public discourse would thus leave many people out of the essential democratic process of public debate.

The most illuminating practice for a democracy would be to have the range of arguments publicly debated. Should religious groups advocate law or policy, they should be held to the same standard as other groups in liberal democracies: their proposals, case by case, must fall within constitutional parameters even if they are faith-based in the minds and language of the confessional group. The requirement is that the proposal be constitutional, not that believers translate their ideas into one or another of society's many discourses.

This book, a small piece of the public discourse, aims to bring the perspectives of "new evangelicals" into play.

Larry Perry, Mississippi/Idaho

LP We come from the South. I was up here [in Idaho] chasing forest fires till my wife said "no more of that." So I started volunteering for her in the church's medical clinic. We came to this church because we were looking for something different. I was raised in the Assemblies of God; my father was a minister. Then I heard the pastor here say something about "authentic reproducible Christians." About that time, the "Sunday school Christians" had really been bothering me. They are good Christians on Sunday and then back out there on Monday doing the same skullduggery. Isn't that a great word — skullduggery.

I have never heard anything in this church that contradicts the Bible. In a lot of churches, they take Scripture and twist it around to what they want. It doesn't say, "Love your neighbor except if you don't like him." I have people here that I know came in swimming from the south [Latin America] — undocumented. But I'm not going to stop loving and feeding them. There are illegals who have killed and illegals who have saved people. I think they should wait their turn [for citizenship] and do it right, but I wish they could get here documented so they don't have to worry about the police. When I was in the fire department, I had a principle: enforce the rule, change the rule to meet conditions, or get rid of the rule. We need to do that with immigration.

It's the same fight that we had under Reagan. He said, close the border. But if you're going to do that, you have to fund it. But people don't want to pay taxes to pay for it. We had budget meetings here open to the public and a guy was screaming about spending too much money. Two months later, his wife dies of a heart attack and he's screaming that there weren't enough paramedics on the ambulances — because there was no money to pay for it!

These unfunded mandates from the government are atrocious. They put so many rules on us in the fire department that you couldn't do 'em. Congress should go into session once every five years and then get out of town because they foul things up. But they should fund what they pass. There are people who say they want smaller government. Then they run into a pothole because the highway district, which they didn't want to pay taxes to, couldn't afford to pave the roads.

MP Should the church work with government on these social issues?

LP Jesus said, Rule 1: Love God with all your heart, soul, and might. Rule 2: Love your neighbor as yourself. That's the job of the church. The Bible talks about feeding the widows and orphans. In the church, we try to lift them out — with food, counseling, medical. We want to help them spiritually, and you can't do that if you don't love them. I have a nephew who's dark-complected; his brother is light-complected, blond hair and blue eyes. The darker one is in construction — he's got $40 million in jobs from New Orleans to Jackson, Mississippi, even in this [financial crisis] economy. Who's smart there? Race has never been a good indicator of intelligence.

We try to do everything we can within the limits of the law. And there is separation between church and state. Jesus said, "Give unto Caesar what's due to Caesar. Give unto God what's due to God." How can you be a Christian and break the law? Law was meant so that people could get along with each other, for the betterment of society.

MP What should you do if you don't like the law, like the law guaranteeing legal abortion?

LP If you're shooting a doctor for performing abortions — that doctor needs prayer, not a bullet. Jesus did not say, "Shoot people you disagree with." He said, "Pray for them." I don't agree with abortion, but I'm not going to put down some poor girl because she had one. There had to be something so fearful in her life for her to do that. I cannot imagine being in the position where you have to have an abortion. But then, I've never been in that position. Some girls are so scared of their dads — "if Dad found out he'd kill me and the boy, too." After economic need, fear is the second most important reason for abortion. I'm not pro-choice; I'm not pro-life. I'm going to pray for someone in that position, for God's perfect will.

We have a woman who works in the clinic for women in crisis [pregnancies] — she's been arrested all over the world, protesting against legal abortion. Her overall strategy is to bring the world's attention to problems; I agree with that. But she is ultraconservative and I don't like her tactics. I'm not going to point my finger in her face, but I think she's wrong about what she's doing and how she's doing it. When you go to a foreign country, you follow their laws. If you go there and break those laws, like to protest abortion, then you're telling them that Christians can't be trusted. Why should they allow Christians in their country? I don't know what I'd do if I lived in a totalitarian country where the law was that I couldn't go into my house and pray. If I had to choose between losing my life or my soul, I think I'd save my soul.

My father was a Southern, conservative Democrat to the right of Rush Limbaugh. My mother was a Republican. I'm a moderate. I think "Democrat" and "Republican" ought to be thrown out. If a Democrat has an idea, the Republicans say it's lousy because the Democrats came up with it. If a Republican has an idea, the Democrats say it's lousy. I try my best to see both sides of an issue. If people are educated and interested in the subject, they might try to see what the right thing would be for the country instead of being polarized.

But I'm just a dumb kid from Mississippi.

Tim McFarlane, California/Idaho

TM I come from a rough background — biker, drug abuser, outlaw. Then I was in construction. My wife and I split up, but she found the Lord in the process. She didn't give up on me and eventually I fell in love with the church. I was saved. Back then, my wife and I didn't want to be members of anything because that wasn't "cool." So Vineyard seemed to fit — no pews, rock music. Later I got hired to be missions director, and one and a half years later I was licensed as pastor. I have no formal training. Everyone on staff has been raised up from within the church.

There are about six hundred Vineyard churches in the U.S. and about one thousand in foreign countries. My job is to develop partnerships among U.S. and overseas churches. Missions work is expensive, so the smaller U.S. churches which can't do it alone can work in a group. We plant churches not to be like us but to be their own identity. We try to understand the culture and contextualize what the Vineyard would be to them. For example, Vineyard music is famous worldwide. The founder of the Vineyard was a saxophone player for the Righteous Brothers. But in Kenya, the worship is entirely different, though our core values are the same — reaching out to the poor, the homeless, praising God for all that's he's done.

We go into an area with a mercy mission — a medical brigade, feeding programs — in the name of God. We tend to everyone — Muslim, Jewish. I am not going to win souls — God will do that. Not by pushing but by example, we try to plant the seed of a church. The commitment is at least ten years — you can't do anything with less. Our Vineyard church is working with five partnerships: Ecuador, the Philippines, Zambia, Chile, and Paraguay.

In many cases, Christians have made a shambles of mission work. Go back to the Crusades; Christians were killing people in the name of God. Give me a break.

In foreign countries, people want to know what we're in it for — the oil, the diamonds? The history has not been good. And you can't go into a village where a man had multiple wives and tell him he can't do that. That's his culture. We let God deal with that. I'm not going to judge. My job is to show the love of Jesus.

I can buy all the "rice Christians" I want. In the third world, people will say anything for rice or money. But for those who join the church, I want the ones who are in it heart and soul. We're very careful: we will not pay a salary to a pastor overseas. But I will help get him training or buy chairs or Bibles for the church. We built a job resource center in Zambia because a pastor there said, "Forty percent of my village are under fifteen; kids are prostituting themselves to get food for their families." We saw we could do job training with just a small building and a few hand-cranked sewing machines and knitting looms. We got the money from the local congregation here in the U.S.

I know what God has called me to do. I believe Christ died on the cross as the only Son of God, who sacrificed his Son for my sins. I don't argue with people who have other ideas. I try to love them as best I can. The approach of the Religious Right would have turned me off: "if you don't, you won't" — if you don't believe as I believe, you won't go to heaven. I'm sixty years old; I was on the other side of the fence for more years than I've been on this side. I came to this church because I'm not real religious. I don't go by the book.

MP Does your mission work with the government?

TM We get no money from the government — too many strings attached. I don't disagree with the government on this. If we don't want to go by their rules, we don't take the money. My overseas ministry gets a third of the tithe from our local church. The benevolence ministry (food, medical clinic) gets a third, and the last third goes to the Association of Vineyard Churches. The Association doesn't tell us what to do; it's a group of autonomous churches that work together. I lean on God; I don't want to lean on the government more than I have to. There's one ministry in our local church, Celebrate Recovery, that did get a [government] grant. Under Bush, we could hire whom we wanted even though we're faith-based. I don't know if we'll get that again.

There are concerns around here about Obama changing the tax laws. People can deduct what they give to the church. We [the church] don't pay property taxes or taxes on anything we give away [to the needy]. We're very appreciative of our tax status. We probably couldn't operate as we do without it. People wouldn't be able to give as much to the church. There's also concern that Obama will change gun laws too. You have people who think the tribulation is here; the Antichrist is taking over. Blah, blah. He's not the Antichrist; he's not going for more government control. Obama has bigger fish to fry. He said it very well: "I've got two wars to fight; I've got a pandemic; I've got an economic crisis. I don't need to bother myself with running car companies or banks. I want them to get back on their feet and run themselves."

MP Do you have Democrats and Republicans in your congregation?

TM Sure. Heck, we have Democrats and Republicans on staff. We're involved in the environment — that's a real shift within Christianity. I'm raising organic chickens at home — that's a shift. Occasionally we'll have someone with the "religious spirit" come through. And that's hard to deal with because then you have someone who says, "God told me this and that, and it says this in the Word." Give me a break. Just go love people.

I've seen God's hand — I've seen people's lives change — in our garden, in the food pantry, with the homeless. I can relate to those guys. They know my past. They see my tattoos. I don't preach to them.

I don't believe that the Vineyard is the only church that'll get you to heaven. Mormonism, Buddhism, Hinduism — God has grace for everybody. There are a lot of things I don't know — what happens to people who commit suicide or who are Buddhists. I hope they go to heaven. There's some comfort in not having to know everything. I've dug thirty-foot water wells with guys who didn't believe what I do, and I love those guys. If God wants to use me to change their belief, that's fine. If not, then, heck, we dug a well.

chapter 2

Freedom of Conscience and
Separating Church from State

A Short History

The Argument from the Devout: 1531-1789

The most common story of freedom of conscience and church-state separation describes a daring rescue mission. It holds that men of political foresight struggled against Europe's monarchies and exclusionary, persecutory churches. Through the reasoned, secular arguments of Britain's Glorious Revolution and the Continental Enlightenment, they saved the West for toleration and democracy. The United States was first to implement these principles, and Europe moved toward them throughout the nineteenth century, establishing robust democracies in the twentieth. Since democratic practice was thought to be the result of victory over the churches, church meddling in government is thoroughly suspect, linked to religious discrimination and the undermining of the democratic system.

Yet freedom of conscience and church-state separation were born not of Deists or agnostic Enlightenment thinkers but of devout dissenters — and not to protect the rational, democratic state from persecutory religion but to protect minority religions from the persecutory state and state churches. Indeed, the established churches had long been political, economic, and police institutions in cahoots with Europe's aristocracies. The Holy See in Rome, for one, had political, police, and military status, and exercised it in wars, political deals, and at times religious persecution throughout Europe. Luther, for another, mandated obedience to the upper estates. Worsening matters for commoners, the 1648 Treaty of Westphalia, ending Europe's wars of religion, territorialized the churches, giv-ing political leaders the right to determine the official faith of their regions (the principle of *cuius regio eius religio,* he who rules chooses the faith). Established churches were now structurally arms of the state.

In the short term, the results were beneficial: the territorialization of religion helped to end religious war. In the long run, however, it was unhelpful to the development of liberal democracies, which respect a variety of beliefs. Territorialization required that, for men to agree on government, they had to agree on faith. Since Europe's territories were religiously diverse, the result of territorialization was continued perse-cution and exile of religious minorities. Equally hobbling for toleration and democratic development was the churches' new role as vassals of the state. Rather than honing an independent, ethical voice, Europe's established churches were busy currying favor with the reigning power to keep the privileged position of state church. Over the coming centu-ries, they worked with monarchist, conservative, and militarist parties, often as co-obstacles to toleration and democratic development. Gov-ernments in turn instrumentalized established or dominant churches through the nineteenth century, supporting them as instruments of so-cial control, which the churches obligingly imposed.

Against this one-church/one-state collusion, devout dissenters began calling for freedom of conscience and church-state separation. That is, these linchpins of liberal democracy came first not from a sec-ular Enlightenment analysis but from a religious one. The Renaissance humanist Erasmus (1465/69-1536) was an early voice. But a more force-ful writer of this period was Sebastian Franck, a sixteenth-century radi-cal spiritualist whose *Chronicle of World History* (1531) declared that even the followers of the radical Jan Hus and the Anabaptists were true Christians. With this flourish, he nearly voided the concept of Chris-tian heresy, a kindness for which Europe was unready.[1] A generation later, Sebastian Castellio too robbed heresy of its punch and made clear claims for freedom of conscience.[2] Demoting heresy from a sin to a dis-agreement among well-meaning men, he was among the first to distin-guish between faith (for God to judge) and action (for magistrates to

1. See the *Chronica* and *Paradoxa ducenta octoginta* (1534) in J. Lecler, *Toleration and the Reformation* (London: Longmans, Green, 1960), 1:175, 176.
2. S. Castellio, *Concerning Heretics and Whether They Should Be Persecuted, and How They Should be Treated* (1554), ed. and trans. R. Bainton (New York: Octagon Books, 1965), p. 129.

judge). Thus men who disagree on faith (beyond human judgment) could nonetheless come to agreement about the proper actions of states and citizens. In this, Castellio adumbrated the idea that church-state separation is the political structure in which intellectual and religious liberty would flourish — an idea he sharpened in his third tract on tolerance, *Concerning the Nonpunishment of Heretics* (1655). There he warns that if the political authorities remained in charge of religious truth, freedom of religion would be impossible. Against inquisitions and persecution, he argued for patience and education. These are Jesus' path, he wrote, and "left free," true religion will emerge — a claim that makes Castellio an early advocate of the marketplace of ideas.[3]

By the next century, ideas such as these had significant footing in Britain. Quakers and the radical, populist Ranters and Levellers argued that the individual's relationship with God could be judged by no man, and thus freedom of conscience was due of all. The Leveller[4] John Lilburne was whipped and imprisoned for his efforts to explain his dissenting beliefs, including the idea that the kingdom of God was spiritual and could not be governed by the state. His colleague William Walwyn argued for freedom of conscience and the marketplace of ideas in nearly full modern voice: erroneous views would fade in time as they failed the test of debate (*A New Petition of the Papists,* 1641). Richard Overton, in his satirical play *The Arraignment of Mr. Persecution* (1645), dared to call for religious tolerance even for Muslims and Jews. 5 This was rather unheard of at the time, and John Milton, among the era's most luminous writers, aspired to a more modest standard. He did however argue against the censorship of ideas in his *Areopagitica* (1644). In his more radical *Treatise of Civil Power in Ecclesiastical Causes* (1659) he called for freedom of conscience on classic Protestant *sola Scriptura* grounds. No priest or magistrate but only the Bible may guide men in their faith, and so no human official may judge belief or enforce a preferred creed. Building on a century of these works, the Quaker William Penn published his *Great Case of Liberty of Conscience* in 1670.

The great summation of this literature came in John Locke's *Letter*

3. Castellio, *Concerning Heretics,* especially pp. 123, 129, 132-35, 222-25, 251-53.

4. The Levellers were a populist group that demanded expanded suffrage, greater democracy, and religious toleration.

5. C. Marshall, *Crowned with Glory and Honor: Human Rights in the Biblical Tradition,* Studies in Peace and Scripture, vol. 6 (Telford, Pa.: Cascadia Publishing House, 2002), p. 148.

concerning Toleration (published in 1689). It was written earlier, under the double shadow of the Huguenot persecution in France and Locke's own political exile to Holland. He fled there to escape the wrath of the British Crown against his patron, the earl of Shaftesbury, who imprudently had criticized it. Locke held that persecution is inconsistent with the loving teachings of Christ and is a ploy for power under the guise of faith or national security. Expanding on Castellio's and Lilburne's distinctions between church and state, he distinguishes between government, which is to secure "civil goods" (life, liberty, security, health, and property), and church, which is concerned with the soul. About government, citizens must come to some agreement. About God, men will disagree. But as no man can be certain of the right path to salvation, none can judge another's beliefs. Each "is orthodox to itself and erroneous or heretical to others."[6] From this Locke argues that churches should be free from state control, indeed "free and voluntary." This is a call for both freedom of conscience and church-state separation.

By the eighteenth century, arguments to separate church from state — to protect the churches — had a solid dossier of support. But these arguments were soon turned on their heads, first in France. Rather than a way to protect minority churches from the state, church-state separation became a way to protect the state from the church. The flip occurred in the buildup to the French Revolution. Since church and state elites had worked together against commoners, religion was seen as monarchy's enforcer and incompatible with rule by the people. France's democratizers responded with a double attack against cross and crown. As they removed the aristocracies from power, so too did they remove the churches. Church-state separation thus became a way to keep the church's hands off France's infant democracy, and religion became suspect as inherently antidemocratic.

Ironically, the territorialization of religion, which at first had empowered established churches, led to their demise. For it left Europe's democratizers, especially in France, with this logic: from territorialization, there are two terms, church and state. Church, a partner to the oppressive state, is incompatible with a democratic one; therefore, for states to democratize, church must be cleaved from state and privatized, and in the end will fade.

---

6. *The Political Writings of John Locke,* ed. D. Wootton (New York: Mentor, 1993), pp. 65, 67, 68, 71-91.

France's story did not immediately generalize to all of Europe, where the process of democratization differed from region to region. In England, for instance, hostilities with revolutionary France made the British more conservative, and British patriotism became framed by the idea that God blesses Britain's efforts against the radicals across the channel. Anticlericalism was thus less a feature of the British Enlightenment and democratization at this time. Yet gradually, through much of Europe, suspicion of religion entered eighteenth- and nineteenth-century cultural currents.[7]

This was not the case in America, where the churches were rarely in league with an oppressive political system. When Americans overthrew their monarchist masters, they had one prong of attack, against the British state — not two prongs, against an oppressive state and a state church. Britain's established church was not America's church. Indeed, America had not a single church but, owing to multifaithed immigration, an ever-increasing array of grassroots, populist denominations — especially after the First Great Awakening of the 1730s and 1740s — a festival of breakaway churches and unorthodox preaching by untrained men (and women). Even in those colonies that had established churches, such as Massachusetts and Connecticut, the need to attract immigrant talent made pluralism a fact of life and weakened the hold of established religion. Unconnected to the Crown or its chosen church, America's churches supported the revolution and republican self-rule.[8] It was the Baptist John Leland who wrote, "Rebellion to tyrants is obedience to God."[9] The Presbyterian Benjamin Rush in 1791 wrote to the Baptist minister Elhanan Winchester, "republican forms of government are the best repositories of the Gospel."[10]

Because of multifaithed immigration and the Awakening's explo-

---

7. Late-nineteenth-century Europe saw a left-wing Christianity that worked with socialist movements; in the twentieth century, progressive churches joined the European New Left. But while these movements saw that helping others was godly work, none departed from the Enlightenment principle that politics is the purview of rational debate, not the imponderables of church doctrine.

8. That is, checks and balances and a three-tiered government: an executive, a legislature, and popular participation.

9. *Life, Journals, and Correspondence of Rev. Manasseh Cutler,* 2 vols. (Cincinnati: Ohio University Press, 1888), 2:66-67.

10. Rush to Winchester, November 12, 1791, in *Letters of Benjamin Rush,* ed. L. H. Butterfield, 2 vols. (Princeton: Princeton University Press, 1951), 1:611-12.

sion of religious groups, America did not share Europe's logic. There were not two terms, "church" and "state," but three: "church," "state," and "civil society" — where much of America's religious experience took place. Since church was not a partner to an oppressive state, it was not incompatible with a democratic one. It did not have to privatize or fade to ensure democratization. Indeed, religion in eighteenth- and nineteenth-century America kept its positive valence, and church-state separation retained a double purpose: not only to protect state from church but also to protect church from state. Said another way, locating religion extrastate put it not on the monarch's side but on the people's, and saved its reputation.

America located its churches in the civil sphere, protected from the state, for reasons idealistic and pragmatic. First, as many early immigrants came in search of freedom of conscience, they retained the nonconformist's interest in shielding their beliefs. For these settlers, faith was the inspiration, not the problem. States (and state churches) were the problem, and these recent beneficiaries of religious freedom wanted to see the state firmly constrained. Roger Williams was perhaps the most passionate seventeenth-century advocate of church-state separation, though his ardor went unappreciated by theocratic Massachusetts, which expelled him in 1635-36. In *The Bloudy Tenent of Persecution for Cause of Conscience* (1644), Williams argued that Jesus' teachings, in contrast to Mosaic law, distinguished between the political and religious arenas. Government pertained to the defense of individuals, property, and peace. The church was concerned with "spirituall and Soul-causes, which could never be decided by man."[11] Thus, he held, individuals should be free to choose their beliefs and churches should be free from the state.[12]

Williams can be seen as a republican *avant la lettre*, and his *Bloudy Tenent*, a sister work to Locke's *Letter concerning Toleration*. Both books had political effects. One was the charter of Rhode Island, which Charles II granted to Williams in 1663, six years before freedom of conscience was inscribed into Carolina's charter by Locke and the first earl of Shaftesbury. The Rhode Island charter guaranteed full religious lib-

11. R. Williams, *The Bloudy Tenent of Persecution for Cause of Conscience* (1644), in *The Complete Writings of Roger Williams* (New York: Russell and Russell, 1963), pp. 153-60, 250, 343.

12. Williams, *The Bloudy Tenent* (1963), pp. 79-81.

erty, holding that "no person within the said colony shall hereafter be in any wise molested or called in question for any difference in opinion in matters of religions."[13] It was also Williams who gave America its famous "wall" between church and state. Complaining about church-state collusion in Massachusetts, he wrote that such mingling punctured "a gap in the hedge or wall of Separation between the Garden of the Church and the Wilderness of the World."[14] When Thomas Jefferson repeated the phrase in 1802, he was cribbing from Williams.

In 1639, Williams underwent adult rebaptism in Rhode Island. He is often considered the founder of the American Baptist confession. As Baptists had long been the whipping boy of Europe's established churches, it's not surprising that they became defenders of freedom of conscience and church-state separation in America. In 1774, as the nation was setting out its founding principles, another Baptist, Isaac Backus, appeared before the Massachusetts and Continental congresses to make sure church would be kept outside the state.[15] He had become alarmed at a Massachusetts tax to support the Congregationalist church — for him a specter of religious establishment that had to be nipped in the bud. After the revolution, yet another Baptist, John Leland, put it plainly in 1790: "The notion of a Christian commonwealth should be exploded forever."[16] An established church was out, and government, he continued, "should protect every man in thinking and speaking freely."[17]

A second, more pragmatic motive for keeping religion separate from state emerged from the rough nature of America's settlement. Early Americans needed every helping hand to survive. To lure the multifaithed across the seas, they advertised a government that neither persecuted nor discriminated by faith. America's "perfect equality and freedom among all religious denominations," Tench Coxe of Pennsylvania declared, would lure Europe's persecuted dissenters; "they will at

13. See J. Wilson and D. Drakeman, eds., *Church and State in American History: Key Documents, Decisions, and Commentary from the Past Three Centuries,* 3rd ed. (Boulder, Colo.: Westview Press, 2003), pp. 30, 31.

14. R. Williams, *The Bloudy Tenent of Persecution for Cause of Conscience,* ed. R. Groves (Macon, Ga.: Mercer University Press, 2001), p. xxiv.

15. See Backus's *Appeal to the Public for Religious Liberty* (1773).

16. F. Church, ed., *The Separation of Church and State: Writings on a Fundamental Freedom by America's Founders* (Boston: Beacon Press, 2004), p. 92.

17. Church, *Separation,* p. 71.

once cry out, America is the *'land of promise.'"*[18] Even the Massachusetts theocracy by the 1640s had to accept non-Puritans to keep the colony going. And even in colonies with established churches[19] and religious tests for office, arguing for religious exclusion became increasingly unproductive in a nation of immigrants struggling to get on its feet. Maryland passed its Religious Toleration Act, applying to all Trinitarian Christians, in 1649. Pennsylvania, Rhode Island, and Carolina were, since their inceptions, experiments in toleration. In eighteenth-century America, religious exclusion was increasingly a losing cause.

A third reason for setting religion extrastate was that this was where most things happened in America. Because of sparse settlement and thin government, people had to do most things for themselves, or in voluntary groups, as little state structure existed to do it for them. As Tocqueville noted, America's economic and social structures developed first locally, in the civil sphere. Only later did state and national structures emerge. So too for the churches. Far from being territorialized from the top down — set up and propped up by the reigning government — churches were increasingly local and populist, and more so after the First Great Awakening. The marketplace of confessions, a distant dream for Castellio, was in America a bazaar.

To be sure, locating religion outside the state in civil society was not the only way to protect freedom of conscience or lure immigrants. A welcoming monarch with a tolerant state church would do as well. In the same century as America's founding, Frederick the Great built up Prussia on just this idea. Religious toleration lured Huguenots, Jews, and other religious minorities into Frederick's lands — to Prussia's great economic benefit. But America's church-state separation was also effective in protecting minority religions and attracting immigrants — and it had the advantage of being codified in law, not dependent on the kindness of monarchs. The First Amendment to the Constitution states that "Congress shall make no law respecting an establishment of

---

18. Merrill Jensen, ed., *The Documentary History of the Ratification of the Constitution,* vol. 18, ed. J. Kaminski and G. Saladino, Commentaries on the Constitution, public and private: 10 May to 13 September 1788 (Madison: Wisconsin Historical Society Press, 1997), pp. 278-85.

19. After America's earliest settlement in Jamestown nearly foundered just three years after its establishment in 1606, London dispatched Sir Thomas Gates to impose martial law and religious observance on the wayward community; nonconformity was a capital offense in seventeenth-century Connecticut and Virginia.

religion, or prohibiting the free exercise thereof" — which roughly means: *"Our many religions flourish in the civil sphere without religious war or crippling persecution. This keeps the peace and the immigrants coming. And government shall not mess this up."* This does not mean that there were no efforts postindependence to maintain established churches in some American states. It just means that those efforts failed.

Freedom of Conscience and Church-State Separation: The Evangelical Contribution

Support for freedom of conscience and church-state separation was found broadly in early America. Yet evangelicals were especially enthusiastic. As dissenters from Europe's established churches, they were — by theology and history — individualist, anti-authoritarian, and suspicious of government. Historically, they had been persecuted by Europe's religious establishment and thus favored church-state separation. Theologically, their emphasis on the individual's relationship with Jesus, individualist Bible reading, and the priesthood of all believers made them insist on freedom of conscience as well.

Indeed, the individualist emphasis created a third demand for freedom of conscience — a doctrinal one — that dovetailed with the political demand (freedom from persecution) and the economic demand (the need for immigrants). The doctrinal demand begins first with individualist Bible reading and the priesthood of all believers, which fueled an animus against established churches and wariness of authorities, including government. With that came evangelical insistence on freedom of conscience, which was explicit — and successful. If Roger Williams in the seventeenth century had to fight theocratic Massachusetts with his Bible-reading, *sola Scriptura* argument, the fight was a downhill battle by the time of the First Great Awakening. The appeal of populist evangelical preaching made it clear to any lingering statists that religion, like much else in America, was grass roots and rather immune to control by the states or state churches.

Evangelical doctrine about salvation also dovetailed with freedom of conscience and church-state separation. With the eighteenth-century popularization of Arminian doctrine by the brothers Charles and John Wesley, the Calvinist emphasis on God's grace was reimagined to accent man's role in his redemption. Arminianism holds that man's free will is given by God's prevenient grace (grace before redemption). Free will allows man to sin — but also to choose Jesus' way and so achieve not only forgiveness but also Christian perfection even in this world. In short, though God moves men's hearts, Arminianism accents man's critical step in salvation: accept Jesus, choose his way, and you are saved. This God-to-man shift gave great importance to individual will and the need to protect it from the pressures of a state or state church. Arminianism became a fundament of American Methodism, the most popular confession of the nineteenth century. (In 1800, there were roughly 65,000 Methodists in the United States, and by 1850 over 1,250,000; in the latter nineteenth century, Methodists increased from 1,250,000 to 5,500,000.)[20] With influence far beyond its members, it both reflected and contributed to America's anti-authoritarianism and to its defense of the individual.

Doctrinal support for church-state separation came also from the evangelical understanding of the human and divine realms. Evangelicals, like most Christians, hold that human governments are part of God's creation to maintain order and keep the peace. Yet the relevant Bible passage, Romans 13:1, states that God orders or organizes governments for his purposes; he does not validate them. All are human and in one way or another fallen. The kingdoms of the world may thus never be confused with the kingdom of God. From the separation of divine and earthly kingdoms, the step to church-state separation is not long. Moreover, God's kingdom, known to man through Jesus' teachings, is the standard by which evangelicals judge human conduct. This standard of necessity sets evangelicals apart from government, which has worldly, self-interested grounds for assessing human events. To maintain their ethical stance, evangelical churches must be extrastate.

Evangelical support notwithstanding, the realization of church-state separation took some time. New York, for instance, held a blasphemy trial as late as 1811. Nonetheless, the Virginia statute of religious freedom was implemented within a decade of Jefferson's penning it in 1777. The 1797 Treaty of Tripoli with Muslim North Africa declared that "the Government of the United States of America is not, in any

---

20. See E. Gaustad, *Historical Atlas of Religion in America* (New York: Harper and Row, 1962), p. 78; E. Gaustad and P. Barlow, *New Historical Atlas of Religion in America* (New York: Oxford University Press, 2001), p. 374.

sense, founded on the Christian religion."[21] Patrick Henry's proposal for a religious tax in Virginia was defeated. Luther Martin's argument for Constitutional recognition of Christianity was rejected. Massachusetts was the last state to disestablish religion in 1833. By the beginning of the nineteenth century, state churches were gone from both national and state governments.

And all to the benefit of the churches. For positioned outside of government, they continued to be seen as a force for good — untainted by political corruption on one hand and associated with optimistic, anti-authoritarian individualism on the other. Church leaders were aware of the extrastate advantage. The Reverend Wainwright of Auburn, New York, whom Tocqueville visited on his legendary journey, noted that churches, if they participated in government, would be treated as political parties were — persuasive to some and attacked by others. But outside government, their influence was transcendent. Lyman Beecher, among the most prominent religious figures of the early nineteenth century, had a chance to test this idea. He fought against Connecticut's plan to disestablish Congregationalism in 1818, fearing it would weaken religion. But within two years, he admitted that church-state separation had led to a religious resurgence. Churches, lacking the imprimatur — and dullness — of being "official," had to make their ideas relevant to the public. "Revivals now began to pervade the state," he wrote, calling disestablishment and civil society religion "the best thing that ever happened to the state of Connecticut."[22]

If Lyman Beecher had to be persuaded of church-state separation, evangelicals, as we've seen, were ahead of him as advocates of civil-society voluntarism and sometimes populist radicalism. Many were antifederalist, antibanker, pro-squatter Jeffersonians, and populist Jacksonians. Ministers were often central in agrarian antilandlord unrest. Some supported black churches and women preachers.[23] Between 1800 and 1840, over one hundred women, mostly Methodist, Free Will Baptist, Disciples of Christ, and Cumberland Presbyterian, were engaged as ministers or itinerant preachers. Evangelical associations — in-

21. "Treaty of Peace and Friendship, Signed at Tripoli November 4, 1796," Yale Law School, Lillian Goldman Law Library, http://avalon.law.yale.edu/18th_century/bar1796t.asp.

22. Wilson and Drakeman, *Church and State*, p. 87.

23. See C. Brekus, *Strangers and Pilgrims, 1740-1845: Female Preaching in America* (Chapel Hill: University of North Carolina Press, 1998).

novative and voluntary — became the backbone of America's civil society. They ran the gamut — supporting free public education and slavery in the South, supporting free public education but opposing slavery in the North. They opposed Sunday mail, the expulsion of the Christianized Cherokee from their land, Chinese foot-binding, and Indian suttee. From 1789 to 1828, the U.S. government spent $3.6 million on infrastructure development while the thirteen leading voluntary associations, many evangelical, spent $2.8 million on their projects. The largest U.S. government operation at this time was the postal service, but by 1850 evangelical churches had double the employees of the postal service and twice as many facilities, and raised three times as much money.[24]

In this anti-authoritarian, do-it-yourself atmosphere, evangelical preaching synthesized the tones of a second Reformation with those of a second Revolution. Orthodoxies might be ignored; a variety of doctrines were combined with each other and with the social causes of the day. Mysticism might be combined with populist politics, biblical literalism with ecstatic experiences. In 1843, the *Methodist Quarterly Review* boasted about being "unsparing iconoclasts"[25] ready to question any received wisdom.

Indeed, the more radically experimental and populist evangelical churches were, the more popular they often became. The number of Methodist churches rose from 20 in 1770 to 19,883 in 1860, a 994.1 multiple of increase. The number of Baptist churches rose from 150 in 1770 to 12,150 in 1860, an 81 multiple of increase. By the middle of the nineteenth century, the evangelical Methodist and Baptist churches accounted for two-thirds of Protestants in the United States.[26] Through the same period, the more traditional Congregationalist churches in-

---

24. M. Noll, *America's God: From Jonathan Edwards to Abraham Lincoln* (New York: Oxford University Press, 2002), pp. 182, 200-201.

25. J. Moorhead, "Prophecy, Millennialism, and Biblical Interpretation in Nineteenth-Century America," in *Biblical Hermeneutics in Historical Perspective*, ed. M. Burrows and P. Rorem (Grand Rapids: Eerdmans, 1991), p. 297.

26. See also R. Carwardine, "Methodist Ministers and the Second Party System," in *Rethinking Methodist History: A Bicentennial Historical Consultation*, ed. R. Richey and K. Rowe (Nashville: Kingswood Books, 1985), p. 134; T. Smith, *Revivalism and Social Reform: American Protestantism on the Eve of the Civil War* (New York: Abingdon, 1957), p. 22; C. Goss, *Statistical History of the First Century of American Methodism* (New York: Carlton and Porter, 1866), p. 106.

creased by a factor of 3.6, Anglican by a factor of 6, German Reformed by 4.7, Dutch Reformed by 4.4.[27]

In promoting their novel doctrines and populist religio-economics, evangelicals relied heavily on the freedom of speech, freedom of religion, and disestablishment clauses of the First Amendment. That amendment was their protection from persecution and their ticket into the marketplace of ideas. "No group," writes Randall Balmer, professor of American religious history at Barnard College, "has profited more from the First Amendment and the disestablishment of religion in America than evangelicals." He notes, "They operated outside of the New England religious establishment in the seventeenth and eighteenth centuries, and the explosion of Baptist growth in the nineteenth century would have been impossible — or, at least considerably more difficult — without the protections of the First Amendment."[28]

After the Civil War, evangelicalism competed with urbanization and industrialization but remained a potent, often radical force politically and intellectually. Between 1860 and 1900, membership in the major Protestant groups, many evangelical, tripled.[29] Continuing their theological innovation, evangelicals applied nineteenth-century Romanticism to Scripture. Romanticism focused on the soul's deepest yearnings as expressed in literature and art. Through its lens, the Bible could be read as a work of metaphorical and poetic truth. This meant, among other things, that each "day" in the biblical creation story could be seen as the symbol of an era, which allowed some if not all evangelicals to accommodate evolution. Also under Romanticism's influence, the classic God-the-judge was replaced by God-the-loving-Father, which was persuasive to an America less stern, more adventurous, and more encouraging than the countries from which many immigrants had come.[30]

In the late nineteenth century, the wretched working conditions

27. R. Finke and R. Stark, "How the Upstart Sects Won America: 1776-1850," *Journal for the Scientific Study of Religion* (March 1989): 30; Noll, *America's God,* p. 166.

28. R. Balmer, *Thy Kingdom Come: How the Religious Right Distorts the Faith and Threatens America — an Evangelical's Lament* (New York: Basic Books, 2006), pp. 185, 61.

29. G. Marsden, *Understanding Fundamentalism and Evangelicalism* (Grand Rapids: Eerdmans, 1991), p. 12.

30. For more detailed discussion of Romanticism in evangelical thought, see D. Bebbington, *The Dominance of Evangelicalism: The Age of Spurgeon and Moody* (Downers Grove, Ill.: InterVarsity, 2005).

under robber baron capitalism spurred evangelicals to greater social activism. Dwight L. Moody, perhaps the most popular preacher of the day, lambasted business for paying starvation wages and he set up schools for young women and men (in that order). He founded the Student Volunteer Movement, which sent thousands of young people to build hospitals and schools overseas as they carried the word of Jesus. Throughout the nation, evangelicals threw their political support behind the populist leader William Jennings Bryan, who ran for president three times on a pro-worker, pro-farmer platform (1896, 1900, 1908). Under the leadership of Walter Rauschenbusch, evangelicals developed the Social Gospel, which ran programs for the poor and provided one of America's earliest critiques of laissez-faire capitalism. "Nations do not die by wealth," Rauschenbusch noted, "but by injustice." The church was obligated "to act as the tribune of the people."[31] Rauschenbusch's book *Christianity and the Social Crisis* was hostile to Jews and Catholics, and reflects the era's naive view that Protestantism would bring wealth, health, and democracy worldwide. Yet, along with Upton Sinclair's novel *The Jungle*, it helped kindle the Progressive Era of economic reform. It influenced the thinking of Martin Luther King Jr. as late as the 1950s.

As before the Civil War, radical views such as these made evangelicals, Baptists in particular, enduring advocates of freedom of conscience and church-state separation — though they were at this point numerous, popular, and in no danger of persecution. To be sure, late-nineteenth- and early-twentieth-century Baptists often harbored anti-Catholic and racist feelings and were active in some causes that blurred church and state. The Sabbatarian movements, for instance, sought state enforcement of Sunday no-work rules.[32] Nonetheless, George Washington Truett, president of the Southern Baptist Convention from 1927 to 1929, proudly claimed disestablishment and religious freedom as "pre-eminently a Baptist achievement." He objected to church reliance on any state power. "God wants free worshipers and no other

31. W. Rauschenbusch, *Christianity and the Social Crisis* (1907), ed. D. Ottati (Louisville: Westminster John Knox, 1992), pp. 265, 284; the book was rereleased in 2007 by HarperOne publishers as *Christianity and the Social Crisis in the 21st Century: The Classic That Woke Up the Church*, with commentaries by Cornel West, Jim Wallis, and Richard Rorty, who is Rauschenbusch's grandson.

32. Ironically, no-work rules based on religious claims dovetailed with the demands of the labor movements, as workers could get at least one day off.

kind. Christ's religion needs no prop of any kind from any worldly source, and to the degree that it is thus supported is a millstone hanged about its neck."[33] By this time, Truett's rejection of church-state intermingling echoed over two hundred years of Baptist and evangelical conviction.

33. C. D. Weaver, *In Search of the New Testament Church: The Baptist Story* (Macon, Ga.: Mercer University Press, 2008), p. 177.

chapter 3

The Evangelical Turn to Conservatism

Reuniting Church and State?

Freedom of conscience, anticapitalist critique, and church-state separation are not the tradition associated with the evangelicals of the last century. According to David Kinnaman and Gabe Lyons, two evangelical researchers, evangelicals are more often associated with opposition to abortion and gay marriage, support for laissez-faire capitalist economics, and a judgmental approach to others.[1] Two shifts in evangelical concerns are responsible, one in the early twentieth century and another beginning in the late 1960s.

The Early Twentieth Century

By the turn of the twentieth century, significant numbers of evangelicals felt that the Social Gospel movement was spending too much time on charity and not enough on saving souls. The concern — a shift from a this-worldly to an otherworldly emphasis or the feeling that a choice had to be made between the two — grew under the influence of Romanticism, which ironically had earlier lent support to social welfare activities. While some evangelicals took Romanticism to mean a loving, fatherly God and forgiveness (leading to charitable activity), others were captured by the drama of Romantic apocalypticism. With the world

---

1. D. Kinnaman and G. Lyons, *Unchristian: What a New Generation Really Thinks about Christianity and Why It Matters* (Grand Rapids: Baker, 2007).

coming to an end, they held, improving earthly conditions was a distraction from the mission to evangelize.

Three new strains of evangelicalism developed under this apocalyptic focus. Premillenarianism held that Christ would return to earth before (pre) the thousand years of peace and prosperity, but until his arrival, the world would decline into disaster. As many souls as possible needed to be saved to prepare for Christ's return. A second strain, dispensationalism, held that history was divided into phases or dispensations. The present one would soon end amid an apocalyptic disaster of the sort described in the book of Revelation. Social and political causes were thus diversions from the proper focus on the soul. Third, Holiness doctrine held that ardent believers could – with enough ecstatic intensity – reach unity with God even in this life. One's focus should therefore be on achieving such a union and not on the mundane world. While there had been a similar idea in Arminianism and Methodism, Holiness doctrine added a twist. Whereas Methodism required some enduring evidence of a person's sanctified state – moral living, for instance – Holiness doctrine proposed the Romantic idea that one could achieve unity with God in a flash, rapturous moment. Reaching it became a focus of the Keswick and Pentecostal movements, and occupation with earthly things was thought trivial by comparison.

The trend away from worldly engagement was reinforced by fear of the new Bible criticism imported from Germany. Relying on new philological and archaeological scholarship, new Bible criticism invigorated some evangelicals but alarmed others, in particular the more populist believers. For centuries, they had gotten along with relatively untutored, literalist Bible-reading by the common man and woman. Suddenly they felt outstripped by elitism. They rejected new exegetical methods amid a general wariness of the modern world and defended their homegrown ways. Ironically, the 150-year tradition of progressive anti-elitism suddenly – in the face of new exegetical methods – set evangelicals in a rearguard action of conserving the past.

Tensions between populists and intellectuals were aggravated by industrialization. Evangelicals in the relatively rural, less developed South and West deepened their resentment against the wealthier, industrial, more cosmopolitan North – an animus that had been substantial since the Civil War. They saw Northeastern cities as corrupted by eastern-European immigration, the Bolsheviks it brought, and after

World War I, with Jazz Age moral decline. Insisting on their simple, up-
right Christianity, they shifted from what had been progressive anti-
elitism toward a conservative, sometimes nativist, stance. From 1910 to
1915, the oil magnates Lyman and Milton Stewart subsidized free distribution of a pamphlet series, *The Fundamentals,* to bring America back to
basics — back to its anti-elitist populist traditions. The series gave the
world the term "fundamentalism."

Divisions among evangelicals played themselves out in the fight
about evolution. Evangelicals, from anti-authoritarian conviction, had
long held that God made it possible for every man and woman to understand creation through means available to all: the five senses,
commonsense reasoning, etc. They embraced a Baconian empiricism,
with its open-ended fact collection and induction from evidence. Such
scientific methods, they held, were man's God-given tools to appre-
hend the world. Under proper empirical inquiry, nature's facts and biblical facts would lead to a common understanding of the universe. Indeed, eighteenth- and nineteenth-century evangelicals had considered
themselves modern empiricists with a hankering for evidence. Their
main philosophical enemy was rationalism, with its reliance on un-
proved first principles rather than on observable, measurable phenom-
ena. "We deal with facts," declared the *Record,* a leading Anglican evangelical newspaper in mid-nineteenth century, not with "the vain
speculations of romancing rationalists."[2]

Knowledge, moreover, was expected to advance with time. Before
Darwin, many evangelicals followed William Paley's argument that
since something as complex as the world suggests a plan or design,
there must be a designer.[3] After Darwin, many evangelicals accommodated his ideas into theirs. B. B. Warfield of Princeton, for instance,
along with Henry Ward Beecher, Lyman Beecher's son and perhaps the
most influential minister of midcentury, developed a Christian Darwinism. Consistent with Christian doctrine dating back to Augustine,
it held that what science discovers is God's plan. Hugh Miller's popular
"day-age" interpretation of Genesis held that each day of the biblical
creation was in fact an "age" of long duration, as Darwin described.
The leading American theological journal, *Bibliotheca Sacra,* after reject-

2. *Record,* January 2, 1863, London.
3. W. Paley, *Evidences of Christianity* (1794).

ing Darwin in 1872, six years later declared that Darwinism "gives us higher and nobler view of the Creator."[4]

Others did not agree, holding to more literalist interpretations of the Bible. Thomas Huxley and John Tyndall, Darwin's popularizers, were trounced in several evangelical publications of the 1870s; Charles Hodge published his broadside *What Is Darwinism?* in 1874. Between 1878 and 1906, nearly every American Protestant denomination endured at least one heresy trial, typically of a theologian who accommodated evolution. Billy Sunday, the most popular preacher at the turn of the twentieth century, campaigned against it with flair. When Prohibition became law in 1919 and temperance was no longer a national issue, routing evolution became a banner evangelical cause. In 1923, George McCready Price published *The New Geology*, which held that God created the world six to eight thousand years ago and used the flood to create older-looking geological formations. Though the reasons for this flinty ruse remained unclear, the book became an anti-Darwinist best seller.

Two years later, in the the attention-getting Scopes trial, evangelicals were lampooned in the press, notably by the writer H. L. Mencken, and made to look like backward provincials unsuited to America's postwar, international role. Bruised by the public mockery, many evangelicals withdrew into their communities until after World War II, when slowly, under the radar of much of the nation, they began to rebuild their numbers and their interest in politics.[5] In 1942, the National Association of Evangelicals (NAE) was founded; within five years, its influence extended well beyond its 1,300,000 members from thirty denominations. Youth for Christ selected one of its young ministers, Billy Graham, as its first full-time employee, to bring evangelicalism to the mainstream. Within a decade, he had. Youth for Christ soon had over a million constituents and held nine hundred rallies in its first year.

From 1965 to the Present

This postwar, revived movement found itself in much the same surprising position as evangelicals had at the turn of the twentieth century.

4. F. Gardiner, "Darwinism," *Bibliotheca Sacra* (April 1872): 288; F. Gardiner, "The Bearing of Recent Scientific Thought upon Theology," *Bibliotheca Sacra* (1878): 65-66.
5. See J. Carpenter, "From Fundamentalism to the New Evangelical Coalition," in *Evangelicalism in Modern America*, ed. G. Marsden (Grand Rapids: Eerdmans, 1984), p. 15.

The anti-authoritarian, individualist populism that had been progressive for two hundred years was suddenly on the defensive — and on the conservative end of the political spectrum. After the 1964 defeat of Republican presidential candidate Barry Goldwater, evangelicals of the Greatest Generation looked around and saw an America threatened by world communism, by Democratic failure in Vietnam, and by antiwar protests — to them, a lack of nerve and sense of responsibility for world freedom. Worse was the "self-indulgent" youth counterculture, the hippies and yippies. Worse still were the civil rights movement and Lyndon Johnson's Great Society antipoverty program, which expanded federal government, gave "handouts" to the poor, and so undermined America's tradition of individualist anti-authoritarian self-reliance.

Against these, evangelicals for the first time joined forces with a political party, the Republicans, to direct the country back to its moral probity and can-do pride — and back, they held, to fighting the most dangerous threat to self-responsibility: godless communism. Because of evangelical support for the armed forces, the United States Military Academy in 1972 gave its Sylvanus Thayer Award to the Reverend Billy Graham for embodying the academy's values of duty, honor, and country.[6]

Yet, at the same time, a different sort of evangelicalism also emerged in the 1960s — or rather, two different sorts. One, among black evangelicals, spearheaded the civil rights movement and had a profound effect on the country. The second, among a small group of mostly white evangelicals, echoed the Social Gospel and found a home in the Sojourners movement. Yet until 2005, this echo of the Social Gospel was muted amid the enthusiasm of what became know as the evangelical right.

What perhaps best characterizes postsixties evangelicalism is irony. In well-meaning efforts to reassert anti-authoritarian, self-reliant moral conduct, evangelicals lost sight of self-reliant, church-state separation and hitched themselves to the authority of the state. The irony emerged as early as 1947, when the Supreme Court ruled that church-state separation applies not only to the national government but also to the states.[7] This put evolution into public schools and took

6. A. Bacevich, *The New American Militarism* (New York: Oxford University Press, 2005), p. 140.

7. *Everson v. Board of Education* (1947).

prayer out.[8] (Students may voluntarily pray, but school and state authorities may not mandate or endorse school prayer.) Evangelicals saw the court's decisions as corrosive to the nation's morals and as Washington's interference with local school boards. Yet to change policy, the churches would have to get involved with schools and possibly get into government — which violated the evangelical tradition of church-state separation. Faced with the dilemma of how to respond — keep church-state separation or prayer — most evangelicals chose prayer. But this meant they were arguing for sectarian activities in public schools and arguing that *government* implement them (further church-state blurring) over the objections of religious minorities — which violated the evangelical tradition of freedom of conscience.

One reason evangelicals found themselves with this dilemma is their earlier ubiquity. Throughout the nation's history, so present had religion been in the public sphere that few had noticed, much less objected, when religion was de facto present in public institutions. And no religion more so than popular evangelicalism. Schools were after all *public,* of and for the people, not *state* schools, as they were called in other countries. They would naturally have whatever the public sphere had, including religion. No one, evangelicals included, had to get into government to put religion anywhere, as it was already everywhere. As long as the two purposes of the neutral state were realized (procedurally unbiased government and freedom to practice one's faith), church-state separation seemed to be working, even with religion's de facto public presence. But this presence was Protestant, often evangelical. After the war and into the 1960s, when minorities called for inclusion in the public arena, the nation could not continue with default Protestant prevalence. Protestant school prayers imposed an unwanted religion on non-Protestant children. Prayer per se imposed on nonbelievers. To ensure religious freedom for all and to avoid untenable pressure on children, prayer could no longer be run by the schoolhouse.

Evangelicals were astonished at the logic: the right to freedom of religion could end in mandating its absence! The astonishment was repeated in the 1973 Supreme Court decision legalizing abortion. The Court held that "life begins at conception" is a religious belief that neutral government could not support. It certainly could not override a woman's civil right to control her body. Evangelicals were flummoxed:

---

8. *Epperson v. Arkansas* (1968).

the neutrality of government, meant to protect each person's moral traditions, led to the practice of immorality. As if to create a perfect storm, proposals to end the tax-exempt status of religious schools were added to the decade's mix. The government held that racially segregated schools, including religious ones, could not retain the tax exemptions they had as nonprofit entities. Loss of this exemption would have been financially crippling, and evangelicals — many of whom found racism repugnant — mobilized to protect the financial viability of their institutions, along with school prayer and the lives of the unborn.

This political mobilization fed into the already-smoldering "culture wars," with white evangelicals and Republicans coming together as the New Right. Evangelicals — antistatist and self-responsible — for the first time made common cause with Republican business interests, which too sought "small government" to limit state interference in the market. However sensible or practical, the coalition moved evangelicals from their position as extrastate advocates to positions inside the Republican Party and government — again, ironically, against antistatism and self-reliance.

For some, church-state separation collapsed. "Dominionists," or "Reconstructionists," set out to recast U.S. law as Mosaic.[9] Dominionism's founder, Rousas John Rushdoony, wrote, "The state has a duty to serve God, to be Christian, to be a part of God's kingdom, or else it shall be judged by him."[10] George Grant, former executive director of the influential Coral Ridge Ministries, further explained, "It is dominion we are after. Not just a voice. It is dominion we are after. Not just influence. It is dominion we are after. Not just equal time. It is dominion we are after. World conquest."[11]

For most evangelicals, however, church-state separation remained as much a part of America as ever. There is nothing illiberal or undemocratic about extrastate, civil society groups — including churches — lobbying, protesting, or electing representatives who share their views. Yet in these years, evangelical advocacy at times lost its traditional caution against becoming mechanisms of political parties or the state.

9. See R. J. Rushdoony, *The Institutes of Biblical Law* (Phillipsburg, N.J.: P&R Publishing, 1973).

10. R. J. Rushdoony, *Thy Kingdom Come: Studies in Daniel and Revelation* (Fairfax, Va.: Thoburn Press, 1978), pp. 39, 194.

11. See G. Grant, *The Changing of the Guard: Biblical Principles for Political Action* (Fort Worth, Tex.: Dominion Press, 1987), pp. 50-51.

That this was true of "the other side" in the culture wars did not make it untrue of evangelicals. In 1992, Pat Robertson, head of the influential Christian Coalition, told the *Denver Post*, "We want . . . as soon as possible to see a majority of the Republican Party in the hands of pro-family Christians."[12] In 1997, Ralph Reed — whom *Time* magazine called "the Right Hand of God" — described his electoral tactics: "I want to be invisible. I do guerilla warfare. I paint my face and travel at night. You don't know it's over until you're in a body bag. You don't know until election night."[13] Robertson and Reed were not unsuccessful: in the first administration of G. W. Bush, evangelicals served as House speaker, Senate and House majority leaders, and House majority whip. This provoked a backlash as many nonevangelicals saw it not as extrastate engagement with government but as slippage into government — or at least as an unduly moist hand-in-glove relationship that would slather America with evangelical mores.

The culture-war tinderbox of G. W. Bush's first term was faith-based social services. While medical and educational religious agencies had long received government funds, certain conditions had pertained: public funds could not be used for religious programming or for coreligionist hiring (hiring only those of a preferred faith, discriminating against other applicants). These were prohibited because they would make the neutral government a supporter of sectarian beliefs (through religious programming) and a discriminator by religion (through coreligionist hiring). While *privately* funded religious agencies may choose to hire only coreligionists for all staff positions, *publicly* funded religious agencies may hire coreligionists only for the positions of priest, pastor, rabbi, imam, etc. — the "ministerial exception" to the nation's nondiscrimination employment laws. All other staff in *publicly* funded agencies must be evaluated on professional merit, not faith.

These long-standing provisions had gone without much objection and were incorporated into President Bill Clinton's 1996 Charitable Choice program, which increased public funds for faith-based social services. The 1996 law read: "No public funds provided directly to

---

12. See Center for Religion, Ethics, and Social Policy, "The Rise of the Religious Right in the Republican Party," Theocracy Watch Web site, February 2005 (Ithaca, N.Y.: Cornell University, 2005).

13. J. Carney, "The Rise and Fall of Ralph Reed," *Time*, July 23, 2006.

institutions or organizations to provide services and administer programs . . . shall be expended for sectarian worship, instruction, or proselytization." But after G. W. Bush's election, pressure emerged to allow religious programming and coreligionist hiring even in publicly funded agencies. Pressure also emerged to change national voucher laws. Some states do not allow vouchers to be used for religious education since vouchers are funded by public tax dollars. After 2000, federal legislation was sought to override these state provisions.

Evangelicals again found themselves in an ironic position. In pressing for publicly funded coreligionist hiring, they seemed to violate their traditions of church-state separation. In pressing the national government to void state voucher laws, they seemed to disregard self-reliant local independence. Nonetheless, Bush declared that even publicly funded religious agencies may engage in coreligionist hiring. His 2002 executive order, the Equal Protection of the Laws for Faith-Based and Community Organizations, stated that the government would partner with agencies that practice it. Prohibiting coreligionist hiring, he argued, would violate a Clinton-era law (1993)[14] that prohibited government from placing "substantial burdens" on religious groups.

The reaction to Bush's executive order was swift and negative. So much so that John DiIulio, first director of Bush's Office of Faith-Based and Community Initiatives, called the Religious Right demands "disastrous."[15] None of those demands — not government funding for religious programming, not coreligionist hiring, and not new voucher laws — were put into law. Indeed, a June 2003 report by the Office of Faith-Based and Community Initiatives repeated that public monies may not be for used religious programming. It stated that religious organizations could apply for government grants only if they "do not discriminate against any person receiving a public service," do not demand "participation in religious activities as a condition for receiving services," and do not use public funds "to support inherently religious activities."[16] The

14. The Religious Freedom Restoration Act.

15. Pew Forum on Religion and Public Life, "John DiIulio Previews How Faith-Based Initiatives Would Change If Barack Obama Is Elected President," September 23, 2008; see also, DiIulio's account of this episode, J. DiIulio, *Godly Republic: A Centrist Blueprint for America's Faith-Based Future* (Berkeley and Los Angeles: University of California Press, 2007).

16. See DiIulio, *Godly Republic,* p. 138.

voucher demands were weakened to the point where one White House official called them "All hat and no cattle."[17] What remained at the end of the Bush presidency was a 2007 memo calling for coreligionist hiring, and a good deal of national confusion.

Indeed, the fracas created the sense that the nation was more divided than it was. Seventy-five percent of Americans opposed both coreligionist hiring and religious programming in publicly funded religious agencies.[18] Both the NAE, politically centrist, and Americans United for Separation of Church and State, politically progressive, agreed that coreligionist hiring is constitutional only in privately funded programs, as the practice had been for decades.[19] Once sparked, however, the political sniping grew into what DiIulio called "a surreal war."[20] Small parishes feared they would be forced to hire atheists and homosexuals while secularists feared that Bush would legalize employment discrimination.

This did not happen in the presidency of G. W. Bush, nor has it in that of his successor, Barack Obama. Yet, in part because of the fracas and in part because of government interest in supporting faith-based social services, questions remain regarding their use of public funds. These questions are among the most pressing of unresolved church-state issues, and they will be discussed, along with five others, in the next chapter.

A Sketch of Religion in America and among Evangelicals

Having come, in our brief historical sketch, to the Obama presidency, I'll end this chapter with an overview of current American and evangeli-

17. DiIulio, *Godly Republic,* p. 134.

18. See the following reports from Pew Forum on Religion and Public Life: "Faith-Based Funding Backed, but Church-State Doubts Abound," April 10, 2001; "Americans Struggle with Religion's Role at Home and Abroad," 2002; *Lift Every Voice: A Report on Religion in American Public Life,* 2002; "Many Americans Uneasy with Mix of Religion and Politics," August 24, 2006.

19. American Jewish Committee and the Feinstein Center for American Jewish History at Temple University, "In Good Faith: Government Funding of Faith-Based Social Services," in *Sacred Places: Civic Purposes; Should Government Help Faith-Based Charity?* ed. E. J. Dionne and M. H. Chen (Washington, D.C.: Brookings Institution Press, 2001), pp. 311-12.

20. DiIulio, *Godly Republic,* p. 133.

cal religious practice. In 2009, much was made of the American Religious Identification Survey,[21] which showed decreases in church affiliation and possibly in American religiosity overall. The number of Americans without religious affiliation has risen from 8 to 15 percent since 1990; the number of atheists or agnostics, from 1 million to 3.6 million.[22] Yet lack of church affiliation has never meant lack of religious belief or practice. In Puritan Salem, 83 percent of taxpayers by 1683 were unaffiliated. Moreover, in the 2009 survey, 20 percent of American "atheists" said they believed in God and 91 percent of the unaffiliated considered themselves religious or spiritual.

Overall, America's religiosity has shown itself to be stable. Surveys taken over the last quarter-century indicate 95 percent of Americans say they believe in God,[23] 85 percent say religion is "important" in their lives, and 78 percent find prayer important. Nearly 50 percent would disapprove if their child married an atheist, while only a third say the same of a Muslim.[24] Forty percent of Americans report weekly religious worship, and there remain over two hundred religious traditions, twenty sorts of Baptists alone.

A third of Americans identify as born-again Christians; between 1988 and 2003, the percentage of Protestants who considered themselves evangelical rose from 41 to 54 percent. Meanwhile, between 1960 and 2003, membership in mainline denominations fell by over 24 percent.[25] Evangelical churches have seen an influx of Latinos, both converts from Catholicism and those who remain Catholic but embrace evangelical, charismatic practices for a more personal relationship with an immanent God. Roughly 54 percent of Latinos are "renewalist."[26]

21. B. Kosmin and A. Keysar, *American Religious Identification Survey* (Hartford, Conn.: Trinity College, 2009).

22. D. Stone, "One Nation under God?" *Newsweek,* April 7, 2009.

23. See Pew Forum on Religion and Public Life, "An Overview of Religion and Science in the United States," November 5, 2009; see also, Pew Forum on Religion and Public Life, "U.S. Religious Landscape Survey," April 19, 2008.

24. P. Edgell, G. Joseph, and H. Douglas, "Atheists as 'Other': Moral Boundaries and Cultural Membership in American Society," *American Sociological Review* 71, no. 2 (2006): 211-34.

25. W. Mead, "God's Country?" *Foreign Affairs,* September/October 2006.

26. See "Separated Brothers: Latinos Are Changing the Nature of American Religion," *Economist,* July 16, 2009; Pew Forum on Religion and Public Life and the Pew Hispanic Center, "Changing Faiths: Latinos and the Transformation of American Religion," 2007.

Among Protestant Latinos, more than half are evangelical, with churches enough to create an umbrella organization, the National Hispanic Christian Leadership Conference, representing sixteen million born-again Christian and 34,218 congregations.[27]

Politically, white evangelicals have been a Republican bloc since the late 1960s. In the mid-1990s, the Christian Coalition, the predominant evangelical umbrella organization of the period, held a majority of leading positions in the Republican Party in eighteen states and had near majorities in thirteen others. In the 1996 and 2000 presidential elections, 62 percent of white evangelicals voted Republican.[28] In 2003, 74 percent supported the Iraq War compared to a little over 50 percent of nonevangelical Americans.[29] Seventy-two percent of evangelicals and 78 percent of "traditionalist evangelicals" believed preemptive war was justified.[30] In 2004, 78 percent of white evangelicals voted for Bush; 75 percent voted Republican in the 2010 midterms. Latino evangelicals are twice as likely as Latino Catholics to vote Republican.

Evangelicals are active at the nation's top universities, as they are in top corporations. Donations to Christian causes by evangelical CEOs and corporate presidents run from $30,000 to $15,000,000 per person, annually.[31] At the universities, the Christian Union, founded in 2002, aims at "reclaiming the Ivy League for Christ." A third of the 101 evangelical elite interviewed by sociologist Michael Lindsay in 2007 had attended one of the nation's twelve most highly selective universities. The college organization Campus Crusade for Christ, founded in 1951 at UCLA, has a staff of 26,000 people active in 191 countries and an an-

27. See www.nhclc.org.

28. M. Hout and A. Greeley, "A Hidden Swing Vote: Evangelicals," *New York Times,* September 4, 2004, A17.

29. S. Austin, "Faith Matters: George and Providence" (Political Research Associates, 2003).

30. F. Stockman, "Christian Lobbying Finds Successes: Evangelicals Help to Steer Bush Efforts," *Boston Globe,* October 14, 2004; J. Green, *The American Religious Landscape and Political Attitudes: A Baseline for 2004* (Washington, D.C.: Pew Forum on Religion and Public Life, [September] 2004), p. 34.

31. For interviews on the evangelical elite, including 101 evangelical CEOs, chairmen, and presidents of large companies (including Pepsi, Johnson & Johnson, and New York Life Insurance), see D. M. Lindsay, *Faith in the Halls of Power: How Evangelicals Joined the American Elite* (New York: Oxford University Press, 2007); see also Pew Forum on Religion and Public Life, "American Evangelicalism: New Leaders, New Faces, New Issues," May 6, 2008.

nual budget of $374 million.[32] Interestingly, its Yale chapter, 100 percent Caucasian twenty years ago, was 90 percent Asian American in 2008.[33]

Evangelical media programming accounts for roughly 85 percent of all religious programming in the United States and 75 percent of religious programming worldwide.[34] Domestically, evangelicals run six national TV networks and over two thousand radio stations. The Christian Broadcasting Network airs in fifty languages and ninety countries. The evangelical *WorldNetDaily* is among the ten most interlinked blogs. As we've seen, Rick Warren's *Purpose Driven Life,* according to *Publishers Weekly,* is the best-selling nonfiction hardback in publishing history. In fiction, Tim LaHaye's Left Behind series of apocalyptic thrillers became one of publishing's biggest sensations, with over sixty-five million sold. In 1998, the first four books in the series held the top four slots of the *New York Times* best-seller list; book ten in the series debuted in the number one slot.

The evangelicalism that moved into politics in the late 1960s has come into its second generation. While the political ethics and priorities of the older generation remain, new institutions and approaches develop, as is expectable in a maturing movement. One is Ralph Reed's new Faith and Freedom Coalition, founded in 2009. It aims at being "younger," more inclusive, and "less strident," with a "fiscal conservative message" on taxes and economic opportunity.[35] Another is "new evangelical" activism, which section II of this book describes. The final chapters of section I will look at church-state issues that remain unresolved in public debate and the courts.

32. "America's Religious Right: You Ain't Seen Nothing Yet," *Economist,* June 23, 2005; L. Goodstein and D. Kirkpatrick, "On a Christian Mission to the Top," *New York Times,* May 22, 2005.

33. Pew Forum on Religion and Public Life, "American Evangelicalism."

34. A. Hunter, *Evangelicalism: The Coming Generation* (Chicago: University of Chicago Press, 1987), p. 7.

35. D. Gilgoff, "Ralph Reed Launches New Values Group: 'Not Your Daddy's Christian Coalition,'" *U.S. News & World Report,* June 23, 2009; A. Sheinin, "Reed to Refashion Coalition," *Atlanta Journal-Constitution,* July 12, 2009.

Mark Batterson, Washington, D.C.

Mark Batterson, pastor at the National Community Church, Washington, D.C., runs a discussion series called "The Elephant in the Church — Everyone's Thinking It but Nobody's Saying It." On November 2, 2008, on the eve of the presidential election, the topic was politics. A video of the discussion was uploaded to the church's Web site; a shortened version of the text appears below.

Most people in our congregation eat, sleep, and drink politics. Some even smoke it — but don't inhale. . . . We made a decision to be apolitical as a church. We don't endorse candidates or parties. Jesus did not come to set up an earthly kingdom. He came to redeem us from sin, to set up a kingdom that would transcend politics, culture, borders, languages. "And the day is coming, when all the kingdoms of this world will be his." Revelation — "and he shall reign forever and ever."

So I'm going to talk about five biblical principles. The first is: Family comes first. Bottom line: We are an incredibly diversified congregation, lots of people on both sides of the political aisle. . . . But, Galatians 3:26-29, "You are all sons of God through faith in Jesus Christ. . . . There is neither Jew nor Greek, male nor female, slave nor free." We have our differences but we're called to love each other despite our differences.

The second principle: We are first and foremost citizens of a spiritual kingdom. Fighting injustice or alleviating poverty or fighting for the sick or for life are not political agendas. They're God's agenda. If the church was doing its job, if we cared about what God cares about, we wouldn't need government to do it for us. Donald Miller, the author of a great book, *Blue Like Jazz,* talks about an initiative from his church in Portland, the Advent Conspiracy. They were fed up with the commercialization of Christmas so they challenged people to quit spending so much money on themselves and give some of it away. They raised enough money to give a five hundred thousand dollar check to the mayor of Portland. How cool is that.

I believe God has strategically positioned people since the

Old Testament in positions of political power to make a difference: Joseph in Egypt, Daniel in Babylon, and Esther in Persia. But it's not about McCain's kingdom or Obama's kingdom. It's about the kingdom of Jesus Christ being advanced on earth.

Principle three: Don't pass judgment on disputable matters. I may not agree with all of someone's politics but I can appreciate their passion. We have a core value in our church: Conformity doesn't equal maturity. Principle four: If you don't vote, don't complain. The Lord said to Moses and Aaron, "I've heard the complaints of these grumbling Israelites." We need to quit complaining and become part of the solution. Final principle: Respect those in authority. Romans 13:1-7. If it's taxes, pay taxes. If it's respect and honor, then respect and honor. We as Christ followers need to operate in the spirit of humility and reconciliation. It changes the tone, the atmosphere. The church should model the unity and diversity that would get things done in a bipartisan way on Capitol Hill. Job 11:6: true wisdom has two sides. If we take the best of both parties we are better off as a country.

DAN LACICH BLOG:
"WHY AMERICA WAS NEVER A CHRISTIAN NATION"

This is a blog posting at *Provocative Christian Living*, by Dan Lacich, pastor of Distributed Sites, Northland Church, Florida, on November 13, 2008; you can find it on the Web at http://provocativechristian.wordpress.com/ 2008/11/13/why-america-was-never-a-christian-nation/.

In the wake of the [2008 presidential] election, all the debates, hype, and turmoil, it is clear that many Christians still do not understand what America is all about and what our place in it really is. I have seen numerous calls for a returning of America to a Christian nation. People; we never were a Christian nation! Was the country in some large way influenced by Christian principles? Absolutely. But it was equally influenced by the philosophical and political theories of European enlightenment which were anything but Christian. Were many of the founding fathers Christian. You bet. But many of them were anything but Christians.

But even if everyone of them was a radical follower of Jesus, that is irrelevant to the question of whether or not this is a Christian nation. What matters is what kind of government they established . . . all religions have equal standing before the law. We are a country designed to be sympathetic to religion but not adhering to or promoting one above another.

The fact is Christianity is a faith best practiced when it is not in power. It is a faith of the exile. For the first three hundred years our brothers and sisters living under Roman rule were outcasts. . . . And guess what? It worked. They changed the Roman world one heart at a time. Our faith is to be counter cultural. We are to be a light to the world. That means that we somehow stand apart, show a different way.

When we are in power, we have the same tendency as other humans. We let it go to our heads and we become intoxicated with power. Even the briefest of looks at the history of Christendom will show that when in power we will coerce and threaten people into conversion in ways that rival the most militant jihadist. That is in stark contrast to the servant lifestyle that Jesus demonstrated and calls us to. . . .

America is not a Christian nation. But it is a nation in which Christians have greater freedom and resources to celebrate and live their faith, as they see fit, than anyone ever before. Even in the "Christian" nations of the past, it was only certain types of Christians who had that freedom. If you belonged to the state church you were safe. If not, you could suffer worse than non-Christians in the same country.

In reality, nations are not Christian. Only living, breathing, men, women, and children are Christians. And we must learn to live our faith as exiles in this world, no matter what government we submit to. If we love the Lord our God with all our heart, mind, soul, and strength, and love our neighbor as ourselves, then many more will fall on their knees and worship Him and whether or not we are a "Christian" nation will be a moot point. Why? because our provocative lives will have changed the world.

Dan and Barbara Lacich, Florida

Dan and Barbara Lacich live in central Florida, where Barbara, who had considered working as a translator at the UN, now teaches Spanish. Their youngest son is studying Mandarin; the middle son is competent in Arabic; their oldest is fluent in German and Spanish; and Dan, a pastor at Northland Church, is studying Afrikaans to help him in his church work in South Africa. One of the things Dan describes about his work is the influence of cultural and language differences on the ability of people and groups to understand each other.

MP Is the mission work in your church today a change from your work in earlier years?

DL The Social Gospel developed at the end of the nineteenth century. Then there was a divorce between two things that the Bible never wanted to divorce: the care ministries and the proclamation of truth. But Jesus was pretty clear that loving God and loving your neighbor are supposed to be together. We're now recapturing something that got lost.

MP Why was it lost?

DL Because of fear. A lot of Christians didn't know how to deal with changes in the culture, with scientific advances, and they reacted in ways that were counterproductive. The generations now are more confident; they don't have to prove themselves. If we live out our beliefs, that will make a difference. Also, the Religious Right hasn't worked out very well. Not only didn't we get what we wanted, whatever that was, but it gave the impression that Christians are just angry people.

BL Who wants to be that?

DL There's a lot of discussion about the post-Christian era. Cultural Christianity is fading away — the day when you went to church because that's what everyone did. Some wrongly assume this means Christianity is losing influence. But the actual influence on people's lives is on the rise because the facade is not there anymore. Before Constantine,

Christians were not in power or the dominant cultural influence; they served from being "the lesser." As Christianity has less organizational influence — the post-Christian era — it faces what believers faced in the first centuries. How did they change the Roman world? It had to do with taking in the babies that Romans cast out, with caring for the sick when plague took over, even losing their own lives. Eventually, people wanted to be a part of that. Even if self-interest is involved — people want to be cared for when they're sick — they also see what happens when they're the caregivers.

MP It's not good for Christianity to be in power?

DL Absolutely not good.

BL It engenders laziness because people think someone else will take care of things — almost socialism: the government, my lawmaker, someone *else* is going to do it so I don't have to talk to my neighbor or be informed and involved. I translate that as, "I want to abdicate my responsibility for impacting those around me. I want to stay in my nice little world and I want everyone around me to be nice and clean with cookie-cutter behavior and morality."

DL That's not to say Christians should not be lawmakers, but if a Christian is going into politics, they have to care about issues of justice, oppression, and integrity — not try to get prayer in the schools again. The Bible asks the question, what is true religion? It answers itself by saying that it is the care of widows and orphans, the poor and hungry. That is simply a shorthand way of saying that what God really cares about is justice and compassion for people in need. It is reiterated in the Bible time and again. Nowhere does it say "you know you are a Christian because you are working to get prayer back in schools." Christian politicians need to be concerned about issues of justice because God is just, or about compassion because God is compassionate. That is the kind of thing that will change the world.

BL I wonder why anyone wants an overarching organization to set the rules, in the schools, for instance. We can't agree on styles of worship from one corner to the next. Why do we think government would have the answer?

DL Let's think this prayer issue through: in fairness to everyone, we should all get a chance. So Monday would be the Baptist day, Tuesday is Presbyterian day, Wednesday is the Jewish day, Thursday is the Hindu day, Friday is Muslim day. Suddenly people realize they don't want that. So how about we don't have any of it and we teach kids to pray at home.

I distinguish between a country influenced by Christian values and a country where Christianity is the religion of the land. Jesus said, "I came not to be served but to serve. Now you do the same." When you're in power, it's easy to be tempted to be served. Look at the incredible greed of major ministry leaders who have million-dollar empires.

Leadership is influence. It should not mean that I'm getting this law passed but rather that I'm making a difference in people's lives. We don't have to agree with someone on every issue in order to work with them on one issue. That's hard for some Christians to grasp. Who knows, maybe working together and showing them the love of Christ might cause them to reevaluate. And there are all the things we will learn from them.

MP Is it new to be partnering with religious or secular agencies you don't agree with?

DL On the abortion issue, our approach is, let's make what progress we can by working together to reduce abortion. That doesn't mean we're giving up our ultimate goal. In work on poverty and homelessness, we're working with the Islamic Society of Central Florida. We're not asking them to tell people about Jesus — we're working together to help the poor. The Director of Outreach for the Islamic Society asked me to give the lecture on Christianity for a world religion class at a local college where he teaches. We have a great relationship. Students in the class ask if I believe you have to believe in Jesus to go to heaven and I answer, "Yes, it's part of what makes me a Christian just like my friend, their teacher, thinks that believing Islamic tenets is what makes him a good Muslim." We laugh about secretly trying to convert each other. But it's a great relationship of friendship and trust.

Honoring the other person is more basic than what our religions are. My friend and I both hold to the idea that we are made in the image of God and how we treat the created reflects what we think of the Creator. If I honor God, I must honor my Muslim friend as someone made in God's image. That's more foundational than how we approach issues of salvation and worship. By more fundamental I mean that before I can ever talk to him about his need for Jesus, he must know that I respect him as someone made in the image of God. My desire for him to know and follow Jesus is then rooted in my love for him as my neighbor and not in some religious competition in which people want to engage.

chapter 4

Church-State Blurrings

For much of the nineteenth century, relatively few questions regarding the rights and responsibilities of churches made it to the courts. First, given the substantial prevalence of Protestantism in America's public sphere, not many noticed, much less protested, if Protestant institutions at times ran afoul of church-state separation. Moreover, laws defining that separation were less elaborated, as fewer cases had been brought to court to provoke clarification. Indeed, in the American federal system, the separation of church and state — a clear obligation on the national government — did not apply to state governments until the Supreme Court ruling of 1947.[1] Before that year, a good deal of religious practice appeared legally in the public sphere, under state and local law. Among the issues that did come under legislative and legal scrutiny were the Sunday mails: May a government agency such as the post office refrain from delivery on the Christian Sabbath, or does that amount to endorsement of religion in violation of state neutrality? But much Christian advocacy — for or against slavery, for public education, etc. — did not prod legal concerns since political activism by civil society groups triggers no constitutional complaint.

    This relatively light level of church-state jurisprudence ended in the late nineteenth century, with mass immigration of non-Protestants. Especially alarming to the Protestant majority were Catholics from southern and eastern Europe, who added to the "papist threat" that

1. *Everson v. Board of Education,* 1947.

Irish immigrants had ostensibly been posing since the 1820s. In the century starting from 1880, anti-Catholic and anti-Semitic laws and practices ended up in court for violating the religious freedom of minority faiths.

In some cases, anti-Catholic animus was cloaked in state neutrality. The Blaine amendments, named after James Blaine, the nineteenth-century congressman who proposed them, was one. Blaine tried to get a constitutional amendment prohibiting the public funding of religious schools. When it failed, his amendment was taken to the state level, where Blaine amendments, as they were called, were incorporated into all but eleven state constitutions across the country. By prohibiting public funding for religious schools, Blaine may have been trying to quiet antagonisms between Catholics and Protestants — since he was seeking Catholic votes. But some of his supporters saw it as a way to keep public funds out of Catholic hands, as Catholics were founding most of the private religious schools. (With default Protestant presence in public schools, Protestants usually didn't see a need for private ones.) Many states retain their Blaine amendments, preventing for instance the use of vouchers in religious educational institutions. Today, these include many Protestant schools as well as Catholic ones — so Protestants who now seek public funding for their schools find themselves blocked by the very amendments Protestants used a century ago to block funds from Catholic ones.

During and after the Second World War, as America hailed itself "leader of the free world" against fascism and "godless communism," two somewhat contradictory movements emerged. One pushed for grounding American politics and culture more explicitly in religion. Though the goal may have been to distinguish America from Soviet godlessness, this movement risked church-state blurrings. The words "under God" were added to the Pledge of Allegiance in 1954. The next year, the phrase "In God We Trust" was required on U.S. coins and currency, after having appeared somewhat haphazardly on coins since the 1860s. It was made the national motto in 1956. Yet at the same time, a second movement aimed at greater government neutrality and greater pluralism in the public sphere. As America presented itself to the world as the alternative to Soviet dictatorship — an alternative where freedom of conscience and equality before the law presided — it became increasingly difficult to ignore minority protest against racial and religious discrimination. Indeed, so damaging was discrimination to U.S. foreign policy that the federal government filed a "friend of the court" brief supporting school integration in the *Brown v. Board of Education* case that ended legal school segregation in 1954. Secretary of State Dean Acheson wrote a letter to the Supreme Court saying that segregation was a "constant embarrassment" exploited by the Soviet Union to U.S. disadvantage.[2]

The same raised expectations for legal and political equality that galvanized the civil rights movement also encouraged religious minorities to protest default public Protestantism. This led to court decisions from the 1940s through the 1960s applying church separation to the states, prohibiting prayer in public schools, and limiting religious activity in public arenas (see chapter 3). And these cases provoked their own opposition — new cases aimed at containing what was seen as overreaching secularism. Since the 1970s, courts have been asked to adjudicate how far neutral government should *accommodate* religious belief and practice. (Should pupils be allowed to conduct religious activities in public schools; should employees, in their offices?) How far should governmental resources *support* religious institutions or activities? (May secular activities in religious schools be publicly funded?) How far should churches become involved in politics? (Should they endorse electoral candidates?)

Areas of Consensus

Below, I'll describe church-state controversies that remain most controversial and pressing, but first I'll sketch the debates for which resolution or consensus has been found, beginning with the matter of taxes and donations. The property of religious nonprofit institutions is exempt from real estate, sales, and other taxes. Religious nonprofit institutions may receive donations that donors deduct from taxable income, thus lowering their tax burden and encouraging charitable donations.

In employment, though the private workplace is governed largely by employers, workers retain robust religious rights. They may not be discriminated against in hiring or job benefits because of religious be-

---

2. D. Bell, *Silent Covenants: Brown v. Board of Education and the Unfulfilled Hopes for Racial Reform* (New York: Oxford University Press, 2004), pp. 65-66.

lief, practice, symbols, or clothing. Moreover, unemployed workers may not be deprived of state unemployment insurance if they refuse jobs that require them to work on their Sabbath.

In the armed services, chaplains are retained in all world religions. Religious groups and services are permitted, and the military may not interfere with the religious practice of its members unless it interferes with the orderly running of the armed forces. In 1986, for instance, the Supreme Court ruled that headgear that isn't army issue and doesn't follow army regulations is not permitted in the armed services. But more recently, this ruling has been relaxed, and religious headgear may be permitted at the discretion of the military.[3] Religious convictions, among others, may be used as exemption from conscription.

In faith-based social service agencies, public funds may not support proselytizing or programs where religious activity, belief, or confessional membership is a condition of receiving aid. Coreligionist hiring in "ministerial" cases — the hiring of priests, ministers, imams, rabbis, etc. — is permitted to all faith-based institutions, publicly and privately funded. Coreligionist hiring for *all* staff is permitted in *privately funded* social services programs. Faith-based institutions may use their facilities for social service delivery without renovating to remove religious icons, change organizational governance, or otherwise secularize their mission statements or organizations. But agencies are not exempt, on religious grounds, from professional performance and health and accountability standards. Voluntary prayer is permitted in all nonprofit social services, including those that receive public funds.

In public schools, the central principles for the role of religion are covered by the 1971 *Lemon v. Kurtzman* Supreme Court decision, which sets out the basic criteria for determining whether church-state separation has been violated. *Lemon* holds that government may support religious activity, including activity in schools, if the support neither advances nor hobbles religion, creates no excessive entanglements between government and religion, and has a secular purpose (for instance, helping disabled students). In public schools, students on their own may:[4] pray and read religious texts, individually or in groups; dis-

---

3. *Goldman v. Weinberger,* 1986; http://caselaw.lp.findlaw.com/scripts/getcase.pl ?court=us&vol=475&invol=503.

4. In 1995, the U.S. Department of Education codified these legal requirements under encouragement from the Clinton White House.

tribute religious literature and proselytize to others who voluntarily accept it; wear religious clothing and symbols; and use school facilities for religious gatherings if these facilities are available for other student gatherings. In addition, public boards of education may lend secular textbooks to religious schools at no cost and public money may be used to pay for computers and to aid disabled students at religious schools. Parents whose children attend religious schools may deduct the tuition costs from their income, thus lowering their tax burden.

Public schools, however, may not require student participation in religious functions; neither may state governments. School personnel and faculty may observe student religious activities but not lead or participate in them, as this may appear as endorsement. Neither schools nor states may reimburse religious schools for salaries, textbooks, or other purchased materials. They also may not exempt children, on religious grounds, from passing required state exams (children educated at home must pass relevant examinations). Special religious school districts are not permitted.

A relatively new area of church-state law involves school-mandated vaccination. In some states, children who, for religious reasons, have not been vaccinated are nonetheless permitted to attend school — even though vaccination is usually required for attendance. The alternative — prohibiting unvaccinated children from attending public school — has led to a rise in homeschooling, as parents often choose to educate their children at home rather than violate religious principles.

In universities, all the above-mentioned student rights apply. Additionally, students may use federal grants at religious colleges and universities, and federal money may be used for building construction.

Unresolved Issues Today

At present, the key unresolved issues in church-state relations include the following: church endorsement of electoral candidates; regulations for the display of religious symbols in public places; "moments of silence" in public schools; the teaching of creationism/intelligent design in public schools; the use of school vouchers at religious schools; and regulations for publicly funded faith-based social services, including coreligionist hiring and conscience-based service refusal (for instance, may a publicly funded clinic, on religious grounds, provide birth con-

trol only to married but not to unmarried women?). The sections below describe the national debate on each issue as background, much as
the rest of section I has provided historical and other background information. "New evangelical" views are described in section II.

Churches and Political Endorsements

Since 1954, churches and nonprofit charities have been prohibited from
endorsing political candidates. This prohibition was put into place to
conform with campaign finance law. The law holds that contributions
to political campaigns are not tax deductible (while donations to
churches and charities are). Thus to prevent people from doing an end
run around campaign finance law — by receiving tax deductions for
their church donations even though those donations are used to support political candidates — churches and nonprofits must refrain from
candidate endorsement. If one wishes to support a candidate, one must
do so in another way.

In 2008, the Alliance Defense Fund challenged the 1954 law, arguing that citizens should be able to express their political preferences by
donating to church electoral campaigns. It also argued that the law unduly involves government in religion since government must examine
church materials to check for improper candidate endorsements. Defenders of the 1954 law argued that citizens may indeed express their
political preferences but not through the churches since campaign contributions may not be used as tax deductions. They held that government is not overly involved in religion because it looks only at political
— not doctrinal — church materials. And they argued that exempting
churches from the 1954 law would mean special benefits to religion,
since all other nonprofit organizations must follow it. And such special
benefits are precisely what neutral government may not allow.

A 2010 case did not help to clarify matters. In *Citizens United*,[5] the
Supreme Court ruled that nonprofit corporations, unions, trade associations, and grassroots groups may support electoral candidates as long
as their efforts are not coordinated with candidate or political party
electoral campaigns. The ruling did not, however, change tax law, which
holds that contributions to candidates are not tax deductible and so

5. See http://www.oyez.org/cases/2000-2009/2008/2008_08_205.

churches may not support candidates if they wish donations to themselves to remain tax deductible. The question is open whether the
courts, in future decisions, will move toward allowing churches to be
both tax exempt, with donations to them tax deductible, and to endorse
or fund candidates. Churches might be allowed to contribute to PACs,
political action committees, which gather funds from a range of sources
and use those funds for a range of political activities, including funding
candidates. Though a nonprofit organization or church might techni-
cally lose its tax-exempt status if its funds were discovered to have been
used for candidate endorsement, tracking church funds through a PAC
is pragmatically daunting. Thus, as a practical matter, court permission
for churches to contribute to PACs would create the possibility of
church funds finding their way to candidate endorsement and electoral
campaign swithout costing the churches their tax-exempt status and
without costing church members their tax deductions.

Religious Symbols in Public Places

Unsurprisingly for a country where religion in the public sphere is
cherished and where 85 percent of the population is Christian, 83 percent of Americans hold that Christmas symbols may be displayed on
public property; 74 percent hold the same for the Ten Commandments.[6] Given the importance of religious expression on one hand and
state neutrality on the other, the courts have been asked to define the
regulations that allow as much public religious expression as possible
without creating the impression that the state is backing the views of
one church or another.

On private property — even private property accessible to the public — owners may display the symbols of their choice. In cases regarding
public property, courts have considered three factors in deciding if a display is to be allowed. First, displays may not be construed as state support for religious belief, though they may acknowledge the role of religion in history or Western culture. In 1989, the Supreme Court reviewed
two public displays.[7] One was a crèche donated by a Roman Catholic

---

6. Pew Forum on Religion and Public Life, "Religious Displays and the Courts,"
June 2007.

7. *County of Allegheny v. ACLU,* 1989.

group to the main staircase of the county courthouse. The second display, set outside a county office building, included a menorah owned by a Jewish group, a Christmas tree, and a sign proclaiming the city's "salute to liberty." The Court ruled the crèche impermissible and the outdoor display permissible because its multiple symbols conveyed tolerance and diversity, not state endorsement of a specific religious belief. In 2005,[8] when two Kentucky counties hurriedly added the national anthem, the Declaration of Independence, the Bill of Rights, the Magna Carta, and the preamble to the Kentucky Constitution to copies of the Ten Commandments hanging in their courthouses, the Supreme Court ruled that the original religious intention behind the Ten Commandments could not be masked by last-minute additions. But that year the Supreme Court did allow a Texas display of the Ten Commandments[9] outside the capitol building because it had been donated by a secular group and had stood for over forty years next to sixteen other statues commemorating significant events in Texas history.

The second factor in determining whether a religious symbol may be displayed on public property involves the nature and intention of the donor — sectarian or not? The third test is social divisiveness. This may be triggered when preferences are given to one religion over another, but it may also be triggered when legitimate religious symbols are removed from the public sphere. The Supreme Court found in the 2005 Texas case described above that the Ten Commandments outside the capitol building passed all three standards: there was no government endorsement of religion but rather of diversity; it had been donated by a secular group with secular aims; and finally, its removal would have created a divisive atmosphere after forty-five years of its message of diversity.

Another question that has come to the courts is, under what conditions may the religious ideas of *private* citizens be permitted in public places? In parks or plazas, considered *open fora* where people are free to express all sorts of beliefs, government may not ban religious (or secular) expression. If it is clear that a display belongs to a private group, it will not be confused with state support for sectarian beliefs. A church, synagogue, mosque, the Ku Klux Klan, and the ACLU may display their symbols and literature in public.[10] This seems clear enough. But the

8. *McCreary County v. ACLU*, 2005.
9. *Van Orden v. Perry*, 2005.
10. *Capitol Square Review Board v. Pinette*, 1995.

town of Pleasant Grove, Utah, noted that this requires government to accept all private displays on public grounds, even displays that offend the local community that elected it. Moreover, a display — unlike a rally or person holding a sign — may stand on public property for long durations and may be construed as governmental.

This issue emerged in Pleasant Grove when its Summum community wished to erect a monument of the Seven Aphorisms in a local park, near a copy of the Ten Commandments. The Summum believe that these seven mystical principles explain the universe and were brought by Moses from Mount Sinai. When the principles were not understood, Moses returned with the simpler Ten Commandments. The city government refused permission to erect the Summum monument, noting that a permanent display would be seen as city endorsement of Summum beliefs. The Summum answered that, on this reasoning, the Ten Commandments could also be taken as city endorsement, and a neutral government may not favor one religious symbol over another.

In 2009, the Supreme Court ruled that Pleasant Grove may decide what permanent displays are erected on city grounds. And this has thrown some confusion into the religious-symbols debate. To avoid the appearance of endorsement of religious symbols such as the Seven Aphorisms, governments want discretion over what is placed on public property. Yet this very discretion allows government to favor some religious displays over others (Ten Commandments over the Seven Aphorisms), which liberal democracies may not do.

Moments of Silence in Public Schools

Public-school prayer has been debated and adjudicated since the 1940s. At present, the law prohibits state- and school-led prayer, though students may pray on their own. A strong public consensus for this position exists as well. Spontaneous prayer, where students pray in an unplanned moment, is under most circumstances allowed, as long as the state and school staff do not lead, plan, or support it, and as long as the prayer does not disrupt educational activities (it need not be permitted in the middle of chemistry class, for instance).

Yet, while some consensus has been reached about school prayer, less consensus exists about moments of silence. On one hand, twenty-three states permit, and thirteen states require, them.[11] A wide majority of adults prefers them to sectarian prayer (69 percent versus 23 percent),[12] and 84 percent of teenagers, ages thirteen to seventeen, favor such contemplative moments over sectarian prayer as well.[13] One reason for this preference is practical: officially sponsored sectarian prayer would require schools or the state to organize prayer for all denominations in order to avoid discrimination, and this is an organizational obligation few want. On the other hand, those who object to moments of silence hold that they are a wedge into returning religious prayer to the public schools.

Since 1985, the Supreme Court has held that moments of silence do not violate public-school neutrality if such moments have a secular rather than religious purpose.[14] While the Court rejected an Alabama moment-of-silence law because its sponsor admitted its purpose was "to return voluntary prayer to our public schools," the Court indicated that it would have allowed the moments of silence had they had a secular purpose. Determining the purpose of such silent moments is not always easy and has led courts to varying decisions. In 2008, for instance, a Texas moment-of-silence law was upheld by the district court, though challengers claimed it aimed at introducing prayer into the schools. The law had, according to the court, the secular purpose of promoting "contemplation, seriousness and reverence," not "to advance or inhibit religion."[15] However, in 2009 an Illinois law requiring a moment of silence was ruled unconstitutional because, in the words of the court, "The statute is a subtle effort to force students at impressionable ages to contemplate religion."[16]

At present, the 1985 standard is being challenged by religious groups who argue for all moments of silence, even if their purpose is sectarian.

11. Pew Forum on Religion and Public Life, "Courts Not Silent on Moments of Silence," April 24, 2008.

12. D. Moore, "Public Favors Voluntary Prayer for Public Schools: But Strongly Supports Moment of Silence Rather Than Spoken Prayer," Gallup poll, August 26, 2005.

13. B. Ott, "School Prayer: Teen Support Hinges on Type; Least Likely to Support Spoken Prayer That Mentions Jesus Christ," Gallup poll, August 25, 2006.

14. *Wallace v. Jaffree*, 1985.

15. *Croft v. Perry*, 2008.

16. M. Robinson, "Illinois Moment of Silence Ruled Unconstitutional," Associated Press, January 22, 2009.

Teaching the Biblical Version of Creation in Public Schools

Since the 1960s, the Supreme Court has ruled that creationism and intelligent design are religious beliefs and may not be taught as science in the public schools. Science, on this view, is a specific mode of inquiry that develops hypotheses and substantiates or disproves them with empirical evidence, as best it can be gathered. Evolution may not be an unassailably proven fact, but it falls within the parameters of scientific inquiry: evolution is a hypothesis that can be tested and disproved by empirical evidence. Therefore, the proper place to discuss it is in science class. The biblical version of creation, like much in life, does not fall within the parameters of scientific hypothesis-testing: the existence of God or God's hand in creation cannot be tested and disproved by empirical evidence. Thus, according to the courts, the proper place for discussing these ideas is not the fairly narrow confines of science classes but in world religion classes, history classes, sociology classes, etc.

Quite apart from court rulings, the popularity of both creationism and intelligent design remains high, along with advocacy for teaching them. Fifty-three percent of Americans believe that mankind has either always existed in its present form, without evolution, or that man evolved under the guidance of a divine force. Only 32 percent say life evolved solely through natural selection.[17] Sixty-four percent support teaching creationism/intelligent design together with evolution, to give pupils both views.

Between 2003 and 2008, creationism controversies erupted in over half of the states.[18] In some, such as Kansas and Pennsylvania, creationism or intelligent design were mandated in school curricula. Other states required curricula that raise questions about evolution through critiques or disclaimers, like one from Georgia, which said that evolution is "a theory, not a fact [and] . . . should be approached with an open mind, studied carefully and critically considered."[19] Texas, Alabama, Florida, Louisiana, Michigan, Missouri, and South Carolina have con-

17. Pew Forum on Religion and Public Life, "Overview: The Conflict between Religion and Evolution," February 4, 2009; Pew Forum on Religion and Public Life, "Public Opinion on Religion and Science in the United States: Views on Science and Scientists," November 5, 2009.

18. Pew Forum on Religion and Public Life, "Overview."

19. *Selman v. Cobb County School District,* 2005.

sidered requiring classes to consider "the scientific strengths and weaknesses of Darwinian theory."[20] The debate has been aggravated by textbook selection. When populous states, which order large numbers of textbooks, require material that highlights evolution's weaknesses (as Texas did in 2007), textbook publishers tend to print these books and not others, affecting the schoolbooks available nationwide and prodding protest from evolution's supporters.

Advocates of creationism/intelligent design hold that, as there is an important controversy about Darwinism, both sides should be taught in public schools. Opponents hold that this may be a good idea for civics classes, but that creationism/intelligent design cannot be taught as science. Regarding evolution disclaimers, supporters note that Texas requires students to critique all scientific theories, not only evolution, by exploring "the strengths and weaknesses" of each. But in 2009, a panel of Texas teachers proposed a change in state requirements: they should no longer explore "strengths and weaknesses" but should "analyze and evaluate scientific explanations using empirical evidence." Eugenie C. Scott of the National Center for Science in Education holds that "The phrase 'strengths and weaknesses' has been spread nationally as a slogan to bring creationism in through the back door."[21] A tie vote in the Texas Board of Education led to the removal of both the "strengths and weaknesses" and "empirical evidence" requirements,[22] but the controversy over creationism/intelligent design in school curricula continues.

School Vouchers

The Alliance for School Choice, an organization that supports school vouchers, reports that 64,079 Americans used these government grants in 2008-9, and that 179,721 students used all school choice programs (which include vouchers, tax credit programs, and programs for children with special needs).[23] Despite their usefulness, vouchers have en-

---

20. See J. McKinley Jr., "In Texas, a Line in the Curriculum Revives Evolution Debate," *New York Times*, January 22, 2009.

21. T. Stutz, "Texas Rejects Effort to Require Teaching of Evolution 'Weaknesses,'" *Dallas Morning News*, March 27, 2009.

22. Stutz, "Texas Rejects Effort to Require Teaching of Evolution 'Weaknesses.'"

23. See www.allianceforschoolchoice.org/UploadedFiles/ResearchResources/ASC _Yearbook_2010_final.pdf.

countered two objections. One is that, as children use them to leave failing public schools for private ones, public school enrollment drops. Because enrollment determines funding, this drops as well, leading to a downward cycle of ailing schools. Better, on this argument, to improve public schools than to siphon funds into private ones. Yet lower-income parents have countered that, while improving public schools is an excellent idea, they are unwilling to sacrifice their children's education to this lengthy process.

The second argument against school vouchers is that they end up supporting religious education in violation of both government neutrality and state Blaine amendments prohibiting the public funding of religious schools. And this, it is feared, will Balkanize the population and weaken student understanding of the benefits of neutral government. As vouchers are relatively small grants, they generally cover religious-school tuition, which is subsidized by the churches and thus low. Since vouchers are usually insufficient for the higher costs of (unsubsidized) private secular education, low-income parents frequently use vouchers to send their children to religious schools. In Cleveland, for instance, 99.4 percent of students using vouchers attended religious schools.

In 2002, ruling on the Cleveland voucher program, the Supreme Court upheld the use of vouchers for religious schools as long as users have the choice of secular private schools as well.[24] This satisfied those who feel religious schools offer a solid education in secular as well as religious subjects, teach good values, and provide children a safe place in which to learn. It alarmed those who hold that, in practice, there is no choice between expensive secular private schools and low-cost, church-subsidized ones. Insofar as parents use vouchers for religious schools, states end up subsidizing religious education. There is also concern that certain adults, such as prisoners or drug addicts in court-mandated training programs, are not in a position to freely choose where to use their training-program vouchers — in secular programs or faith-based ones.

The core of the 2002 *Zelman* case was: Can public money be used in procedurally neutral programs that in practice benefit religion? This question was raised again in 2011, when the Supreme Court let stand an Arizona program that creates scholarships for disadvantaged children

---

24. *Zelman v. Simmons-Harris*, 2002.

to attend private (often religious) schools.[25] Arizona taxpayers can earn a tax credit when they donate funds to scholarship tuition organizations (STOs), nonprofit groups that use taxpayer contributions to offer scholarships at private schools. Challengers to the program noted that, in practice, much public money went to religious institutions, over 50 percent in 2009, and that many recipients were not disadvantaged but, rather, middle class and already attending religious schools. Additionally, some of the STOs limited scholarships to students wishing to attend religious institutions. Advocates of the program held that it meets the 2002 *Zelman* standards: it has a secular purpose, directs government funds to parents rather than schools, covers a broad class of beneficiaries, and offers students a meaningful choice between secular and religious options. The Court ruled that challengers to the program lacked standing to bring a suit. Though it was a technical ruling that did not assess whether the actual flow of Arizona funds violated church-state separation, it is considered support for the program's advocates. The ruling may limit future challenges to tax provisions that directly or indirectly benefit religion, such as the special tax laws that govern housing for clergy.

Regulations for Faith-Based Social Services

Public Funding for Religious Programming and Coreligionist Hiring Currently, 69 percent of Americans support government funding for religious social services, such as job training, hospitals, and drug-treatment counseling. The sharpest drop in support for such funding occurred, interestingly, among white evangelicals, down from 77 percent in 2001 to 65 percent in 2009.[26] The most controversial aspect of this sort of funding is whether public grants can be used by agencies that hire only coreligionists (thus discriminating against other job candidates). Since the 1964 Civil Rights Act, discrimination on the basis of religion has been prohibited in all workplaces, private and public. But a "ministerial exception" was provided for houses of

25. *Arizona Christ School Tuition Organization v. Winn*, 2011. See http://www.oyez .org/cases/2010=2019/2010/2010_09_987; *Arizona Department of Revenue v. Winn*, 2011. See http://www.supremecourt.gov/opinions/10pdf/09=987.pdf.

26. Pew Forum on Religion and Public Life, "Faith-Based Programs Still Popular, Less Visible," November 16, 2009.

worship so that they may hire ministers only from within their faith (that is, they may discriminate against people of other religions). A 1972 clarification allowed faith-based agencies to hire only coreligionists for all staff — if they do not take public monies. In effect, then, privately funded institutions may discriminate in favor of coreligionists in all staff, but publicly funded institutions may discriminate in favor of coreligionists only for ministerial staff.

In practice, most social service agencies neither use religious material in their counseling nor engage in coreligionist hiring. Among agencies that move welfare recipients into jobs, for instance, only 2.9 percent hire only coreligionists and only 6.9 percent give coreligionists preference in employment.[27] This practice reflects public opinion. Seventy-four percent of Americans oppose coreligionist hiring in public-funded social services, and only 33 percent of white evangelicals support it. Sixty-three percent of Americans oppose government funding for agencies that proselytize or use religious materials in counseling; only 33 percent of white evangelicals support it.[28]

There is no experimental evidence to date that faith-based social services are more effective than secular ones, though some case studies show religious service providers with results superior to those of secular agencies.[29] Additionally, engagement in religion shows a positive correlation with socially productive effects — from lowering hypertension and suicide to lowering street crime and school failure. But it is not clear that these benefits are caused by religious belief or other factors, such as stronger communities or more stable family life. Homes that are highly unstable — because of substance abuse, crime, death, or separation — are also less involved with church than more stable families. The better medical and psychological conditions found in more religiously engaged homes may come from greater family stability rather than from specific religious teachings.[30] It is also possible, however,

---

27. J. DiIulio, *Godly Republic: A Centrist Blueprint for America's Faith-Based Future* (Berkeley and Los Angeles: University of California Press, 2007), p. 178.

28. Pew Forum on Religion and Public Life, "Faith-Based Programs Still Popular, Less Visible."

29. Nelson A. Rockefeller Institute of Government, "Taking Stock: The Bush Faith-Based Initiative and What Lies Ahead, the Final Report by the Roundtable on Religion and Social Welfare Policy," June 11, 2009.

30. See B. Johnson, *Objective Hope: Assessing the Effectiveness of Faith-Based Organizations: A Review of the Literature*, Center for Research on Religion and Urban Civil Society,

that religious teachings promote more stable family life and so may contribute to socially productive effects.

In the legal debate about public funds, faith-based social services ask if refusing public funds only to religious agencies constitutes discrimination against religion. Government does not refuse funding because of variations in secular service provision — it does not give funds to Montessori kindergartens but refuse Piagetian ones. Is state neutrality preserved if government funds Montessori kindergartens but not Methodist ones? Linking the type of counseling to the type of counselor, agencies that favor religious approaches wonder how they would implement them if employees came from many confessions or from none at all. For instance, an agency may hold that telling addicts that Jesus loves them helps build self-esteem and enables addicts to give up short-term highs for long-term health. What is Methodist about a clinic if the counselors do not hold these Methodist beliefs? In his 2010 Executive Order, Fundamental Principles and Policymaking Criteria for Partnerships with Faith-Based and Other Neighborhood Organizations,[31] President Obama retained the policy of evaluating instances of coreligionist hiring on a case-by-case basis, leaving open the standards for that evaluation and thus leaving open the political and legal debate.

Questions about coreligionist hiring will become more heated if religion classes are added to public school curricula. Though religious instruction in public schools has been prohibited as a linchpin of church-state separation, it is being considered as a way to raise religious literacy, promote pluralism and tolerance, and provide an understanding of religious imagery in history, art, and literature. Can schoolteachers be expected to know enough about all religions to teach them? Or should schools hire members of the confessions? Must they hire members of all religions, and if not, which ones must they hire?

As if these questions weren't sticky enough, they become stickier when we consider enforcement. One key way to repair the damage of employment discrimination is through lawsuits against discriminating institutions. Since a 1968 Supreme Court ruling, citizens may sue the government if they discover that it has participated in workplace dis-

---

Manhattan Institute and University of Pennsylvania, 2001; J. Levin and H. Koenig, eds., *Faith, Medicine, and Science: A Festschrift in Honor of Dr. David B. Larson* (Binghamton, N.Y.: Haworth Pastoral Press, 2005).

    31. See http://www.whitehouse.gov/the-press-office/2010/11/17/executive-order-fundamental-principles-and-policymaking-criteria-partner.

crimination — for instance, by funding an agency that practices coreligionist hiring.[32] Yet a 2007 court ruling limits this possibility of redress.[33] It states that citizens may sue the government only if the funding was authorized by a legislature (national or state). Funding of coreligionist hiring by any other means is thus unassailable. As a result, the Kentucky Baptist Homes for Children was allowed to fire a lesbian employee — whose lifestyle, the organization said, did not conform to Baptist teachings — because its public funding came not from legislative but from executive sources.[34]

Coreligionist Admissions While coreligionist hiring applies to staff, coreligionist admission applies to students and membership in private associations. The Boy Scouts went to court in 1998 to exclude homosexuals and atheists from membership. The Supreme Court agreed,[35] ruling that voluntary organizations, privately funded, may maintain their own membership standards. Because members are allowed freedom of association under the Constitution, the Boy Scouts are not bound by antidiscrimination laws covering government, businesses, public schools, and public accommodations such as restaurants and hotels. (For the same freedom-of-association reasons, the Irish community parade in Boston was allowed to refuse participation by gay Irish groups.)[36]

In 2009, a California court similarly ruled that a private Lutheran high school may maintain its own admission standards and reject gay students. Though California antidiscrimination laws are stricter than federal law and apply even to private, voluntary organizations like the Boy Scouts, the court held that the purpose of the Lutheran school was to instill religious values in its students, who along with their parents know the school's values when they enroll. Unlike public schools and other private organizations in California, the court held, private religious schools are not bound by state antidiscrimination laws and may admit only students who meet their criteria. Moreover, the court continued, compulsion to admit homosexual students would violate the school's religious freedom.

32. *Flast v. Cohen,* 1968.
33. *Hein v. Freedom from Religion Foundation,* 2007.
34. *Pedreira v. Kentucky Baptist Homes for Children,* 2008.
35. See http://www.oyez.org/cases/1990-1999/1999/1999_99_699.
36. See http://www.oyez.org/cases/1990-1999/1994/1994_94_749.

Religiously Grounded Service Refusal Questions regarding conscience-based (or religiously based) service refusal pertain both to publicly funded institutions and to individuals who work in them. If publicly funded agencies may opt out of services that contravene their
religious beliefs — such as dispensing birth control to unmarried couples — does that constitute government endorsement of that belief? To
maintain its neutrality, may government make performing such services a condition of receiving public grants? If adoption agencies place
children with heterosexual but not gay couples, does this constitute
discrimination, which government may not fund?

One argument holds that, if one takes government funds, one
must follow government antidiscrimination laws. Another holds that
having certain religious beliefs — that homosexuality is *not* a sin, for instance — cannot be a condition of employment or receipt of government funds. The Boston and San Francisco Catholic Charities closed
their adoption agencies rather than follow antidiscrimination laws and
place children with gay couples. The Boston agency offered to refer gay
couples to other organizations, but the courts ruled this legally insufficient.[37] In 2010, San Francisco Charities sued the city of San Francisco
for violating the Charities' religious freedom.[38]

In his last month in office, G. W. Bush issued a policy allowing
employees in medical facilities — from janitors to surgeons — to refuse
aspects of their jobs that contravene their religious beliefs. While the
U.S. Council of Catholic Bishops and the Family Research Council ap-
plauded the policy, those opposed asked whether it would allow conservatives to block medical procedures they dislike by taking jobs in
agencies that provide those procedures and then abstaining from their
jobs on religious grounds. Seven states sued to prevent the policy's implementation because of its disproportionate impact on low-income
women who use publicly funded health clinics. Wealthier women have
greater options in choosing physicians, but if physicians in public clinics cease providing certain services, poor women have little choice of
where to go to obtain these legal medical procedures. The Reverend

37. A. Surdin, "Calif. Court Considers Medical Rights: Justices Weigh Whether
Doctors, Citing Religion, Can Refuse to Treat Some Patients," *Washington Post,* June 19,
2008; see also M. Stern, "Will Gay Rights Trample Religious Freedom?" *Los Angeles Times,*
June 17, 2008.

38. Surdin, "Calif. Court Considers Medical Rights"; Stern, "Will Gay Rights
Trample Religious Freedom?"

Carlton Veazey, president and CEO of the Religious Coalition for Reproductive Choice, said the ruling "denies women the right to follow their conscience and make decisions according to their religious and moral beliefs."[39]

Veazey put his finger on the complexity of this issue: in protecting the consciences of health-care providers, the Bush policy may have violated the consciences of patients. Moreover, it may create chaos at service agencies. To prevent discrimination by religion, employers may not, in the hiring process, ask about candidates' religious beliefs. Yet by not asking and so potentially hiring people who will abstain from work on religious grounds, they risk the operation of their agencies — ironically by protecting the religious freedom of job candidates.

To summarize the key issues regarding faith-based agencies: there is some consensus at present that government funds may not be used for religious programming. But opposition remains, holding that religious programming is effective and expresses the values of faith-based institutions, which should not face discrimination. The issues of coreligionist hiring and religiously based service refusal have not found consensus.

39. M. Berger, "New Health Regulation Permits 'Conscience' Exceptions," Religion News Service, December 18, 2008.

chapter 5

The Möbius Strip

Ironies of State Neutrality toward Religion

The project begun centuries ago by Sebastian Castellio, Roger Williams, and other pleaders for church-state separation has yielded nuanced legal and governmental practices. Yet it has also produced ironies that early modern writers would have hardly imagined.

One is that religion would be restricted by the very efforts to make it free. A central aim of state neutrality toward religion is to prevent government from interfering with religious practice. It is a position supported even by nonbelievers, to protect minority beliefs. To further this goal, not only governments but also the agencies they fund must remain neutral toward religion. Otherwise, states could get around the requirement of neutrality by funding outside agencies to discriminate for them. Ironically, however, the very requirement of neutrality constrains religion. It dictates that, when an agency takes government funds, its programming and hiring must conform not to church tenets but to the state's. Faith-based agencies are no longer free to practice as they please. Faith-based agencies may hold, for instance, that God's love helps troubled youth build self-esteem so that they do better in school. They may hold that this loving message can be conveyed only by people who believe it. They may not want to hire people who don't. But the requirement of neutrality prevents such agencies, if publicly funded, from following their beliefs. Religious practice is constrained by, of all entities, government — the one agent that in liberal democracies may not constrain religion.

This irony is furthered when one compares government regulation of secular and faith-based agencies. The state does not discriminate in the programming of secular agencies (unless they break the law), and secular agencies do not forgo government funds because of their counseling preferences (Freudian, behavior modification, etc.). Is the state neutral if it prohibits religious approaches in publicly funded agencies but allows all secular ones? State neutrality toward religion is meant to ensure that government treats all religious and secular entities impartially. But as it stands, the obligation on government to remain impartial has led to partiality. It places constraints on religious programming that are not placed on secular programming.

This is a paradox of our First Amendment. It creates a religious exceptionalism, where government may espouse and support political, economic, and social views of all sorts — indeed it must, to function as government — but it may not advance religious ones. Religion is, constitutionally, an exceptional category. This is meant to prevent discrimination against religion. Yet, religious exceptionalism, to protect religion, has led to restrictions especially on the practice of religion.

These paradoxes and ironies will arise wherever a neutral government cooperates with religious agencies. Yet the cooperation itself presents another irony: antistatist reliance on the state. The Religious Right became popular in the 1970s in part because of its call to self-reliance — in opposition to hippy self-indulgence and "big government" civil rights and antipoverty programs. It sought a return to the nation's traditional, individualist self-responsibility, to "small government," and to independent, voluntarist, civil-society institutions. Yet from the 1980s on, the Religious Right sought government support for religious practices — such as prayer in the schools — in public institutions. It relied on the state to institutionalize religious values, such as teaching creationism in public schools, and thus it invited some church-state intermingling — which is forbidden in order to protect freedom of religion.

Inviting the state to support religion reveals not a failure of religious freedom but its success. In the experience of early modern writers, state mingling in religion meant religious persecution. Today, it means help. Those who invite government to support religious practice are so confident of their religious freedom that they assume state aid will be benign. Government will not discriminate, much less persecute. This is a remarkable testament to freedom of conscience and its firm place in current society and law. After spending centuries trying to get the state out of church affairs, the heirs of Roger Williams so trust the state's impartiality that they invite it back in.

It is possible that these ironies cannot in principle be solved. In practice, the democratic experiment of the last four hundred years has been an attempt to maximize state neutrality without hobbling religious practice, and to maximize religious freedom without damaging state neutrality. In the next section, we'll see the variety of ideas and practices that are emerging among "new evangelicals" to keep this balance, as well as the contradictions and difficulties that this entails.

ROBUST RELIGION WITHIN LIBERAL DEMOCRACY

America's "New Evangelicals"

If there is racial injustice in your community, you have to speak to that. If there is educational injustice, you have to do something there. If the poor are being neglected by the government or being oppressed in some way, then you have to stand up for the poor. . . . We are interested in the poor, in racial reconciliation, in global poverty and AIDS, in the plight of women in the developing world.

Bill Hybels, in D. Kirkpatrick, "The Evangelical Crackup," *New York Times Magazine,* October 28, 2007

RC Obama's faith-based outreach isn't going so well. I don't mean
Josh Dubois [head of Obama's Office of Faith-Based and Neighborhood Partnerships]. It goes back to Obama and his perception problem. Obama has to actually go to church to persuade people he's not
a Muslim.

MP Why?

RC He's not comfortable talking about it. It's his desire not to repli-
cate the errors of the Bush administration; he doesn't want to appear
to be exploiting the religion factor. But he's bent so far backwards that
his image doesn't conform to who he is. Forty percent of Republicans
think he's a Muslim. Some of that is just wishful thinking; they don't
like the guy; they don't like his policies. I'm not saying he's an evangelical; by his own words, he said he's not an evangelical. But he's a believing Christian.

Some are accusing him of a falsehood. They are constructing an
image to suit their political and ideological agendas. One of the Tea
Party leaders, Mark Williams, in 2009 called Obama "an Indonesian
Muslim turned welfare thug, and a racist in chief."[1]

MP They're tarring Obama because they don't like his policies or his
race?

RC Both. For some people it is racially motivated or tinged, but not for
all. During the 2008 election there was a high-profile evangelical leader
on a conference call with other leaders who are part of the Arlington
Group. That leader said, "You don't need to worry about this. Evangelicals won't vote for a black man." That is firsthand knowledge from a
member of the Arlington Group board, himself an African American.

---

1. The remark was made on CNN's *Anderson Cooper 360;* in 2010, Williams was expelled from the National Tea Party Federation after he posted a racist blog, which Federation spokesman David Webb said was "clearly offensive."

But the majority of people who don't like Obama are motivated by opposition to his policies.

MP Is this — Obama's policies, opposition to his policies — linked to why you started the New Evangelical Partnership for the Common Good in 2010? Why was this the right time to do it?

RC I was told at the National Association of Evangelicals [NAE] that my ideas were too radical or liberal. But the ideas I expressed on *Fresh Air* [the National Public Radio program whose interview with Cizik sparked his departure from NAE] were views of the evangelical *center*, with the exception of one issue — gay civil unions. If that's too radical for the existing organization, then there's something wrong with the existing organization. According to the Public Religion Research Institute, 52 percent of white evangelicals in California now oppose Proposition 8, which prohibits same-sex marriages. That's a shift; 13 percent have changed their minds. What that says is, there is a movement of change occurring.[2]

MP Why has that been happening?

RC It's occurring independent of even our leadership, as much as we would like to think we're giving voice to it. It's a spiritual awakening to an agenda broader than the concerns that people say they know was too narrow.

Our goal at the New Evangelical Partnership is to have a witness by an evangelical organization that is not subservient to partisanship and ideology — not subservient but above it or independent of it. That is healing rather than divisive, loving rather than angry. We're trying to tap into a methodology for evangelical political engagement that says politics isn't a zero-sum game where somebody else has to lose in order for us to win. The goal is to enhance the common good as much as to enhance the evangelical cause. As we espouse policies of the common good, the evangelical reputation will also go up because people will see that we're about justice for all.

2. In 2010, Public Religion Research Institute reported that 59 percent of white evangelicals no longer hold that Proposition 8, passed in California in 2008, "was a good thing." See http://publicreligion.org/objects/uploads/fck/file/CA%20Survey%20Report%20FINAL.pdf.

We also sense that there's a great need to empower a new generation of evangelicals around a broad agenda. The goals of the broad
agenda are described in a document I put together when I was at the
NAE called *For the Health of the Nation*. We want to offer leadership to do
that. Even the rightist types who are still in the NAE now say, "You're
right: the agenda has to be broader than a narrow litmus test of opposition to abortion and gay marriage." They may not agree on civil
unions but they agree that there needs to be a broader agenda. So
there's no pushback from the NAE on that question. Leith Anderson
[NAE president] wouldn't allow it — though some conservatives won't
go as far as nuclear weapons reduction. I've been showing a film
around the country about loose nukes, called *Countdown to Zero*. A
friend took it to Focus on the Family[3] and asked if they would become
a cosponsoring organization for a free screening in Colorado Springs.
They said it wasn't their issue. What they could've said is, "If it's good
enough for Chuck Colson,[4] it's good enough for us" — because he's
lent his name to the film. But we're going to show it in Colorado
Springs and we're going to invite all the pastors.

MP In the years since Obama has been elected, has there been, among
evangelicals, a move away from the broader agenda that you've been
talking about? Was there a move in one direction in 2008 and now, in
2010, a move in the other?

RC To a certain extent, interest in evangelicals accompanies interest in
the Religious Right. The "big" press is interested in outcomes — who
influences the election. So they don't care about all the evangelical or-
ganizing or about grassroots progress. They care about the vote. So the
Tea Party has all the public attention around an election.

---

3. An evangelical nonprofit organization, founded in 1977, which advocates socially conservative public policy. Its mission is "nurturing and defending the God-
ordained institution of the family and promoting biblical truths worldwide" through
its daily radio broadcasts, magazines, videos, audio recordings, free resources, and family counseling; see http://www.focusonthefamily.com/about_us/broadcasts.aspx.
   4. Convicted and incarcerated for Watergate-related charges in the 1980s; founded
Prison Fellowship ministries upon his release; is the author of over twenty books; has received fifteen honorary doctorates and in 1993 was awarded the Templeton Prize in the
field of religion. He donated this prize to Prison Fellowship, as he does all his speaking
fees and royalties.

But around the country, there is a gradual earthquake shift that is occurring. Evangelical colleges, for instance, with a few exceptions, are in the midst of an enormous shift, which will not be felt immediately in elections but which will bring evangelicals into a greater place of influence in society. These are young people who are a lot smarter and less naive about how society operates, and they are committed — not to burnishing the evangelical image but to solving problems here and abroad. Not about making a statement but making a difference. You can go up to Houghton College and you've got four hundred students in a cultural studies major. They learn the languages, culture, religion, and they're intent on going overseas, to make a difference about poverty, AIDS, etc.

I was asked last year to judge the stories written on creation care in all the publications in the Evangelical Press Association. I gave the number one and number two awards to writers at two dispensational colleges, Biola and Dallas Theological Seminary. In each institution, the college or seminary was shifting its entire institution to the new green economy. The president at Biola drives a Prius. They're shifting at Dallas in all the ways you would wish Harvard was. I ran into Charles Ryrie [of the *Ryrie Study Bible,* the premier dispensational Bible], and he said, "Of course I agree with you on the environment. I go swimming every day to take care of my body. Of course we should also take care of this earth. Just don't use Genesis 2:15 because it's pre-flood." I said, "But there's a systematic theology after that." He said, "Of course there is: use it all." Here was a dispensationalist and two dispensationalist schools. . . . Once I was controversial saying what I did about the environment. Today, not so much.

But of course, there are more controversial subjects. At the New Evangelical Partnership, we're proposing a reframing of family planning. That's a third-rail hot button for many conservatives. But I believe that younger evangelicals can understand that family planning does not equal abortion. On abortion reduction, maternal health, on girls' and women's rights, this country has been pursuing a policy dating back to 1980 called the Mexico City Policy, which punishes the very people whom we call brother and sister. I'm convinced that evangelicals can make the shift away from a policy that is anticontraception to procontraception. After all, we're not Catholics.

With that kind of policy, you wouldn't have Religious Right groups without impunity charging Republican lawmakers to vote against family planning programs. You would have evangelicals going overseas who are willing to acknowledge publicly what they now acknowledge privately: that maternal health which includes family planning is essential to women's livelihood. You can't say, "We'll take care of poverty, HIV, and climate change" but ignore that women's access to family planning is a critical component to their survival. Moreover, for white evangelicals in their affluence in America to say to poor women in the global south, "You don't have the same rights as we have," is worse than hypocrisy. It is approaching a level of condescension and arrogance that no evangelical should speak.

We have these issues right here in the District of Columbia, where the AIDS rate is as high as in sub-Saharan Africa. In D.C., there are eight Planned Parenthood clinics and one pro-life, crisis pregnancy clinic. So what's your strategy: Defund the agency that gets most of the clients? We shouldn't defund Planned Parenthood; we should have our volunteers assist them. You can't go there to undermine the purpose of the clinic. But when you reckon with the fact that more than half of all abortions are by women who are having a second abortion or more — the statistics come from the Guttmacher Institute[5] — then you know that, to reduce abortion, you have to engage with women in need whose lives bespeak an imbalance. They wouldn't be doing this to themselves if something wasn't out of kilter — whether it is because of their relationships with men or whatever else. So when I say "volunteer," I'm saying, volunteer by asking, "What can I do to help people who have an obvious need?"

Rather than defund Planned Parenthood, why don't we write the rules for funding to include specific kinds of programs aimed at that clientele? What leads a woman to get into a position where she's using abortion as a form of birth control? These are not teenagers but adult women. Rather than go through the rigmarole over who votes for life and who votes for choice, why don't we figure out who would vote for alternatives to abortion? Let's go after people who won't support alternatives — Republican or Democrat — and say, "We're going to target you if you don't supply the funding that's needed for women in crisis."

MP It's going to come down to some money because, according to the Guttmacher Institute, three-quarters of women who have abortions

5. http://www.guttmacher.org/pubs/gpr/10/2/gpr100208.html.

cite financial inability to support a child as their reason.[6] That means support not only till birth but afterwards — in day care, job training, medical care, etc.

RC If you want to cut the abortion rate, cut the poverty rate. If you want to be pro-life, you have to create these programs.

MP Evangelicals around the country tell me the same thing about helping women in crisis pregnancies — but that government is the last entity you want providing that help. They say they'll do it instead, through ministries.

RC No. Go talk to the women who run the evangelical crisis pregnancy clinic in D.C. Nearly an argument broke out between [NAE president] Leith Anderson and a woman who works there when she said, "We go to pastors and ask for their help and they won't help us. They won't even give us verbal support." Anyone who says, "*We'll* do it," is dreaming. It doesn't happen that way. The one crisis pregnancy clinic here is underfunded, undervolunteered; it's in a crisis of its own. The only way you'll reduce abortion is through the existing system.

This is one reason why I don't believe that the Tea Party agenda of cutting government programs conforms with evangelical reality. Thirty-six percent of Tea Partiers are white evangelicals. According to the Public Religion Research Institute, whose board I sit on, the Tea Partiers comprise 11 percent of the general population. So white evangelicals who are also Tea Partiers are a third of 11 percent — not a big percentage — while evangelicals overall comprise 16 percent of the total population [figures vary according to the definition of evangelical and thus, who is included in the count].

But in any case, the general population doesn't buy what the Tea Partiers are saying. Now the Tea Parties are not exactly a flash in the pan, but remember this: Tea Partiers aren't just antigovernment; they're antipolitics because they don't believe in compromise. And people who don't believe in compromise are eventually going to be disaffected and drop out. Besides, it's not how politics works. So whether the Tea Party becomes a broad political movement, all these candidates, far left and far right, ultimately have to deal with reality. Com-

6. http://www.guttmacher.org/pubs/fb_induced_abortion.html.

promise is part of the process — for Tea Partiers too. Once they're in Congress, they're going to have to work with — compromise with — mainstream Republicans who've been elected many times, like Mitch McConnell in the Senate. And those Tea Partiers are going to have to persuade their voters that they're really not compromising? . . .

I've worked in this town since 1980 so I've seen the political pendulum swing back and forth. No big surprise when the Democrats lose one of the houses. Reelections depend on it. Obama can run against the Republicans who've taken over.

At the New Evangelical Partnership, we're creating a C-4 [nonprofit organization that can engage in political work] and we're going to get involved if not in electoral races then in legislative work.

MP Are you getting a response from the public?

RC We're public only seven months. We don't have — like the Tea Parties — someone who gave us an anonymous million-dollar gift. George Soros isn't giving us any money. But we have more visibility than we expected to have by this time.

MP Are most of your donors small donors? From any area in particular?

RC Small donors from all over. We have projects that we raise foundation funds for. We have proposals, for instance, at Plowshares for our events on nuclear weapons reduction. I talked about our proposal on family planning. We have Christian-Muslim engagement. On Earth Day 2010, in Morocco, we created the Casablanca Institute. It aims to continue the conversation that began in 2004 with Muslim leaders on climate change, weapons proliferation, poverty, and other issues. The institute includes people such as the president of Al Akhawayn University and former diplomats in Morocco on the board. The point is to build interfaith dialogue not for dialogue's sake but for engagement on issues. I told Samuel Huntington that he didn't understand evangelicals if he thinks there's going to be a hundred-year war. So he said, "I don't understand evangelicals." That kind of religious war is not in the cards. And it doesn't further what evangelicals want.

The New Evangelical Partnership is also going to do a criminal justice program, with a focus on juvenile justice. I got introduced to this the hard way. My sixteen-year-old was drug-tested and spent thirty days in the detention center on a false drug charge. I also have a young kid from the Caribbean living in our home who got involved with the criminal justice system. I'd like to do a project on reversing the criminalization of youth, because that's what's going on. For a lot of judges, the solution to a problem is incarceration. But there ought to be a way, in a faith-based initiative, for nonviolent offenders to skip incarceration and do probation and restitution. Many judges already do community service but along with incarceration — they do both — and it's the introduction into the criminal justice system that is so bad for kids when they go in for thirty days.

When evangelicals think that they'll start a ministry, they don't realize how large the dimensions of the issue are. My son had an awful experience in part because he wasn't afforded a simple change in the law that would be very helpful: whenever you have a kid who's been found to be positive on a drug test, you mandate — especially if the kid disputes the test — a follow-up chain of custody test [a strict monitoring process to prevent tampering with the sample or the results of drug testing]. My son's probation office told me, "Drug tests don't lie; teenagers lie." I said, "Give him another test" — same result. Even a third. But we went to the hospital for a chain of custody test. The next morning we went to an emergency center for another test but the doctor just went onto the hospital computer and said, "Your son hasn't used any drugs — clean on every count." What was going on?

I went to an OSI [Office of Special Investigations] meeting in Chicago and these guys said, "Welcome to our world. This happens all the time all around the country." How do we fix it? They said, the chain of custody test. But they also said, "Don't be deceived. The reason why the states and probation officers don't want to mandate it is because the probation officers get more money the more kids they supervise, and the state gets money for its prison system by building more prisons."

The way you change this is to get a purple state like Virginia [formerly Republican, increasingly mixed in party affiliation] to shift its policies. Then you go to the national state legislature convenings to talk with other states about rolling back this incarceration trend. We're going to try it in Virginia, where I live. I know enough legislators there with seniority, one of whom had a son of his own who was repeatedly incarcerated for marijuana. He knows that incarceration is counterproductive.

If evangelicals are identified with the common good, with doing things that help everybody, others won't say, "I don't want to live next to that kind of person." When you do national surveys about who people think evangelicals are, they are seen as people who hate abortion, hate gays, blah blah. And I have a lot of young evangelicals who say, "We're with you but we don't like the term 'evangelical.'"

We use it because you can't change it unless you claim it from within. Many evangelicals have had pastors who've allowed them to think one way for a long time because it was so easy. Now people in the congregations are saying, "We're not satisfied with your simple definition of being an evangelical, which is to profess Christ and go to church."

I'm not averse to saying that the deeper you go into Jesus, the less judgmental you become.

MP How do you explain the anti-Muslim animus among evangelicals?

RC There are people with a vested interest in stoking it, who want to turn Islam into the new evil empire. Some of it is that they need to have an opponent. Some of it is ignorance, or bigotry. Some are involved in Christians United for Israel or with the dispensational emphasis on the role of Israel in redemption — and some of those folk have anti-Muslim attitudes. Some of their leaders are insufficiently sensitive to the ways in which their policy recommendations have contributed to anti-Muslim fervor.

It's hard to pinpoint one cause, except there is at heart a relationship deficit. In 2008, I did a poll of the NAE board, 120 Christian leaders, and not one of them would profess to having one Muslim friend or acquaintance. That's a relationship deficit! If you don't have one friend of another faith, you're going to be insensitive in ways you don't even know you are.

But it can be spoken to. You have to speak out against it. Silence isn't an option. I'm confident that there are enough people who oppose that sort of thing. We even had Franklin Graham [Billy Graham's son], who won't give up his "Islam is an evil and wicked religion" shtick, but even he said, you can't burn the Koran [when a small Florida church threatened to do so on the 2010 anniversary of the September 11 attacks].

MP Where is the New Evangelical Partnership on Israel?

RC We're among those who believe we need a new, balanced foreign policy on Israel and Palestine. We would support a two-state solution. There is the idea that Israel is way up here at the top of evangelical priorities. But on the laundry list of issues in the Pew 2008 Religious Landscape Survey,[7] it's not. It's down the list.

There is a process of maturing on foreign policy among evangelicals and it'll be reflected in a less dispensational view of Israel policy. I've been to White House briefings in the past where evangelicals stood up and said to the staff assistant to Elliott Abrams [Deputy National Security Adviser for Global Democracy Strategy under G. W. Bush],[8] "Tell Mr. Abrams he's doing a good job, but if the president compromises and supports a two-state solution, God will bring him down."

I've changed my mind about interfaith dialogue. I used to say, I don't do interfaith. September 11 changed my mind. We — evangelicals — have to deal with foreign policy issues. We have to do this for the sake of the movement, for the sake of our personal reputations, for the sake of the gospel. We have to engage with religious communities abroad. My predecessor at the NAE, whose funeral I spoke at a few weeks ago, never in my knowledge of the eighteen years I worked with him, went overseas, aside from Hawaii. When he was stepping down in 1996, the NAE held an event called "A Statement of Conscience on Worldwide Religious Persecution." Over one hundred Christian leaders signed the statement. It was the first foray into the international terrain and it became the rallying cry that led to the passage of the International Religious Freedom Act in 1998.

We need a balanced foreign policy not only on Israel/Palestine but overall. America has resorted to policies that prop up dictators and regimes that in the long run haven't served American interests well. Now evangelicals have a reputation as players on the international front. We started with the International Religious Freedom Act (1998), then the Victims of Trafficking and Violence Protection Act (2000), the Prison Rape Elimination Act (2003), then PEPFAR, U.S. President's Emergency Plan for AIDS Relief (2003), the North Korean Human Rights Act (2004), and then the Darfur Accountability and Divestment Act (2007). We're going to be critical players in implementing the new START

7. http://religions.pewforum.org/reports.

8. Abrams was also Assistant Secretary for Inter-American Affairs under President Reagan, a key player in the Iran-contra affair.

[Strategic Arms Reduction Treaty, the nuclear arms reduction treaty between the United States and the Russian Federation]. There were four Republicans on the Senate Foreign Relations Committee who voted for it in 2010 — Johnny Isakson, Richard Lugar, Bob Corker among them — on what should be a bipartisan vote. But we evangelicals are going to Colorado Springs, in the shadow of NORAD [North American Aerospace Defense Command],[9] to host the movie *Countdown to Zero* with Muslim leaders from the Middle East, who'll be in the discussion after the screening.

You have Tea Partiers and others ready to wage war not only against Muslims but also against the former Soviet Union. Look at the new contract for a new ABM [antiballistic missile] system. Fight a nuclear war with Russia? Are you kidding me? Billions for a new ABM system? — and they say they want to cut the deficit and balance the budget. And they also want to cut taxes for the wealthiest 1 percent of Americans. This is lunacy! It's an internal contradiction; it can't be done. That's voodoo economics if I've ever heard it.

The report *Engaging Religious Communities Abroad* — we call it a new imperative for U.S. foreign policy — is something I've been doing with R. Scott Appleby and others for the Task Force on Religion and the Making of U.S. Foreign Policy sponsored by the Chicago Council on Global Affairs. Obama asked the task force to analyze U.S. foreign policy and make recommendations. There'll also be reports from the Department of Defense and other offices, and they'll all be collated for recommendations for the Obama administration.

Our assessment is that we need structural changes within the government to understand what's happening. The success in Iraq was seriously hampered by a failure to understand religious movements. In our report, we outline these religious trends, chief and foremost that religion has a new political salience. We also need changes outside governments as well, in NGOs, academia, and other intermediaries who can play a role in the civilian engagement that has to occur in places like Pakistan and Afghanistan.

We can't spend two billion dollars per week on this war in Afghanistan. We can't afford it. The only option is a different form of engagement in the twenty-first century.

---

9. NORAD is run by the United States and Canada to provide aerospace warning, air sovereignty, and defense.

chapter 6

The "New Evangelical" Landscape

An Overview

In October 2008, as the nation was preparing to vote for president, evangelicals were undergoing what evangelical theologian Scot McKnight called "the biggest change in the evangelical movement at the end of the twentieth century, a new kind of Christian social conscience."[1] Evangelical concerns were broadening from abortion, gay marriage, and electoral wins to poverty relief, environmental protection, and immigration reform.

One sign of this change was the way evangelicals viewed church involvement in elections. Nearly the same proportion of white evangelicals (64 percent) as religiously unaffiliated Americans (68 percent) held that it was *not* the role of churches to endorse political candidates. Among those who attend church at least once a week, 63 percent opposed candidate endorsement.[2] Among those for whom opposition to gay marriage was politically key, 50 percent disagreed with candidate endorsement — up from 25 percent in 2004. Among those for whom

---

1. Scot McKnight teaches at North Park University, Chicago; see D. Kirkpatrick, "The Evangelical Crackup," *New York Times Magazine*, October 28, 2007; see also R. Sider, *Rich Christians in an Age of Hunger: Moving from Affluence to Generosity* (Nashville: Nelson, 1977); R. Sider, *Just Generosity* (Grand Rapids: Baker, 1999); R. Sider, *The Scandal of Evangelical Politics: Why Are Christians Missing the Chance to Really Change the World?* (Grand Rapids: Baker, 2008).

2. Pew Forum on Religion and Public Life, "Americans Wary of Church Involvement in Partisan Politics," October 1, 2008.

opposition to abortion was key, 49 percent opposed candidate endorsement — up from 33 percent in 2004.[3]

Such shifts were emerging not among an elite but across the demographic and geographic range. By 2008, the devout who identified themselves as outside the Religious Right came to 25 percent of the adult population. Making up this group were the Religious Left, at 9 percent (the Evangelical Left, the Catholic Left, and new, evangelical emergent churches); "red letter Christians" (who red-line Jesus' words in the Bible as a guide to progressive politics), also at 9 percent; and religious centrists, those with liberal theology and moderate-centrist politics, at about 6 percent.[4] The National Association of Evangelicals (NAE), reflecting a center bloc of the "new evangelical" range, includes 45,000 churches from fifty denominations. The Willow Creek network, an evangelical forerunner in poverty relief and environmental protection, has 12,000 churches from ninety denominations in forty-five countries. The Vineyard church network, internationally known leaders in poverty relief and environmental protection, has 1,600 churches worldwide.

One group not included in these shifts or in this book is the historically black churches, which led the civil rights movement and the next forty years of minority community development. "It was religion that got us on the buses for the Freedom Rides," John Lewis, among the leaders of the 1965 civil rights march in Selma, Alabama, notes. "We were in Selma that day because of our faith."[5] Hardly a speech of Martin Luther King's failed to link political rights and Christian faith. The historically black churches often hold conservative views on abortion and gay marriage but tend toward progressive positions on the economy, including government aid to the needy. As a result, the black evangelical vote is strongly Democrat (over 90 percent). The historically black churches have also been among the most consistent, long-term providers of private, faith-based social services and have most extensively bridged across racial and religious lines. While cooperation between white and black evangelicals has increased significantly since the

3. Pew Forum on Religion and Public Life, "More Americans Question Religion's Role in Politics," August 21, 2008.

4. Pew Forum for Religion and Public Life, "Assessing a More Prominent 'Religious Left,'" June 5, 2008.

5. J. Meacham, *American Gospel: God, the Founding Fathers, and the Making of a Nation* (New York: Random House, 2006), p. 192.

1990s, the history and politics of the black churches form their own tradition, which demands its own study. A number of works begin such an investigation.[6]

Explaining religio-political shifts among white evangelicals since 2005, John Green, leading analyst at the Pew Forum for Religion and Public Life, said, "It may have something to do with the perception that's shared by many people, not just by young evangelicals, that the Republican Party didn't manage the government well."[7] For many evangelicals, the gap between Jesus' instructions to love and serve and certain of Bush's policies — his use of torture, for instance — grew alarming. Moreover, Jesus joined no political party or government. Thus, for increasing numbers of evangelicals, the role of those who follow him is not to be the state but to remain outside it, serving society and advising government when it is unjust. The view gained ground among evangelicals that being in government does not necessarily lead to the kingdom of God or the Christian path.

"New evangelical" explorations of a different path came on the heels of broader national shifts. Over the last forty years, ideas about sex, the environment, pluralism, and global connectedness changed in the heartland as in coastal cities. Evangelical experience of globally interlocked economies and family life (divorce, gay relatives, etc.) began to raise questions about the approaches of the 1970s-1990s. Positions that seemed "middle of the road" then seemed, by 2005, unnuanced or unresponsive to new conditions. The Internet and YouTube and social networking sites allow people to see environmental disasters and the faces of the third-world poor; evangelicals, like anyone else with access to a computer, communicate with people unlike themselves. In 2009, Richard Land, president of the Commission on Ethics and Religious Liberty of the relatively conservative Southern Baptist Convention, voiced no objection to Obama's inclusion of atheists in his speeches: "We are," Land said, "a very pluralistic nation."[8]

6. See C. P. De Young et al., *United by Faith: The Multiracial Congregation as an Answer to the Problem of Race* (New York: Oxford University Press, 2004); M. Noll, *God and Race in American Politics* (Princeton: Princeton University Press, 2008); D. Perry, *Breaking Down Barriers: A Black Evangelical Explains the Black Church* (Grand Rapids: Baker, 1998).

7. Pew Forum for Religion and Public Life, "A Post-election Look at Religious Voters in the 2008 Election," December 8, 2008.

8. L. Meckler, "Obama Walks Religious Tightrope Spanning Faithful, Nonbelievers," *Wall Street Journal*, March 24, 2009.

Political Effects: Civil Society Activism, Party Adhesion, Issue-by-Issue Policy Assessment

The "new evangelical" shift from emphasizing political wins to emphasizing civil society activism — what Richard Cizik describes as a "gradual earthquake"[9] — was visible by 2006, when David Kuo, former deputy director of Bush's White House Office of Faith-Based and Community Initiatives, lambasted evangelicals who were instrumentalizing Jesus for party politics — who were "taking Jesus and reducing him to some precinct captain, to some get-out-the-vote guy."[10] "Suddenly we were reminded," an office worker and evangelical in the Midwest said, "Caesar — governments — are fallen; they will sin and you can never tell when. Christians have to be with the Gospel, not with the party, and they have to go to DC to argue for those who have no voice."[11]

A second political effect of evangelical change is party adhesion. Though evangelicals had been a Republican bloc for nearly forty years (as we've seen, with 62 percent of white evangelicals voting Republican in the 1996 and 2000 presidential elections, 78 percent in 2004), in 2009, 35 percent identified as Democrats, 34 percent as Republican, and the remaining third as independents.[12] Yet the significant change in party adhesion was not a shift to the Democratic Party — unlikely in any case because of opposition to abortion and traditional evangelical preferences for self-reliance and small government. Rather, it was to more of an issue-by-issue assessment of policy — more Democrat on environment and economic justice, more Republican on abortion, more independent on government involvement in the market. This sort of fine-tuning poses little difficulty in social service projects as "new evangelicals," like other citizens, need declare no party allegiance in their educational, environmental, or anti-poverty efforts. Yet in voting, where one chooses along party lines, some evangelicals find themselves with an internal schism. If the abortion issue were even somewhat resolved, by extensive investment in abortion reduction for instance, some of the glue that binds evangelicals to the Republican Party might weaken. As Richard Land noted, "If that issue [abortion] were taken off the table,

9. Interview with the author, September 28, 2010.
10. D. Kuo, *Tempting Faith: An Inside Story of Political Seduction* (New York: Free Press, 2006).
11. Interview with the author, April 26, 2009.
12. D. Stone, "One Nation under God?" *Newsweek*, April 7, 2009.

then other issues get oxygen, issues where evangelicals are not nearly as certain that Republicans offer the best answer. Issues like economic justice, racial reconciliation, the environment."[13]

Land's prediction was evident in 2010, when 75 percent of evangelicals voted Republican in the midterm elections in dissatisfaction with Democratic economic policy. But evangelical leaders agreed with Obama on eighteen policy issues including immigration reform, abortion reduction, the importance of fatherhood, the Strategic Arms Reduction Treaty (START) to reduce nuclear weapons, and the new health care bill (even where there was disagreement about certain provisions). Announcement of that agreement was a headline article in the December 2010 NAE newsletter.[14] The NAE itself encouraged members to write to congressional representatives in support of START and the Dream Act, which allows undocumented young people to earn citizenship by attending college or serving in the military.

Indeed, issue-by-issue policy assessment has been evident since Bush's second term. Owing to the disarray in Iraq and Afghanistan, to the Bush administration's use of torture, and to its thin response to environmental degradation, evangelicals began to view the Republican platform more critically. While in 2002, 87 percent of white evangelicals aged eighteen to twenty-nine approved of Bush's performance, in 2007 the figure dropped to 45 percent. Among older white evangelicals, support dropped from 80 percent in 2002 to 52 percent in 2007. Between 2001 and 2005, the percentage of young, white evangelicals who considered themselves Republicans was consistent at 55 percent; in 2007 it was 37 percent.[15] The financial collapse of 2008 deepened evangelical critique. Marvin Olasky, editor of the evangelical magazine *World* and adviser to Bush when he was governor of Texas, noted, "There was a time when evangelical churches were becoming largely and almost exclusively the Republican Party at prayer. To some extent — we have to see how much — the Republicans have blown it. . . . The ball now really is in the Democrats' court."[16]

13. Quoted in S. Tomma, "Influence of Christian Right in the GOP Wanes," McClatchy Washington Bureau, September 30, 2007.

14. http://www.nae.net/news-and-events/525-evangelicals-concur-with-obama-on-multiple-issues.

15. D. Cox, "Young White Evangelicals: Less Republican, Still Conservative," Pew Forum on Religion and Public Life, September 28, 2007.

16. Quoted in Kirkpatrick, "The Evangelical Crackup."

Democrats picked up the challenge. In 2005, Democrats in Congress set up the Faith Working Group. The Democratic Party developed the Faith in Action (FIA) committee of religious advisers to liaison between the party and America's devout. Starting in 2007, the Obama campaign included a point person, Joshua DuBois, a black Pentecostal pastor, for evangelical outreach and "faith policy." In 2008, the Democrats asked the evangelical ministers Tony Campolo and Joel Hunter to help write the Democratic Party platform on abortion reduction. The platform now reads: "The Democratic Party also strongly supports a woman's decision to have a child by ensuring access to and availability of programs for pre- and post-natal health care, parenting skills, income support, and caring adoption."[17] The 2008 Democratic nominating convention was the first to open with a religious service and include a caucus for people of faith.

Disappointed by Bush and looking at policy more case-by-case, "new evangelicals" began to respond — to listen to what political actors outside the Republican Party were saying. In 2006, Rick Warren, pastor at California's influential Saddleback megachurch, invited Obama to his conference on AIDS. In 2007, he invited Hillary Clinton. Willow Creek invited Bill. In 2008, Warren invited both McCain and Obama. Leah Daughtry, a Pentecostal minister, served as chief of staff to Howard Dean, chairman of the Democratic National Committee. She ran the 2008 Democratic Convention, which nominated Obama. Pro-Obama evangelical leaders and political action committees emerged. Mara Vanderslice founded the Matthew 25 Network, a pro-Democrat, evangelical political action committee that ran $500,000 worth of commercials on Christian radio stations in battleground states. One read: "Imagine a president who stands for this, 'For I was hungry and you gave me something to eat. . . . I needed clothes and you clothed me, I was sick and you looked after me, I was in prison and you came to visit me' (Matthew 25:35-36)." Kirbyjon Caldwell, the influential Houston pastor, gave his support to Obama, though he had given the benediction at both of Bush's presidential inaugurations and presided at the wedding of Bush's daughter in May 2008. Another prominent leader, Wilfredo De Jesús, pastor at New Life Covenant Church in Chicago and staunch opponent of abortion and gay marriage, supported a Demo-

17. See T. Murphy, "Evangelicals, Catholics Applaud DNC's Abortion Language Change," *Religion News Service*, August 12, 2008.

crat, Obama, for the first time in his life.[18] After he was elected, Obama invited Rick Warren to give the invocation at the presidential inauguration. Bishop T. D. Jakes, who draws thirty thousand to his Dallas church, gave the sermon at the private service earlier that morning. In his first months of office, Obama assembled a group of religious leaders as advisers on faith-based social services. They included Jakes, Joel Hunter, Kirbyjon Caldwell, Otis Moss Jr., an icon of the civil rights movement, and Jim Wallis, of the evangelical Sojourners group. Jakes, Wallis, and Hunter are political independents. Moss and Caldwell endorsed Obama.

With the economic recession running into 2011, evangelical criticism of Obama mirrored the nation's. On one side was criticism from progressives. In June 2010, a coalition of religious groups convened in Washington to urge Obama to compromise less with fiscal conservatives and give more to stimulus spending. Complaints were voiced about Obama's scuttling of the public option in his health care program, the only loose requirement on banks to use their bailout money for loans that would spur the economy, and Obama's failure to close Guantanamo Bay prison.[19] David Gushee wrote, "In President Obama's first month in office, he signed Executive Orders that sought to dismantle the practice of torture that had become normalized during the Bush/Cheney administration; however, he has not been thorough enough in investigation nor tough enough in prosecutions. . . . Joining with other people of faith, prophetic evangelicals must continue to call the United States to accountability."[20] The 2010 Gulf oil spill raised additional concerns among evangelicals — from Jim Ball of the Evangelical Environmental Network to the Southern Baptist Convention,

---

18. J. Kennedy, "Preach and Reach: Despite His Liberal Record, Obama Is Making a Lot of Evangelicals Think Twice," *Christianity Today,* October 6, 2008. Openness to Obama and the Democrats was noteworthy among evangelicals outside the South and among younger evangelicals (ages eighteen to twenty-nine); see Religion & Ethics NewsWeekly/United Nations Foundation, "Religion & Ethics Newsweekly/UN Foundation Survey Explores Religion and America's Role in the World," October 22, 2008; see Pew Forum on Religion and Public Life, "A Post-election Look at Religious Voters in the 2008 Election."

19. F. Alfonso III, "Religious Left, Disillusioned with Obama, Coming to D.C.," *Religion News Service,* June 9, 2010.

20. D. Gushee, "Shalom," in *Prophetic Evangelicals,* ed. Peter Goodwin Heltzel, Bruce Ellis Benson, and Malinda Elizabeth Berry (Grand Rapids: Eerdmans, forthcoming).

whose July 2010 statement declared that humanity's "God-given dominion over the creation is not unlimited, as though we were gods and
not creatures." It called for "energy policies based on prudence, conservation, accountability and safety."[21]

On the other side was the conservative and Tea Party critique that
taxes under Obama remained too high, that the stimulus program
made the deficit unsustainable, and that Obama's "big government"
approach would overregulate the very private market activities that create economic growth. This was the more substantial evangelical critique, which also carried majorities in all major voting blocs.

In summing up the political effects of the evangelical shift since
2004, it's worth noting that voting Republican or Democrat in any
given election raises no threats to liberal democracy, and this book is
not primarily concerned with it. It is concerned instead with political
and party independence, policy assessment (the aims of evangelical activism), and the means to achieve political aims — all key to democratic governance.

If the research for this project suggests anything, it is to refine
our categories. For forty years, evangelicals were associated with the
Republican Party, opposition to abortion and gay marriage, and at
times attempts to use the state to impose religious views on the nation. Since 2005, "new evangelicals" are still associated with the Republicans and opposition to abortion but also with poverty relief, immigration reform, and environmental protection rather than with
attempts to penetrate government.

Effects on Activism: Poverty Relief, Conflict Resolution, Immigration Reform, Human Rights, HIV/AIDS, Health Care, Environmental Protection, and Racial Reconciliation

In 2006, Terry Fox, a twenty-year organizer of anti-abortion and antigay
activity in Wichita, Kansas, was asked to step down as pastor of his
megachurch because his activism was no longer "pertinent" to the congregation's new efforts against poverty and environmental degrada-

20. J. Flesher, "Green Religion Movement Hopes Gulf Oil Spill Wins Converts,"
Huffington Post, July 7, 2010.

tion. Within three months, two other Religious Right preachers left Wichita as well.[22] In 2007, when the head pastor died at Coral Ridge Presbyterian, a Florida megachurch with ten thousand members and a TV/radio/Web site audience of three million, the church determined not to hire another pastor of the same religio-political cloth. It broadened its program to include climate change, human rights, poverty, and other social justice issues, and it closed the church's political arm, the Center for Reclaiming America for Christ.[23]

In 2008, 60 percent of evangelicals held that government should do more to help the poor, even if this meant increasing the national debt.[24] Regular church attendance correlated with poverty relief, environmental protection,[25] and the belief that diplomacy rather than military strength was the best way to ensure peace.[26] Putting diplomacy into practice, over one hundred evangelical leaders and the Yale Center for Faith and Culture answered a letter in 2007 from leaders in the Muslim world.[27] Signers to the evangelical letter included NAE president Leith Anderson, Jim Wallis of Sojourners, and Rick Warren. The evangelical letter began by "acknowledging that in the past (during the Crusades, for instance) and in the present (in the excesses of the 'war on terror'), many Christians have been guilty of sinning against our Muslim neighbours." It asked for the "forgiveness of the All-Merciful One and of the Muslim community around the world," and it suggested that "our next step should be for our leaders at every level to meet together and begin the earnest work of determining how God would have us fulfil the requirement that we love God and one another."

The "new evangelical" focus on poverty relief continues the centuries-old tradition of evangelical charity and reinvigorates its more progressive aspects, so vibrant through the nineteenth century. On the

22. Kirkpatrick, "The Evangelical Crackup."

23. D. Gehrke-White, H. Sampson, and A. Veciana-Suarez, "Coral Ridge Presbyterian Puts Politics Aside for Now," *Miami Herald,* August 28, 2007.

24. Pew Forum on Religions and Public Life, "Analyzing the Fall Campaign: Religion and the Presidential Election," September 9, 2008.

25. By 2008, 54 percent of evangelical churches held that greater environmental protection was worth the cost; see Pew Forum on Religion and Public Life, "U.S. Religious Landscape Survey," April 19, 2008.

26. Pew Forum on Religion and Public Life, "U.S. Religious Landscape Survey."

27. Yale Center for Faith and Culture, "A Christian Response to 'A Common Word between Us and You,'" 2007.

more traditional end, Bush in 2004 — under evangelical prodding — increased foreign aid to $19 billion, up from $7 billion under Clinton. Aid to Africa alone rose 67 percent. Evangelicals have been active in trying to end the war in the Sudan. Samaritan's Purse has been particularly strong there (its hospital there has been repeatedly bombed). Its leader, Franklin Graham, son of Billy Graham, was among those who pushed Bush toward negotiating the Sudan peace in January 2005.[28]

World Vision, founded in 1950 and the largest Christian aid organization, aids 100 million people in nearly 100 countries. Its annual budget of over $1 billion comes from governmental and private sources, including donations from 4.7 million Americans. Its microcredit program supports over 440,000 projects in 46 developing countries. Other major evangelical relief agencies include the National Hispanic Christian Leadership Conference, which emphasizes poverty relief and immigration reform. The Association of Evangelical Relief and Development Organization has since 1978 provided a wide range of aid and training to people of all races, religions, and ethnic groups through its forty-seven member groups worldwide. The International Justice Mission, founded in 1997, now with a $10 million budget, focuses on human rights, slavery, sex trafficking, forced labor, rape, illegal detention, and police brutality. Christian Churches Together, a broad ecumenical coalition across the Protestant, evangelical, Catholic, and Orthodox churches, was founded in 2006 and issued its initiative against poverty in 2009.

Parachurch organizations like those above work alongside individual churches such as Rick Warren's, where between 2004 and 2009 over 9,000 members left their homes to serve the poor in 146 nations. Warren's 2007 HIV/AIDS conference featured not only Hillary Clinton but also the first ladies of Rwanda and Zambia.[29] His PEACE[30] coalition links hundreds of first-world congregations with sister churches in developing regions to combat poverty, disease, illiteracy, corruption, and conflict. One PEACE effort raised the number of health care pro-

28. W. Mead, "God's Country?" *Foreign Affairs,* September/October 2006; A. Hertzke, *Freeing God's Children: The Unlikely Alliance for Global Human Rights* (Lanham, Md.: Rowman and Littlefield, 2004).

29. Pew Forum on Religion and Public Life, "The Future of Evangelicals: A Conversation with Pastor Rick Warren," November 13, 2009.

30. PEACE stands for Promote reconciliation, Equip ethical leaders, Assist the poor, Care for the sick, and Educate the next generation.

viders in a Rwanda region from 1 doctor in 2007 to over 1,400 trained community health care workers in 2009. Warren explains: while there was only 1 doctor, there were "826 congregations in this thing. Now, where would you like to get your meds distributed? [A hospital] two days' walk, [a clinic] one day's walk, or five minutes away?" Churches could be the distribution centers for "not only health care, [but] for everything else."[31]

These programs fall fairly well within the traditional evangelical scope. But "new evangelicals" also take positions that more conservative evangelicals would not. Indeed, the evangelical political spectrum has so broadened that the progressive Jim Wallis has found himself criticized for not being progressive enough. *Street Prophet* blog, for instance, wrote that Wallis had compromised too much in his work with bipartisan groups. Wallis, who used to be about as far left on the evangelical spectrum as one could get, is now outflanked.

Among the less traditional arenas of activism are immigration reform and universal access to health care. Because these are controversial, they provoke intrachurch debate and are not always easy positions for organizations to take. In 2010, the NAE, the New Evangelical Partnership for the Common Good, and the Southern Baptist Convention, among other organizations, issued statements supporting comprehensive immigration reform including a path to citizenship for undocumented migrants.[32] But the Southern Baptist Convention also noted that their statement divided the Baptist constituency between supporters and those who feel illegals are lawbreakers who jump the line over applicants for legal immigration and take advantage of American social services.

Also raising not a few eyebrows was the excoriation from Kay Warren, a key AIDS activist and Rick Warren's wife, chastening evangelicals for the "sinful absence and puny efforts" in fighting HIV/AIDS in the past. She and her husband ask not "How did you get sick?" — as though the illness might be appropriate punishment for sin. They ask instead, "What can I do? How can I help you?" Some contended that the church's mandate was spiritual, not social or medical; Kay Warren

31. Pew Forum on Religion and Public Life, "The Future of Evangelicals."
32. National Association of Evangelicals, "NAE Ad Urges Bipartisan Immigration Reform," press release, May 13, 2010; A. M. Banks, "Evangelicals Find New Unity on Immigration," *Huffington Post,* July 13, 2010; C. Echegaray, "Baptist Leader Richard Land Backs Citizenship for Illegal Immigrants," *Tennessean,* June 8, 2010.

said, "I completely disagreed. This is historically at the heart of our Christian faith."[33]

In 2004, the NAE released a watershed document detailing its aims, which David Gushee, professor of Christian ethics at Mercer University, called "a major breakthrough. . . . It is hard to overstate the significance of the new balance and holism that this move represents."[34] The document, *For the Health of the Nation: An Evangelical Call to Civic Responsibility*, calls for a fair legal and economic system "which does not tolerate perpetual poverty. Though the Bible does not call for economic equality, it condemns gross disparities in opportunity and outcome that cause suffering." The word "outcome" is noteworthy. It would not likely be accepted by economic conservatives or the Religious Right, who hold equality of opportunity in procedurally open markets to be sufficient for productive and just economies. Yet equality of opportunity may yield significant, long-term inequalities in outcomes, which the NAE finds unacceptable. It therefore supports not only a liberal economic system and private property but also *structural* improvements in health care, nutrition, education, job training, and immigration.[35] In a significant departure from Republican (and certainly Tea Party) policy, with which evangelicals have been associated, the NAE holds that structural change requires efforts not only by faith-based and civil society groups but also by government. In its 2011 "'Lowering the Debt, Raising the Poor' Resolution,"[36] the NAE called "on the President and Congress to address the national debt in a way that protects and lifts up the poor" because "non-security aid to the world's poor receives only 1 percent of the federal budget" and thus if aid is cut to reduce the deficit, "Private programs, including those run by NAE member organizations, are unlikely to be able to make up the difference." Interna-

33. J. Serjeant, "US Evangelicals Strive to Change Attitudes on AIDS," Reuters, November 28, 2007.

34. D. Gushee, *The Future of Faith in American Politics: The Public Witness of the Evangelical Center* (Waco, Tex.: Baylor University Press, 2008), p. 240.

35. In 2009, NAE president Leith Anderson and other evangelical leaders issued a statement asking Obama to provide adequate finances to implement immigration laws and reduce the "enormous" waiting time for immigrants applying for legal status; see M. Vu, "Evangelicals Make Case for Welcoming Immigrants," *Christian Post Reporter,* April 1, 2009.

36. See http://www.nae.net/news/543=press=release=nae=board=approves=lowering =the=debt=raising=the=poor=resolution.

tionally, the NAE calls for improving nutrition, providing clean water and health care, and preventing or reducing HIV/AIDS, slavery, sex trafficking, and rape. It seeks fair trade economic policies rather than liberal, free-trade only.

Even less traditional than these antipoverty efforts was the 2008 *Evangelical Manifesto*,[37] signed by over seventy evangelical leaders, which offers a harsh critique of the "cheerleaders for those in power and the naïve sycophants of the powerful and the rich." It calls for the "expansion of our concerns beyond single-issue politics, such as abortion and marriage, and a fuller recognition of the comprehensive causes and concerns of the Gospel . . . engaging the global giants of conflict, racism, corruption, poverty, pandemic diseases, illiteracy, ignorance, and spiritual emptiness, by promoting reconciliation, encouraging ethical servant leadership, assisting the poor, caring for the sick, and educating the next generation."

"Reconciliation" is a key word, meaning a coming together in mutual respect, after hostility or persecution, to work toward a better future. It does not extend to "social justice" or "distributive justice," which holds that those who have been deprived of opportunity should be ensured not only improved opportunities but also compensation for past injustice, in the form of better living conditions and assistance out of poverty, which is considered a "right." The idea of assistance as a "right" fits poorly with America's tradition of individualist self-reliance, and neither the NAE nor the *Evangelical Manifesto* supports it.

Yet some "new evangelical" leaders work with modified "social justice" ideas because, as Gushee explains, "Shalom means economic justice — everyone has the means necessary to work successfully to meet their material needs, and no one is permitted to take away from anyone either the means of production (mainly land) or the goods it produces."[38] Wallis; Ron Sider, founder of Evangelicals for Social Action; his colleague the late Diane Knippers; and Joel Hunter, on Obama's 2009-10 advisory council, endorse not only aid to the needy but also an overhaul in "how the numerous goods of society are divided."[39] Hunter writes, "The question from a biblical standpoint for a

37. *Evangelical Manifesto: A Declaration of Evangelical Identity and Public Commitment* (Washington, D.C.: Evangelical Manifesto Steering Committee, 2008).

38. Gushee, "Shalom."

39. R. Sider and D. Knippers, *Toward an Evangelical Public Policy* (Grand Rapids: Baker, 2005), p. 165.

Christian to consider is . . . 'Will this legislation or candidate result in the kind of redistribution of wealth that strengthens all of society?'"[40] Hunter is an interesting man. In 2006, he turned down leadership of the Christian Coalition because it was unwilling to expand programming sufficiently to include poverty relief and environmental protection, which Hunter considers an evangelical mandate.

Further still from conservative evangelicalism are the "emergent churches," groups often of younger believers who meet in unorthodox places such as bowling alleys, movie theaters, and private apartments to pray, study, and develop ministries to the needy. The Barna Group,[41] which provides statistical and survey research for evangelical organizations, estimated that participants in "emergent churches" by 2006 came to over twenty million. One group, National Community Church, meets in Washington's Union Railroad Station, local coffeehouses, and movie theaters to reach the homeless, staffers on Capitol Hill, and anyone else coming through. Its core values have the combination of playfulness and devotion to the gospel that characterizes "emergent" groups: "Expect the unexpected, Irrelevance is irreverence, Playing it safe is risky, Pray like it depends on God and work like it depends on you, Everything is an experiment, Maturity does not equal conformity, and It's never too late to be who you might have been."

Central Community Church in Las Vegas works with the homeless, the addicted, prisoners, and sex workers in America's "sin city." Its pastor, Jud Wilhite, titled his book on his ministry *Stripped: Uncensored Grace on the Streets of Vegas*. Prison Fellowship Ministries was founded by Chuck Colson after his release from prison for obstruction of justice in the Watergate scandal.[42] It works with gangs and substance abuse in prison, and prepares men for more productive lives on their release. xxxchurch.com reaches to the more provocative end of the "emergent church" spectrum. It works with actors in the pornography industry as well as with people who feel their sexuality has been distorted by pornography. Founder Mike Ethur writes, "Jesus wiped away the tears of the prostitutes, held the hands of the outcasts, and touched the

40. J. Hunter, *A New Kind of Conservative* (Ventura, Calif.: Gospel Light Publishing, 2008), p. 94.

41. http://www.barna.org/.

42. Colson is the author of over twenty books, has received fifteen honorary doctorates, and in 1993 was awarded the Templeton Prize in the field of religion. He donated this prize to Prison Fellowship, as he does all his speaking fees and royalties.

wounds of the sick and crazy. . . . Porn stars or preachers, gay or straight, Republican or Democrat . . . we are all in need of this stunningly beautiful thing called grace."[43]

43. D. Kinnaman and G. Lyons, *Unchristian: What a New Generation Really Thinks about Christianity and Why It Matters* (Grand Rapids: Baker, 2007), p. 203.

Vineyard Church, Boise, Idaho

Boise is located in what Idahoans call the "banana belt," that sliver of land that gets slightly less snow than its surroundings. It was rancher country, and space and freedom are prized still. The Vineyard Church, 95,000 square feet, is located on twenty-two acres of what used to be the Boise airport. It is surrounded by trailer parks and communities of immigrants, both legal and undocumented, mostly from eastern Europe, Mexico, and the Balkans. The parishioners are largely working and lower-middle class. Few earn over $50,000 per year (the American median income is $47,000). Nonetheless, donations can be significant. The church raised $66,000 in one offering to build a training center in a Zambian village and $100,000 in another, for church ministries.

A small community of Karen refugees, unwanted by both Thailand and Burma, has found its way from Southeast Asia to Boise. Some are Christian, many Buddhist. To all, the church offers English classes and training in such things as résumé writing and job-interview skills. It offers a Sunday worship service in the native Karen language.

Vineyard's environmental protection program has become a model for churches around the world. Other church ministries include Sunday food distribution to the homeless and a food pantry that distributes over 15,000 food boxes a year. The Ministry on Human Slavery combats labor exploitation and sex trafficking in and outside the United States. The men's ministry hopes to reduce spousal abandonment and divorce. Celebrate Recovery addresses substance abuse, and the overseas missions aim at helping developing-world churches. Of particular pride to Boise Vineyard is its organic garden, tilled by two hundred volunteers, that produces over 31,322 pounds of food for over 1,800 families (over 6,260 people). Sharmin Reynolds, among those who oversee the garden, is learning what vegetables are important to the Karen community.

Church ministries are run by volunteers or by pastors who may have begun with little formal training but have developed expertise in their ministry areas. One pastor is a Hebraist; books in Hebrew are scattered around his office desk and library. The traditional Jewish doorpost marking, the mezuza, is fastened to his office door, and two Hebrew inscriptions have been etched onto the office wall: translated, they read, "Thou shalt love thy neighbor as thyself" and "Hear, O Israel, the Lord thy God, the Lord is One."

The church health clinic, run without state funds, is staffed by doctors who volunteer time and money for medication and equipment. They are not necessarily church members or Christians, though most are. The clinic provides free medical help to roughly one thousand of the uninsured each year, and arranges for free medical treatment for conditions too serious for the clinic to address. Neither citizenship nor confession is a condition of care, though prayer is available for those who wish. Linda, who oversees the clinic, notes, "We can't say, 'Jesus loves you; I hope you get well; goodbye.' We have to be the hands and feet of Jesus, and love people by helping them. In principle, it's great if someone gets converted, but conversion is not what this clinic is about." There have been few, if any, requests from patients that conflict with clinic policy or the consciences of the doctors, such as requests for narcotic drugs, contraception for unmarried couples, or abortion. A second church clinic, also funded without government aid, provides prenatal care and other support services for pregnant women.

Parishioners at Vineyard are self-reliant types, insistent on freedom, especially from government, and thus on church-state separation. They generally hold conservative positions on social issues, opposing abortion, adultery, premarital sex, and homosexuality. But their self-reliance sculpts their views toward a frontier type of tolerance: each of us makes his own way with the Lord.

JOE INGRAO, PASTOR, VINEYARD-BOISE

JI I was born in Rochester, New York, moved to Altadena, California, in 1961 with my family. I am the oldest of four children. My father was Sicilian; my mother was from Naples. They were both born in America. My family was originally Ingram but they moved from England to Sicily to work in the coal mines [and changed the name to Ingrao there]. My grandfather Alphonse sailed alone with the other Italian immigrants to America when he was thirteen years old. As he and his father worked, they sent money back to Sicily so the rest of the family immigrated to America. I was raised, baptized, confirmed, and married as a Catholic.

Here at the Vineyard Christian Fellowship–Boise I oversee the

ministries for marriage, counseling, men, the incarcerated, and Celebrate Recovery. Celebrate Recovery is a twelve-step recovery program
with Jesus as the "higher power," and we link Bible verses to each one of
the program's twelve steps. It covers everything — depression, food addiction, drugs, and sexual issues, parenting, how to be faithful — hurts,
habits, and hang-ups. In the men's ministry, we try to equip men to be
men of character, godly men. Men are pretty standoffish as a gender. We
try to break down barriers. We hope they begin to feel that this is a community where they can say, "I can trust Joe, and maybe I can trust God."

I was a sexual addict for thirty-five years, addicted to pornography
and self-gratification. It controlled my life. I'm transparent with the
guys: I say, "I've had that struggle; I've been able to put it aside for eighteen years." By the late 1980s, I'd tried everything. I wanted to be a mil-
lionaire by age thirty-five. I wanted a beach house. But none of this came
about. I hated my addictions so much; I was prisoner to my own choices.
Then God spoke to me and said, "Let's try it my way for a few years." I
said, "I not only want you, God, to save me; I want you to be my Lord." In
1992, I quit pornography and self-gratification. It's not without struggle.
But if I could do it, anyone can. That's why I'm a pastor now. I have no
formal college or Bible school, but after seven years working with Celebrate Recovery, the senior pastor felt I had the right skills to administer
the program. Imagine, me, a guy with just a high school education.

The teaching at Vineyard is not that you're the only sinner. All
have sinned. In fact, when I go into the prisons, I tell the men: "The
only difference between you and me is that you got caught." How many
times did I drive drunk? The message is: God has hope for you. Just as
you are he loves you. In the prisons, we may bring in a part of the Bible
to teach; we bring in parenting classes, Celebrate Recovery, financial
classes. . . . We try to prepare them for the transition to leave prison.
And we build friendships.

We're working with two Catholic churches now to bring Celebrate Recovery to their members. We work with secular and nonprofit
organizations, like Healthy Families Network — it involves Catholics,
Mormons, Protestants, and nonbelievers in service programs. We're
not out to change people to become Protestant. If someone says, "Hey
— you've got something special; what is it?" then I can tell them about
how Christ changed my life. But we leave the rest to God.

MP Your ministry got a government grant?

JI Yes, it was called the Access to Recovery initiative by the Bush administration. Some people were skeptical that governmental strings would be attached so that we couldn't say "God" or "Jesus" or use the Bible. But we believed our governor, who said that would not be the case; we just had to keep government funds separate from church funds. I think we were one of thirteen states to get the grant, out of fifty. We were honored.

MP How did you hire people for this program?

JI The money that goes to the government comes from taxes. Are some taxpayers faith-based? Shouldn't a portion of tax go back to faith-based work? That includes Muslim, Sikh, and Hindu faith-based work. I was in business for seventeen years; getting a job is a lot about relationships: Are you qualified and are you transparent with me? It's the same here. If I had someone who was a church member and someone, also qualified, who is not a church member, I'd hire the church member because we have a relationship. If I knew someone who was Jewish or Catholic and he was qualified and I had a relationship with him, I'd hire him.

My desire is to accept people where they are right now. I cannot stand Fox News and [Sean] Hannity sometimes. I'm not sure they're not doing more harm than good. If someone comes to me and asks about abortion or homosexuality, I can tell them how I feel and what the Bible says. But it's not anybody's job to change them — it's God's job. We're not supposed to judge people. I don't like the extreme left and I don't like the extreme right.

This Vineyard church is set in the "radical middle" between evangelicals and Pentecostals. We don't agree with some people's view of church, religion, or some of their gods, and hopefully they'll hear enough truth in our meetings to choose this middle lifestyle rather than extremes on either side, left or right. But it's their choice. I try not to judge. God is the judge.

chapter 7

"New Evangelicals"

·······································

Underlying Beliefs

As is expected in any group that spans a political range, underlying beliefs also vary. Yet there remains a family resemblance among "new evangelical" basic tenets. This chapter will outline positions developed by community leaders, organizations, and congregations rather than those debated in academic or theological institutions. As these are widely available, they serve as a framework for individual and community activism.

American evangelicals have generally not taken the evangelical search for an "inner" spirituality to mean withdrawal from the world. The conditions of frontier settlement (where authorities were scarce) and later migration to poor urban ghettos (where authorities also were scarce) mitigated against withdrawal and encouraged self-reliant society building. Yet, not only pragmatic conditions but also evangelical doctrine mitigated against withdrawal. On the evangelical understanding of the gospel, Jesus was too a new society builder. Immanent as well as transcendent, he had this-worldly intent to model a new way of living in the *polis*. In this, he was political — but not in the way of traditional politics.

Jesus' political intent is latent in the annunciation and obvious in the crucifixion. The birth narrative alludes to a political Jesus, a nonviolent rebel preaching a counterculture. As Luke tells it, Mary speaks to her cousin Elizabeth immediately after the annunciation: "He [God] has brought down rulers from their thrones but has lifted up the humble. He has filled the hungry with good things but has sent the rich away empty" (Luke 1:52-53). These are the provocative goals that are heritable, so to speak, to her divinely begotten son. A few passages later, Luke describes the birth of John to Elizabeth and Zacharias. Zacharias cries out, "He has raised up a horn of salvation for us in the house of his servant David (as he said through his holy prophets of long ago), salvation from our enemies and from the hand of all who hate us" (Luke 1:69-71). In the context of midantiquity, this could have meant only freedom from Rome, whose rulers could not have been happy with this seditious family.

These passages were written by Luke for Theophilus, when Christians were a suspect group and Luke was under some onus to avoid the impression that Christians were political rebels. If this is the toned-down, apolitical version, what would an uncensored one sound like?

When Jesus is born, Herod's order to murder the Hebrew infants suggests something of the political threat felt by Rome. Thirty-three years later, the authorities certainly thought Jesus had political intent, for which he was crucified. Political sedition was the only charge over which Pontius Pilate could preside. Had he not thought Jesus' message political, he would have had no standing to try him, as mere heretics or prophets were outside his jurisdiction. At trial, Jesus did nothing to persuade the assembled that Pilate's political view of the situation was wrong.

It is sometimes argued that Jesus was apolitical, as he did not aim at overthrowing the Roman government. His trial and crucifixion were thus not only immoral but also illegal, as Herod's reach extended only to political rebellion. This view is surely correct if one means that Jesus intended no violent revolution. But if one considers Jesus' idea of societal overhaul, his work was indeed political. The scholar John Yoder writes,

> [T]he events in the temple court and the language Jesus used were *not* calculated to avoid any impression of insurrectionary vision. Both Jewish and Roman authorities were defending themselves against a real threat. That the threat was not one of *armed,* violent revolt, and that it nonetheless bothered them to the point of their resorting to irregular procedures to counter it, is a proof of the political relevance of nonviolent tactics. . . . Jesus' public career had been such as to make it quite thinkable that he would pose to the Roman Empire an apparent threat serious enough to justify his execution.

Jesus was, Yoder sums up, "the bearer of a new possibility of human, social, and therefore political relationships."[1]

It is also argued that the conservative *Haustafeln* — the lessons
found, for example, in Colossians (3:18-4:1), Ephesians (5:21-6:9), and
1 Peter (2:13-3:7) — too suggest an apolitical Jesus. These seem not to
recommend even a social overhaul, much less a political one. They follow tradition and admonish wives to submit to husbands, children to
obey their parents, and slaves to obey their masters. Yet those arguing
for a political Jesus counter that the provocation of the *Haustafeln*
comes in the second half of each lesson: husbands are required to love
their wives "as Christ loved the church and gave himself up for her"
(Eph. 5:25-33). Fathers should not "exasperate [their] children" (Eph.
6:4). To masters the writer says: "Treat your slaves in the same way. Do
not threaten them, since you know that he who is both their Master
and yours is in heaven, and there is no favoritism with him" (Eph. 6:9).
Relative to the ethics of the day, the obligation of the powerful to the
weak was socially, politically, and conceptually revolutionary.[2]

Moreover, the political argument continues, the *Haustafeln* carry a
radical message in their structure. They are written in pairs, husband-
wife, parent-child, master-slave. By contrast, in contemporary Stoic
philosophy, morality was grounded in individual status; because one
was a slave owner, father, or husband, one behaved in certain ways. The
moral demand of the *Haustafeln* comes from the relationship, not individual status. It is the relationship that Jesus is after. Relationship is
the place, the context, in which one may treat others justly, where one
may serve others. And this may have vast political effect.

The ideas of relationship and service run through Scripture.
When Jesus ends his forty-day fast, he feeds not himself but those
around him. He washes the disciples' feet. At the Last Supper he de-
clares, "The kings of the Gentiles lord it over them. . . . But you are not
to be like that. Instead, the greatest among you should be like the
youngest, and the one who rules like the one who serves. . . . I am
among you as one who serves" (Luke 22:25-27). Mark reprises: "Those

---

1. J. Yoder, *The Politics of Jesus* (Grand Rapids and Cambridge, U.K.: Eerdmans,
1972), pp. 49, 50, 52, emphasis in original.
2. Claims have also been made that the apostolic *Haustafeln* in any case come not
from Jesus but from existing Jewish law and Stoic philosophy; see F. C. Baur, "Arguments Restoring *Haustafeln* to Jesus' Vision," in E. Hoskyns and N. Davey, *The Riddle of
the New Testament* (London: Faber and Faber, 1947, 1957).

who are regarded as rulers of the Gentiles lord it over them, and their high officials exercise authority over them. Not so with you. Instead, whoever wants to become great among you must be your servant, and whoever wants to be first must be slave of all. For even the Son of Man did not come to be served, but to serve" (Mark 10:42-45).

At least part of the mandate to serve others emerges from the Jewish idea of Jubilee (Lev. 25; 27; Num. 36). Every fiftieth year, debts are forgiven, slaves are manumitted, property taken as debt repayment is returned, and the soil lies fallow. The virtue of debt forgiveness is repeated in Matthew 6:12, in the Lord's Prayer, which reads, "forgive us our debts as we have also forgiven our debtors." The verb is *aphiemi* (from the Greek *opheilema*), which denotes financial debt. The more usual translation, "Forgive us our sins/trespasses . . . ," which broadened the concept to other wrongs, was suggested by Matthew in a gloss to say that what applies to debts applies to other transgressions *(paraptoma)* as well. That is, the first meaning pointed to financial debt.[3] (The broader use is found also in the well-known passage in Luke 4.) The mandate to forgive debts appears also in the parable of the merciless servant. A manumitted slave refuses similar generosity to another slave, demanding that the slave repay him his debt. In the end, the manumitted man is punished for his lack of generosity, arrested, and sold back into slavery for his own debts (Matt. 18:23-25, 35).

The Jewish Jubilee required not only the interest on loans to be forgiven but also the principal. By Jesus' time, financial mechanisms had been developed to circumvent this requirement, as debt cancellation had the effect of discouraging credit and hobbling the economy. In the Sermon on the Plain, Jesus offers his response to this loophole: it's out of the question[4] and moreover preempts greater reward: "If you do good to those who are good to you, what credit is that to you? Even 'sinners' do that. And if you lend to those from whom you expect repayment, what credit is that to you? Even 'sinners' lend to 'sinners,' expecting to be repaid in full. But love your enemies, do good to them, and lend to them without expecting to get anything back. Then your reward will be great" (Luke 6:33-35).

---

3. F. C. Fensham, "The Legal Background of Mt. vi:16," *Novum Testamentum* 4 (1960): 1; A. Trocme, *Jesus and the Nonviolent Revolution* (Scottdale, Pa.: Herald, 1973); Yoder, *The Politics of Jesus,* p. 62.

4. This was the response as well of the Mishnaic and talmudic rabbis, who strove to preserve the debt relief and manumission of the Jubilee.

A more radical redistribution of capital is found a few passages later: "But seek his kingdom, and these things will be given to you as well. . . . Sell your possessions and give to the poor" (Luke 12:31, 33). Traditionally, this passage has been interpreted as the "counsel of perfection," a special injunction to those called to monastic orders. The rest of us need only tithe. Yet Jesus is unsatisfied with 10 percent. "Woe to you Pharisees, because you give God a tenth of your mint, rue and all other kinds of garden herbs, but you neglect justice and the love of God" (Luke 11:42). To be sure, Luke is the Gospel most concerned with social justice and, one might argue, exaggerates Jesus' concern with the *polis* in this life. But those claiming a social-justice Jesus note that the emphases of the other Gospels are no reason to wriggle out of the social-justice injunctions in Luke. If that were the case, one could argue that Luke is an excuse to wriggle out of the other Gospels. They must, on this view, be taken together.

Throughout the Gospels, the ideas of the Jubilee are furthered to service-unto-sacrifice. In life, Jesus served lepers, the hated tax collectors, and prostitutes. In death, he chose crucifixion rather than to recant his mission of a just society, and rather than use violence to achieve it. He rejected both the force of government and the force of rebellion against it. He might have staged a revolt after feeding the masses or cleansing the temple. The crowds backed him and the Roman legion was thrown off guard. Yet he didn't. Thus, while the cross means many things, it is also a call to serve-unto-sacrifice, as Jesus did.[5] John recalls Jesus' assurance to those who fear persecution for their radical service: "If the world hates you, keep in mind that it hated me first" (John 15:18).

Such service would be the hallmark of Christian communities, which would better the world not by might but by, in Yoder's phrase, "revolutionary subordination."[6] Christians would accept their socioeconomic roles and political subordination to government, as Jesus did (1 Pet. 2:18; Eph. 5:22). But *revolutionary* subordination is neither passivity nor weakness. One is never a subordinate in the usual meaning of the word. Rather, each man is equally near to God, one is always a peer with something to offer. One may always act — even toward the powerful — in

---

5. Also central in the evangelical understanding of the cross is the idea of substitutionary atonement, wherein Jesus' death atones for our sins.

6. See Yoder, *The Politics of Jesus,* pp. 185-87.

ways that change the world. Christians would thus not withdraw into alternative communities but live differently within society, promoting the dignity, freedom, and equality of each person (1 Cor. 7:20; John 17:15-16). In this sense, Christian living would be politically revolutionary. It would be, as Jesus said, "salt" and "light" — light in the sense of guide, vision, beacon; salt in the sense of preserving from decay, cleansing from impurity, and as something valuable to the community (salt was a form of pay for Roman soldiers; both the words "salary" and "salvific" have this as a root). Indeed, if all people dedicated to service withdrew from society or eschewed politics, the *polis* would be left entirely to scoundrels. It makes no sense to claim this as Jesus' intent. Christian living would involve neither force nor retreat but patience — neither the spear nor seclusion in the desert but service. By quiet modeling, community practices of equality and service might spread.

Revolutionary subordination, though challenging, is not beyond human capacity because mankind partakes of God's nature: "because in this world we are like him" (1 John 4:17).[7] Thus, mankind may be asked to serve as Jesus did: "See that you also excel in this grace of giving. . . . For you know the grace of our Lord Jesus Christ" (2 Cor. 8:7-9). We may be asked to forgive as drastically as Jesus did. "Be kind and compassionate to one another, forgiving each other, just as in Christ God forgave you" (Eph. 4:32). We may be asked to suffer as Jesus did: "How is it to your credit if you receive a beating for doing wrong and endure it? But if you suffer for doing good and you endure it, this is commendable before God. To this you were called, because Christ suffered for you, leaving you an example, that you should follow in his steps" (1 Pet. 2:20-21).

A substantial argument against taking Jesus' ideas as political — as promoting societal overhaul — is that the church, in its earliest days, developed a politics considerably more conservative than his teachings. The late-nineteenth-century theologian Ernst Troeltsch influenced a century of scholars with his work on the early-church shift from an ethic of love to an accommodationist ethic appropriating Stoic natural law. As the church gained upper-class adherents and

---

7. Humankind may share even in the phenomenon of resurrection. "If the Spirit of him who raised Jesus from the dead is living in you, he who raised Christ from the dead will also give life to your mortal bodies through his Spirit, who lives in you" (Rom. 8:11).

sociopolitical power, Troeltsch held, it both supported status quo social institutions and developed its own, including patriarchal, social,
and class hierarchies; a church bureaucracy; and a priestly class in
place of the priesthood of all believers.[8] Paul in particular is cited as
one who moved the early church from a sociopolitical emphasis to a
more inner, spiritual one that left socioeconomic and political structures as they were. He stressed the importance of reconciling with God
through grace, and he advocated this-worldly reconciliation of individuals, not social overhaul.

Yet on the evangelical view, these complaints miss the mark. It is
true that Jesus' teachings were framed by the expectation of an apocalypse that did not materialize. But this does not mean that they teach us
— absent apocalypse — only about spiritual, not sociopolitical, renewal.
Why not consider Jesus' proposal seriously: a community that follows his
ways of service and sacrifice will be persuasive and slowly change mankind? To be sure, the early church developed mundane societal regulations when the apocalypse did not occur and daily life went on. But it's
not clear that those regulations revoke Jesus' radical vision. On many an
evangelical view, not only Jesus but also many communities in the pre-
Constantinian church practiced revolutionary subordination, a means
of sociopolitical change based on equality, generosity, and nonviolence.
It is this early-church model that remains the Christian obligation.

As for the reading of Scripture where Jesus, the *polis*-reformer, is
superseded by Paul, paradoxically both spiritualist and church-
institution builder — this is for many evangelicals unnecessary. Paul,
like Jesus, says that God's radical love reveals itself when man loves his
neighbor, the stranger, sinner, and enemy. God's radical force emerges
both in the private arena (care of the family and slaves) and in the political sphere (care for the poor, treatment of enemies, and rejection of violence). Many evangelicals thus see no conflict between Jesus' and
Paul's teachings. Jesus' actions during his life *are* what divine grace
looks like when it is on earth. The man who preached this-worldly service *is* the Jesus of next-worldly grace, with whom one seeks to be justified. Jesus' call to a life of service has a this-worldly benefit and is an
otherworldly glorifying of God. We are to let our light shine before
men, so that they give praise to our heavenly father (Matt. 5:16). On this

8. See, for instance, *The Social Teaching of the Christian Churches* (1912; Louisville:
Westminster John Knox Press, 1992).

view, Paul and Jesus faced different circumstances and had different emphases, but they did not gainsay each other. The individual partakes of God's love when she accepts Jesus as her savior (a Pauline emphasis). But godly love, expressed in service, can change the world. When we love and are generous with each other, we witness God's love of us and our spiritual bond to him. Spiritual grace (God's love for us) and social justice (our love for each other) are of a piece.[9]

*   *   *

What are the implications of these doctrinal principles, service-unto-sacrifice and revolutionary subordination, for the relationship between church and state? To begin with, the Bible sees all earthly powers as self-interested and fallen — they are neither the kingdom of God nor capable of service-unto-sacrifice. Yet they are unavoidable if crime and chaos are to be checked. There is no exception made even for oppressive states in Paul's linchpin passage about government (Rom. 13:1-7): "Everyone must submit himself to the governing authorities . . ." Compared to bad government, chaos, it seems, is the worse alternative. This might be a Hobbesian reading of Paul, but more likely Hobbes's *Leviathan* is a Pauline reading of power. Under ordinary circumstances, government is to be obeyed, lest society run amok.

Having explained the need for government, Paul continues, "for there is no authority except that which God has established. The authorities that exist have been established by God." This "establishing" (or "ordering" of governments, in some translations) suggests no justification of a particular power, as all are humanly inadequate. It suggests only that God organizes powers for his purposes. Thus, the Christian aim is neither to destroy government nor to claim any one government for God. Christians are to obey most positive law, as Jesus did and as Jews in the Roman Empire were called to do by both Jesus and Paul: "He who rebels against the authority is rebelling against what God has instituted, and those who do so will bring judgment on themselves" (Rom. 13:2).

This raises the question of resistance against unjust governments. In the classic example of the problem, Jesus taught, "Love your enemies and pray for those who persecute you" (Matt. 5:44), yet governments or-

9. Yoder, *The Politics of Jesus,* pp. 103-6.

der us to combat. War is one of the most important decisions a state makes, yet it grossly transgresses Jesus' injunction to eschew violence. Traditionally, the contradiction between loving one's enemy and obeying the state, which "does not bear the sword for nothing" (Rom. 13:4), has been explained by the public-private distinction. The injunction to obey the state refers to the public arena, the army; Matthew's injunction to love one's enemy refers to the private arena.

But this doesn't wash. Rome's subject peoples, Hebrews included, were not expected to join the emperor's military, so the public arena of war could not be the one in which people obey the state. Moreover, the sword in the Roman world was not a weapon of war (as spears, lances, and bows were) but rather the "sword of justice," against violence and crime. When the Bible says that the state "does not bear the sword for nothing," it does not mean that the state never goes wrongly to war and thus Christians should march blindly to the drum. It means that the state's use of force in daily life — in civil and criminal law, to control crime and chaos — is not frivolous and should be followed. Even on those occasions when the sword was used in war, it was a defensive, not offensive, weapon, used to protect one's homeland from invading armies.

Thus, taking together Jesus' call to obey the state and yet to love one's enemy, we have the mandate to abide by positive law as far as possible and to follow the government in a defensive war against an enemy invasion, when the sword might be used (Rom. 13:4, 7). Aside from that, Christians are not bound to follow the state blindly into war but rather to follow Jesus' love, thus transforming human relations by loving even the enemy.

On the evangelical view, this is not a recipe for rubber-stamping the status quo. Indeed, given the transformative nature of Jesus' vision, it makes little sense to claim Romans 13:1-7 as an invitation to political passivity or the appeasement of unjust governments — though it does mean that one should not use violence in resisting them. The placement of Romans 13:1-7 in Scripture — wedged between Romans 12 and the rest of Romans 13 — argues against an appeasing or accommodationist interpretation. Romans 12 calls Christians to nonconformity and social transformation, to use their various talents to serve the lowest of society and to bless their persecutors.[10] The rest of Romans 13 en-

---

10. "Do not conform any longer to the pattern of this world, but be transformed by the renewing of your mind. . . . We have different gifts, according to the grace given

joins Christians to love their neighbors as they love themselves, and it reprises the last five of the Mosaic commandments (prohibiting murder, theft, false witness, adultery, envy). Readers of the Bible must hold either that Romans 13:1-7 was inserted haphazardly into the text with no connection to its surroundings, or that the passage is linked to its context.

If we take a contextual reading as more likely, Romans 12 and 13 together have this to say about the relationship between church and state: Christians should use their skills and talents to serve their enemies and society's lowest, even if it makes them seem peculiar and nonconformist (Rom. 12). They should not refuse to defend their homeland when enemy armies invade, but shouldn't waste talent and energy undermining local law, which may lead to chaos (Rom. 13:1-7). On the contrary, they should obey the mundane rulers and use their talents to love their neighbors and eschew violence, greed, envy, and corruption. Thus they will change the world (Rom. 13:8 till the chapter's end).

In the phrase "love your neighbor," "neighbor" remarkably includes all nations. Twenty-first-century thinkers tend to believe that multiculturalism is a modern topic, under discussion perhaps since the eighteenth century, when international trade reached proportions unseen since antiquity. But Jesus lived in that earlier global empire, and he mandated love. This inclusiveness has implications for several political arenas, from domestic discrimination to immigration and trade with the developing world. The theologian Hendrikus Berkhof notes, "To reject nationalism we must begin by no longer recognizing in our own bosoms any difference between peoples. We shall resist social injustice and the disintegration of community only if justice and mercy prevail in our own common life and social differences have lost their power to divide."[11]

Revolutionary subordination and quiet modeling of service and sacrifice are well and good as long as government doesn't demand that

---

us. . . . Share with God's people who are in need. Practice hospitality. Bless those who persecute you. . . . If it is possible, as far as it depends on you, live at peace with everyone. Do not take revenge, my friends, but leave room for God's wrath, for it is written: 'It is mine to avenge; I will repay,' says the Lord. On the contrary: 'If your enemy is hungry, feed him; if he is thirsty, give him something to drink. In doing this, you will heap burning coals on his head.' Do not be overcome by evil, but overcome evil with good." Rom. 12:2, 6, 13-14, 18-21.

11. H. Berkhof, *Christ and the Powers* (Scottdale, Pa.: Herald, 1962), p. 42.

Christians violate their principles or government itself doesn't grossly violate them. Under such circumstances, noncooperation or resistance is appropriate as it blocks injustice nonviolently and with as little law-breaking as possible. This was effective when the Jews protested against the idolatry of Caesar's image being spread throughout Jerusalem, as the first-century Jewish historian Josephus describes. When Pilate readied to massacre the protestors, they declared they would accept death rather than commit idolatry. Pilate paused. The images were hauled back to Caesarea. A few years later, having learned little, Gaius Caligula wanted a statue of himself to be worshiped in Jerusalem. Again the Jews gathered in large numbers, and their willingness to die persuaded the consul Petronius to intercede on their behalf. (The classic reprises of this resistance in the modern era are familiar: Gandhi's independence movement, the Danish resistance to the Nazi Holocaust, and the American civil rights movement, among others.)

Nonviolent protest does not always work. It did not, for instance, when Pilate used the temple treasure to build his aqueduct. The Jews protested, and he killed them. In the end, it also did not work in Jesus' own life. He knew his call for nonviolent, transnational service-to-others would bring the state down upon him. But he paid it little mind. They would kill him; so what? He was still right. If others followed his vision, he promised they too would be right. In holding his ground, Jesus not only drew attention to his vision but also undermined the status quo — all without lifting a finger, as Paul adroitly analyzed.[12] He "made a public example" of his persecutors. By forcing them to reveal their fear of him, he exposed their opposition to service and Jubilee-type wealth redistribution. He revealed them for the powermongers that they were, and he eroded their authority over what is just and right. He "triumphed over them." He "disarmed" the powers, not by arming himself[13] but by puncturing their legitimacy.

12. Berkhof, *Christ and the Powers*, pp. 30-31.
13. Eph. 6:14-18 describes the Christian weapons as "the breastplate, shield, helmet and short sword," all defensive equipment, in contrast to the lance, bow, and spear. Thus Christians do not go into the world offensively but defend their beliefs: "Stand firm then, with the belt of truth buckled around your waist, with the breastplate of righteousness in place, and with your feet fitted with the readiness that comes from the gospel of peace. In addition to all this, take up the shield of faith, with which you can extinguish all the flaming arrows of the evil one. Take the helmet of salvation and the sword of the Spirit, which is the word of God."

When nonviolent protest is ineffective, Christians have another, harsher option: leaving, as Joseph and Mary fled to Egypt when the Hebrew infants were being murdered. One might consider the effect on Nazism if in the 1930s, large numbers of German Christians had left the country. This sort of thing is extremely difficult, but on the evangelical view, Christianity is not supposed to make life easy, just better.

In sum, "new evangelical" political thought begins with the idea that no fallen, human government is God's kingdom. Though we are to obey this world's rulers, the two realms remain far apart. From this separation between the kingdoms of God and the world, the separation of church and state is not a long leap. Moreover, if one tries to effect change by political or military efforts, one must compete as players in these arenas do. And in such a game, the means are never Christlike. The better Christian option is neither withdrawal from public life nor aggressive imposition of Christian ideas. Rather, it is a Christian community that obeys positive law in all but extreme circumstances, defends its country under the extreme condition of invasion, and spends most of its time serving those within the church, the stranger, and the enemy. From this revolutionary subordination and service, civil society activism is also not a long leap. Finally, Jesus' vision of how people should live together is an eternal guide. Though one may never impose one's beliefs, the obligation to love one's neighbor and enemy, to serve the needy and stranger, is the standard by which to assess human governments and criticize them when they fall short.

Tri Robinson, Idaho

The Vineyard Church in Boise, Idaho, is described in chapter 6. Here is Senior Pastor Tri Robinson discusses the theology and practice of its service to others.

TR When Jesus first started his public ministry he went to his hometown of Nazareth. He entered the [synagogue] and was handed the scroll of the prophet Isaiah to be read before the people. He opened it to what we know today as Isaiah 61. He read, "The Spirit of the Lord is on me, because the Lord has anointed me to preach good news to the poor. He has sent me to bind up the brokenhearted, to proclaim freedom for the captives . . ." and so on. It was a well-known messianic passage, and after he had finished he announced that he was the Messiah, and that in a manner of speaking Isaiah's words would be his job description.

The point is, if healing the brokenhearted, setting the captives free, and ministering to the poor was his job description, then we believe it is ours as well. This kind of ministry is more needed in the context of today's world than ever. For example, we live in a world where many are held captive to addictions and extreme poverty and even such atrocities as human trafficking. Here at the Boise Vineyard we hold the conviction that Christians must express the heart of God by helping to be part of the solution to human suffering and world crises.

The world is becoming more hostile every day, not just in man's inhumanity to man, but environmentally as well. In Matthew 25 Jesus exhorted his followers to minister to the extreme poor when he said, "I was thirsty and you gave me something to eat . . . ," telling them (and us) that to provide clean water for the thirsty is ministry. I never fully understood this passage until my wife and I experienced the extreme poverty in Zambia, Africa, a few years ago. It was there that we became aware of just how much of the world's fresh water is undrinkable, and how it is literally killing people.

MP Does this reflect a shift in church activism?

TR I have a personal perspective on why much of the church in America has been negative toward issues of social justice and ministries such as environmental stewardship. I believe the pushback started as far back as the seventies during the Jesus movement. During that time there was a huge emphasis on eschatology (the study of the end times). We believed that things like plagues, increased violence, and natural disaster were birth pangs of the last days before the second coming of Jesus. We thought that they were just a part of God's plan. As a result, we put our emphasis on evangelism (getting people to heaven) rather than diving into the crises that caused human suffering.

During that time, some Christians felt that they could better control social change through politics than through ministries of compassion, and as a result the Religious Right was formed. Things rapidly became polarized between what was perceived to be liberal and conservative agendas. Everyone took sides and was willing to die for them. Issues such as social justice and the environment somehow fell on the liberal side of the line, and many churches turned their backs on them.

As a pastor I do not believe that telling people how to vote is my job but rather presenting the kingdom of God in such a way that people will want to return to the valid ministry of Jesus. People love our church because we do care for the poor and partner with other agencies that share our conviction on these matters.

MP What kind?

TR We work with groups like the Boise Rescue Mission and City Lights (a women's shelter). These are Christian groups, but we also work in the local jails and prisons. We have worked with agencies like the Forest Service, Fish and Game as well as a secular environmental conservation group. I was asked to speak at this conservation group's convention a few years ago even though we have clearly been on opposite sides of the abortion issue. They recognized that I authentically cared about the importance of the environment and overlooked the thing that polarized us.

I don't want to be perceived as their enemy even though we don't see eye to eye on every issue. I have even met with our local ACLU leader here in Idaho. I do tend to get angry at the ACLU because I believe they have been illogical about many things I am passionate about. But, I also discovered that by spending some time together we could agree and connect on many other important issues. They care about people, but because of their misconception of who Jesus is, they have seen the Christian church as irrelevant to their cause.

This country was founded on the Christian faith but we are clearly a secular nation now, and to be effective we need to understand it. I do believe every Christian should vote. I think it is an American responsibility, but I never tell our people who to vote for. I believe if they have God's heart they will figure it out for themselves.

I, for one, would hate to lose my freedom to openly express my faith in a nation that once honestly meant it when they said, "In God we trust." The truth is that the way things are going, I fear even losing our nonprofit tax status. This would really damage our ability to care for the poor to the degree that we do. I will admit that there are probably some churches that may not deserve it. Churches were originally granted nonprofit status because they were the nation's welfare agency, and if we are doing what Jesus called us to we still would be. Honestly, I do believe we can do it much more effectively and at a fraction of the cost of government agencies because much of the work is done by volunteers with a heart to serve those in need.

In the case of receiving grant money for specific outreach ministries, it has mostly come through other Christian organizations. But the largest portion of our financial provision is collected in our Sunday offerings. As stewards that are accountable for the funds we have been given, we have learned to operate with little to no waste. We try to use every penny wisely because we have so few of them.

MP Okay. You don't take government funds so that you can preserve a religious approach in your ministries. Is that the same for coreligionist hiring?

TR If we had to hire people who didn't share our values, it wouldn't work. We do what we do because of a biblical mandate and a heart to serve God. Outside of that, we would have little motivation.

MP If someone has your values but isn't in your church?

TR We have teachers in our elementary school who aren't members here and neither is one of our accountants, but they do share our faith in Christ. And, though not on our church payroll, we have worked with Jews and Catholics alike on the environmental issues and have more than once asked a Jewish rabbi to lead us through a seder service.

MP You have said if we take abortion off the table . . .

TR . . . then we can focus on other things. Please understand that abortion is a huge factor for us, especially when it comes to choosing who to vote for. But, I also see that the environment is killing people, especially young children. Over 80 percent of infant mortality in the developing world is water-related. For me that is a "sanctity of life" issue also. In fact our i-61 Ministry — formerly called "Re:Form," www.i-61.org — has been trying to work on every front. ("i-61" stands for Isaiah 61.) There are seven circles in i-61: world hunger, health, environmental decline, human trafficking and social injustice, illiteracy, corrupt leadership, and spiritual deadness. We are in the process of building schools and ministries to prepare people to work in all seven areas. It is our desire to be a model for churches across the country who share our heart for these things. Many pastors are afraid of these ministries because of the stigma of liberalism — which is really crazy in my thinking since they are all so clearly biblical issues.

MP Do you partner with groups to reduce abortion?

TR We do, but only those that share our heart to minister in the compassion of Jesus. We actually provide facility space here on our campus to one such agency. But, here is the thing. We believe it is an injustice to tell a young girl who is pregnant, broke, and scared not to have an abortion if we're not willing to stand with her through her crisis. At the clinic we house, Stanton Health Care Clinic, they provide not only counseling but also pre- and postnatal care for those women (many young girls) who find themselves facing an unexpected pregnancy. Through the services provided at the clinic, they lovingly take these young girls by the hand, walking them through the entire process, while providing invaluable support to them as they choose the path of bringing a little one into the world. In the past, many have done otherwise when confronted with this type of situation, and all in the name of Christianity. Unfortunately it may not have expressed the love of Jesus but rather a spirit of condemnation.

Frankly I am saddened that there have been some from our camp that have operated out of an antagonistic judgmental spirit. We must stick to our convictions, but we need to teach our people to embrace and operate in the fruits of the Spirit — love, peace, patience, kindness, goodness, and self-control. It's not just what we say, but also the heart in which it is said. I am grieved at the mean-spiritedness that often comes through some of those who have airtime. Sometimes I think Christians perceive these people as apostles rather than the radio and TV commentators that they really are. We as Christians should be in the trenches serving the broken world instead of reacting and arguing with those we disagree with about the reasons and causes of the crises.

Concerning politics, it would be great to see a movement evolve with the righteous values of the conservative right blended with the idealism and heart for the poor of the liberal left.

MP What does that mean in practice?

TR That's the hard part, isn't it? Here is the deal. Change requires what I call a ripple effect. For example, I tell people, "We will never change the global environment if we don't first change the environment of people's hearts." One of the main characteristics of becoming Christlike is to become others-centered. If I authentically have Christ in my heart, I gain a new worldview. I see others as more important than myself. I clean up the toxic waste in my heart and it affects my thinking, which in turn changes my motives. I no longer have the idea that "I want mine and I want it now" but instead desire to preserve things for the sake of future generations. I tell people if you want your kids to value environmental stewardship, tell them to clean up their rooms. First our attitudes change, then our practices change. We paint our houses and mow our lawns as much for the sake of our neighbors as for our own satisfaction. As we care about our own world around us, eventually we begin to care about the planet for the same reason. It all has to start in the heart. That's why I've dedicated my life to the only thing I know of that changes hearts — and that's Jesus.

I do struggle with things like the current [Obama] administration's stimulus package simply because I don't think it's going to be good for future generations. In the long run, I think it will simply bring more future financial bondage. Personally I think it would be better to sacrifice now in an effort to deal with our national debt rather than to impose that on our grandchildren and their children. It's just not forward thinking.

MP What would you say to a gay couple in a stable, loving relationship?

TR A gay relationship is not what the Bible spells out as being stable or right. For that reason it's not okay for me, but then neither is any adulterous relationship. It's like divorce; the Bible says God hates divorce, but what we must understand is — he in no way hates those who are caught in it. He so loves them that he sacrificed his life for them. He just hates the stuff that takes away from wholeness and spiritual and emotional health. That's Isaiah 61, "He came to heal the brokenhearted."

MP What about conscience-based social service refusal?

TR I believe it is absolutely wrong to not allow doctors the right of refusal to perform abortions if it goes against their convictions. For one thing, we will lose many good doctors if this is forced upon them. Many will opt to give up their practice if they are made to go against their religious and ethical convictions when it comes to the sanctity of life and preserving it.

MP Teaching creationism or intelligent design in public schools?

TR I used to be a secondary school science teacher before I entered the ministry. I taught it both ways and let my students make up their own minds. I think that's part of the intellectual process. I for one actually came to my belief in God through science. I can't see how anyone can closely look at the creation and miss that fact that there must be a creator. Darwinism is a theory. The Bible is based on faith. When a theory attempts to undo or disprove faith, that's a problem for me. The fact is, though, from my own experience I believe God is much bigger than the bias of a teacher. If parents and the church are doing their job effectively, children will eventually discover the truth concerning God and the universe no matter what the world throws at them.

MP Moments of silence in schools?

TR Honestly I think in this day and age prayer in schools is a nonissue. A family has to take their responsibility seriously when it comes to teaching faith and values. When I sent my kids to public schools, I sent them to get an education. Frankly I didn't want non-Christian or even nominal-Christian teachers leading them in prayer or teaching them the Bible.

MP Religious symbols in public places?

TR It's ridiculous to take those away. A framed copy of the Ten Commandments in a courtroom is a statement that our country cares about justice and was established in godliness. If nothing else, it is a historical document. It is another case of the small, loud minority imposing their prejudice on the majority.

MP What about other religions having their symbols?

TR Forcing a population to take down religious symbols is discrimination and the thought of it offends me. Historically every time a government has forced that issue on its population it has lead to socialism, communism, and in the end, bondage and pain.

JOHN ASHMEN, COLORADO

John Ashmen is president of the Association of Gospel Rescue Missions (AGRM), which is headquartered in Colorado Springs, Colorado, home to many organizations of the Religious Right.

I live in Colorado Springs, a city of 400,000 people and headquarters for about 120 national and international Christian organizations. Because it has so many ministries, some people refer to the place as the Evangelical Capital of North America. How they all ended up here is an interesting story, but I see the mass gathering as more of an opportunity for synergy than a cause for celebration.

Focus on the Family is probably the most widely known Christian organization in the Springs, as we call it. Focus has a unique niche in the evangelical community, but the agenda of Focus is not necessarily the agenda of the other ministries in town. Quite often I'm asked if my organization vigorously opposes abortion and gay rights the same way Focus does.

Unfortunately, in the Christian parade, abortion and gay rights have become the two sides of a big bass drum that is beaten so loudly nobody can hear the sweet strains of the gospel. We need to back off on that heavy pounding if we want people on the sidewalks to hear the redeeming melody that is Jesus.

Regarding the paradigm shifts in Christian organizations — denominations, parachurch organizations, and megachurch movements have all had their turns in the driver's seat of global ministry. Today, ministry is cause-driven. And it is youth-led and technology-enhanced. This paradigm shift is befuddling many of the long-standing, heavily structured religious institutions.

What I mean is that you rarely hear people say they are called to foreign missions; you hear them say that they are about AIDS orphans or clean water. And they don't wait to jump through all of the hoops that the big sending agencies require. They look online to see who's doing what, Tweet or text their desire to engage, and pull up Priceline to get a cheap ticket to the action.

Another wrinkle in the blanket of Christianity these days that some people can't seem to iron out is evangelism methodology. Asbury Seminary professor George Hunter does a great job of contrasting the traditional "Roman style" with the unconventional "Celtic style" in his book *The Celtic Way of Evangelism: How Christianity Can Reach the West . . . Again.* The Roman style — characterized by presentation, decision, and fellowship — that fit so well with the modern era does not seem to be the preferred method of postmoderns I meet. The Celtic style — characterized by fellowship, worship, and commitment — is seen as not only a normal progression for a twenty-first-century mind, but something that Jesus himself embraced with his disciples.

One of the things that makes the Celtic style so compatible with our current culture is that a basic Bible knowledge that most people had thirty years ago — like knowing some of the Ten Commandments, who Jesus was, what the apostle Paul did — is pretty much nonexistent today. Certainly people can come to terms with the claims of Jesus and commit to following him after hearing a simple presentation; it happens all the time. But most folks today need to journey with the gospel for a while — to see how it plays out in the life of someone they trust. The Celtic style has hospitality written all over it: it's about joining in, observing and even participating in worship, asking questions, making mistakes, really finding out what it means to follow Jesus.

When you think about it, Jesus never asked his disciples to commit to something or sign on a dotted line before he pulled them into his circle. He simply said, "Follow me." He meant live with me, listen to my words, watch me, try doing what I do. And when you really get my message, my spirit will make it clear to you . . . and you'll change the world.

Never before has there been a generation more passionate about changing their world for the better. Today's young, active followers of Jesus have a deep desire to do something significant and lasting; they simply need to have specific direction and ongoing encouragement.

The things taking a hit because of this exciting fervor are the more traditional church activities. For example, I recently asked a friend whose kids have always attended a well-known Christian camp if his youngest daughter was registering for the next session. He told me, "I can't get her to go. She says, 'Dad, I can't sun myself on the beach and play games and eat all of that food when there are kids my age in Haiti who still don't have roofs over their heads.' And she's twelve years old!"

My friend admits that his daughter is probably getting her cues from a nineteen-year-old down the street, but she still does a great job championing the message: for some, a Christian camp is no longer a summer option; it's a moral choice.

At AGRM, we recognize the contagious passion young people have to make a difference in their world. They come from dissimilar backgrounds but collectively feel spiritually mandated social responsibility regarding "the least of these" as described in Matthew 25. We believe their perspectives are valid, and that their energy, wedded with the wisdom of those more experienced, could start a revolution of compassion that would fully awaken the church to action in this critical area of personal conviction.

That's why we have the vision statement we do: "AGRM will foster and feed a movement of diverse, energetic disciples who will see the practice of hospitality to the destitute as both a catalyst for life transformation in Jesus and a fundamental expression of their Christian faith, thus propelling the church into the lead role in society's quest to alleviate homelessness."

The Association of Gospel Rescue Missions has its North American roots in post–Civil War New York City soil. By the time the twentieth century rolled around, an informal federation of people helping the destitute and addicted was forged. In 1913, it became formalized as the International Union of Gospel Missions.

Gospel rescue missions have a long history of providing lifelines for those drowning in the waves of adversity and the undertow of addiction. For more than a century, they have been keeping watch on the waterfront of despair, and countless thousands of men, women, and children have been saved in every sense of the word.

Rescue mission used to be about that long line of men winding around the block looking for "three hots and a cot." They were men — almost always — who were functional at one time, but because of an addiction to drugs or, more often, alcohol, they became dysfunctional. They came to the rescue mission and found redemption in Jesus that led to a reorientation for life. And then with rehabilitation through the mission's programs, many worked their way back to functionality.

Over the years, rescue missions have also served unemployed veterans, abused runaways, mentally unstable outcasts, the desperately poor, and refugees — basically, all people to whom Jesus said, "Come to me, all you who are weary and burdened, and I will give you rest." And now, with the staggering increase in homelessness and so many close to homelessness, rescue missions are constantly busy and needed more than ever before. The single women with children who will be knocking on the door of a rescue mission tonight represent the fastest-growing segment of the population seeking services.

AGRM is still North America's oldest and largest network of independent crisis shelters and rehabilitation centers offering radical hospitality in the name of Jesus. Currently in AGRM, we have about 275 member missions, representing most of the first- and second-tier cities on the continent. A few of our members are small start-up works in third-tier cities or rural areas that offer just a day shelter and meals, but most are complex, multifaceted operations with short- and long-term addiction recovery programs, job training, transitional housing, and more. On the high end, a mission could have an annual operating budget of $30,000,000 or more. And interestingly, if AGRM's member missions were one organization, over the past dozen years, the collective annual donations would consistently place it in the top ten charities in America.

AGRM's missions employ the shelter concept, which isn't real popular right now, particularly in Washington. The current push is "housing first." Proponents want to forget the continuum of care. They believe that if you just give someone a house, all of his or her issues will eventually get worked out. I believe that if you put a homeless person in a house, you get just that: a homeless person in a house. If you don't address the reasons people are homeless — which in many cases, not all, revolve around addictions, limited education and job skills, mental stability — you end up spending major taxpayer dollars with embarrassing results. One of our member mission directors told me about a man who recently graduated from his addiction recovery program. The man used to have a homeless voucher obtained with HUD [U.S. Department of Housing and Urban Development] funding. The mission director asked him how he lost his free housing. He answered, "Well, when you're using crack and you invite your drug dealer to live with you, that's kinda what happens."

There are no required programs or strings attached to [HUD] homeless vouchers, and authorities have strict limitations regarding checking up on people. It doesn't take a Ph.D. to figure out that this plan has some serious problems.

Regarding the challenges of changing AGRM — as you know, with a hundred-year-old organization you have a hundred years of tradition, which isn't all bad, but also a hundred years of structure, which isn't all good. Structure upon structure tends to make you rigid and rickety. The AGRM board hired me — the first person to lead the association who had never led a rescue mission — to set a course for future relevance in a sea of complicated societal change.

The image that a lot of people have of a rescue mission is a hundred hungover men slouching in a chapel while a heavy-handed preacher describes in detail God's terrible wrath for the wayward. The meatloaf is cooking in the next room — and everybody can smell it — but nobody gets any until after the altar call. Let's be honest, if someone is hungry and you suggest that they turn to Jesus as part of a prelude to supper, they will gladly turn to Jesus or do jumping jacks or renounce the Red Sox, as long as it means meatloaf for the moment.

While that image unfortunately still lingers in some minds, a grace-based model is what's emerging in today's rescue missions in city after city. The life-changing gospel is still being imparted to the guests, but to guests who have just showered and are wearing fresh, warm clothes and have a full stomach. The image being projected is no longer "repent and then come get something to eat," even though that was never actually the case. Instead it's "have something to eat because the God who has given me a deep love for you wants you to be not only physically renewed but also spiritually renewed through his Son, Jesus." In short, it's about choosing to play the abundant-life card instead of the hell card.

At AGRM we are helping missions rethink quality. For years, organizations that have worked with the poor and have no fees for services — they depend entirely on donations — have found it easy to justify meager facilities. I believe that pious shoddy is still shoddy. Quality is critical. We are putting heavy emphasis into our revised certification program that emphasizes regulatory conformity, cleanliness, best practices, and the like. And it's starting to pay off. I can take you to rescue missions where the lobby looks like a relative's very inviting living room, where the accommodations are like an Ivy League college dorm, and where you'll likely ask for the recipe for dinner's main course.

Underlying this is a new emphasis on hospitality. I've already alluded to this several times. The New Testament church was spread through the ministry of hospitality, and it is something that today's church needs to reclaim. I'm not talking about entertaining, where you get the carpets shampooed and the furniture dusted and invite somebody from church over for dinner. Entertaining is inviting people into your house. Hospitality is inviting people into your life, and letting them know that no "room" is off limits — what's yours is theirs. It is only an understanding and practice of radical Christian hospitality that will eventually move the church back to its intended role — a role that will influence the poor, ease the government's burden, and represent the heart of Jesus.

chapter 8

"New Evangelicalism" in Practice

Political and Economic Activism

> *A story about separation of church and state: "He said 'Marry me.' She said, 'No.' And they lived happily ever after."*
>
> Joel Hunter, *A New Kind of Conservative*

With the model of the church as law-abiding but politically radical in its "revolutionary subordination" — its focus on service and justice — "new evangelicals" take a number of positions on social and political activism. Though there are other typologies of evangelical groups,[1] the one below looks at "new evangelical" positions regarding the state, the economy, and unresolved church-state legal issues — reflecting this book's overall concern with religion's compatibility with liberal democracy and economic fairness.

The positions sketched below are signposts along the range of approaches; individuals and groups fall between them and move among them. They do not correspond to denominations; indeed, many "new

---

1. One, often-used, is the assessment of theological and political positions along liberal or conservative lines. "New evangelicals," however, do not easily fall into these categories. Leah Daughtry, the Pentecostal minister who coordinated the 2008 Democratic nominating convention, is pro-choice but believes both creationism and evolution can be taught in public schools. Richard Cizik, head of the New Evangelical Partnership for the Common Good, opposes abortion but supports environmental protection, poverty relief, and coreligionist hiring. As I am interested in evangelical relations with the state and the economy, the typology here is based on those.

evangelical" churches are nondenominational. Neither do they align with Democrat-Republican politics or with classic left-right economic divisions — one result of "new evangelical" issue-by-issue policy assessment. "New evangelical" groups, for instance, which operate entirely in the private, nongovernmental sphere, are not necessarily neoliberal Republicans but may support the Democrats on the environment, immigration, or poverty relief. Similarly, though the "evangelical left" sounds somewhat socialist or social-market in orientation, their positions on poverty relief and abortion are not necessarily more "left" than those in other clusters. What sets them apart is their historical role since 1970. The term "evangelical left" has been in popular use for forty years, so I have left it undisturbed.

In one cluster are those who develop their domestic and international programs in civil society, without state involvement or funding. In the second are those who at times partner with government and so must discuss the regulation of their agencies with the state. Also described is how this politically engaged group nonetheless maintains its independence from government and political parties. In the third cluster are those who, like those in the first, work mostly in civil society but are more "countercultural." Sometimes known as "emergent churches," they are groups of often younger believers who meet in unorthodox places such as bowling alleys, skating rinks, or private apartments to pray, study, and minister to the needy. One might think of them, to use an imprecise analogy, as an evangelical version of the 1960s — radically for peace and the world's have-nots but without the sex and drugs. (Rock 'n' roll is okay.) Last are the actual evangelicals from the 1960s, the older (white) "evangelical left," who have seen a renaissance since 2005.

For coherence and clarity's sake, I've selected one or two voices as representative of each cluster. A section at the end of the chapter describes how "new evangelicals" look back at the politics of the 1970s through 2004.

Activism without State Involvement

Church-State Basics

The Minnesota pastor Gregory Boyd is representative of "new evangelicals" who believe that political power is always fallen and thus cannot be the Christian way. Noting, for example, that the United States rescued Kuwait from Saddam Hussein in 1991 but did nothing to stop the 1994 massacre in Rwanda, Boyd holds that America, like all political entities, looks out for its own self-interests.[2] Thus "America has never been, and will never be, a 'Christian' nation in any significant sense," though the idea has been popular since the country's founding. "Among other things," Boyd explains, "America, like every other fallen, demonically-oppressed nation (see Lk. 4:5-7; 2 Cor. 4:4; I Jn. 5:19; Rev. 13), is incapable of *loving* its enemies, *doing good* to those who mistreat it or *blessing* those who persecute it (Lk. 6:27-35). . . . The sooner the label 'Christian' gets divorced from this country, the better. It provides hope that someday the word 'Christian' might actually mean 'Christ-like' once again."[3]

One good thing, Boyd notes, that "came out of the failures of the Bush years is that they helped Christians ask: is it wise of people of faith to jump on board with a political regime? Because if your regime tanks, you just tanked your gospel."[4] The idea that Christians should gain political power to correct governmental evils makes Boyd wary: "I believe a significant segment of American evangelicalism is guilty of nationalistic and political idolatry," worshiping political wins rather than Jesus' teachings. He notes that Jesus accrued no political power in his day. The Constantinian turn led to "centuries of barbaric bloodshed — in Jesus' name." Indeed, "the Christian version of the kingdom of the world was actually the *worst* version the world has ever seen because it not only shed blood, it shed it under the banner of the cross!"

During the Bush years, tactics to enmesh church in state pushed Boyd to dismay and then resistance. "In the [2004] election [campaign] of George W. Bush, there was enormous pressure put on pastors to 'steer the flock' in a particular direction. That caused the whole hubbub about me because I wouldn't do that. I see that as idolatry pure and simple."[5] Rather than direct his congregation to vote for Bush, Boyd preached a series of sermons on the differences between the kingdoms of God and the world. One thousand members left his church in protest, a blow in personnel and resources. Boyd held his ground.

2. G. Boyd, *The Myth of a Christian Nation: How the Quest for Power Is Destroying the Church* (Grand Rapids: Zondervan, 2006), p. 89.

3. G. Boyd, "Don't Weep for the Demise of American Christianity," *Christus Victor Ministries* (blog), April 8, 2009.

4. Interview with the author, May 4, 2009.

5. Interview with the author, May 4, 2009.

Boyd's alternative to the kingdoms of the world is the kingdom of God, witnessed on earth by the church community as it follows Jesus. Christians, on his view, are "resident aliens" with an outsider's look at the status quo. "The Kingdom has always thrived — and really, *has only* thrived — when it was on the margins of society. The Kingdom is, by its very nature, a 'contrast society.'"[6] Christian society practices not "power over" but Jesus' "power under." "You can take particular aspects of the culture," Boyd suggests, "and ask, what does it mean to be the kingdom *vis a vis* that particular issue. Take diversity. One of the things we're called to do, following the example of Jesus, is to tear down racial, ethnic walls . . . to be part of the 'one new humanity' that Jesus died for (Ephesians 2:14), where people can come together, worship together, serve together, love one another."[7] Boyd asks, why shouldn't wealthy congregations make it their project to build affordable housing for the needy?

The ministries run by Boyd's church include food and clothing for the poor, job-skills development, job-transition help, emergency financial grants, English as a second language, substance abuse programs, gay-lesbian-bisexual-transgender support, counseling, youth programs, making life more Jesus-like, and aid to local immigrants. In some programs, it works with other churches and partners with city agencies for battered women and the homeless — though it remains financially and administratively independent. Overseas, it works with several ministries to aid children in Haiti; with the Harbor, to aid orphans in Russia; and with Esperanza Viva, to run an orphanage, school, and church in Mexico. Individual parishioners work with local churches in Bulgaria, with public health care in Haiti, with medical missions in Cameroon and Malawi, with children's homes in eastern Europe and Honduras, with agricultural development in Mozambique, with abused and abandoned children in the Philippines, with church and community development in Burkina Faso, with Bible translation in Indonesia and Malaysia, and with evangelical churches in the Netherlands and France.

In this approach to service, Boyd shares ground with Tony Evans, a prominent African American pastor in Dallas and founder of the Urban Alternative, which — through community rather than state action

---

6. Boyd, "Don't Weep for the Demise of American Christianity."

7. Interview with the author, May 4, 2009.

— addresses urban poverty, drug addiction, racism, crime, and poor education. "The church," Evans holds, "is the answer to welfare. . . . Once
we ask the government to take over things like charity, medical care,
and education, government is going to tax us excessively."[8] Neither Evans nor Boyd suggests that government is exempt from reducing injustice but rather that reliance on government makes people feel exempt.
"Power under" assumes personal activism and empathy even for those
one may disagree with, such as homosexuals or women who have had
abortions. Boyd asks, "how can we individually and collectively sacrifice for and serve women and their unwanted children so that it becomes feasible for the mother to go to full term? . . . Are we willing to
bleed for *both?*"[9]

War and Militarism

Since going to war is among a nation's most important decisions yet is
rarely compatible with Jesus' call to peace, "new evangelical" attitudes
toward it will be described separately.

Following Jesus' teachings to love one's enemy, Boyd rejects the
idea of "just war," noting that people are always apt to think their interests justify violence. Boyd recalls a megachurch July 4 celebration after
the 1991 Gulf War: the militaristic sermons about God blessing America and the montages of cross, flag, and fighter jets were met by cheers
from the congregation. He wonders how "this tribalistic, militaristic,
religious celebration" differed from one "carried out by the Taliban
Muslims raising their guns as they joyfully praised Allah for the victo-
ries they believed 'he had given them' in Afghanistan?"[10]

The Christian mandate, on Boyd's view, is to resist oppression.
Though Romans 13 requires that Christians follow positive law, it does
not require participation in the government's violent activities (see
chapter 7).[11] This sets Boyd at the pacifist end of the "new evangelical"

---

8. T. Evans, *What a Way to Live!* (Nashville: Nelsonword Publishing, 1997), pp. 418,
426.

9. Boyd, *The Myth*, p. 143.

10. Boyd, *The Myth*, p. 88.

11. Participation in Rome's army (which was not a citizens' army but a mercenary
one) was not the practice in Jesus' time, so he could not have been referring to it in injunctions to obey the state. The "sword," moreover, was a defensive weapon; see chapter 7.

range, with others like Bill Hybels, who opposed the 2003 invasion of Iraq. Boyd suggests four standards for a Christian assessment of conflict: understanding the motives of one's enemies and their points of legitimacy; understanding the motives of one's own government (securing resources for one's lifestyle?); evaluating the information one gets from one's government; and assessing government efforts to resolve the conflict nonviolently. When one concludes that a war is unavoidable, one cannot glorify it but must plead for God's forgiveness as one can never justify the killing of innocents. Radically, Boyd wonders even if the Civil War was the only way to end slavery. Could a nonviolent way have been tried?

Unresolved Issues: Church Endorsement of Candidates, Religious Symbols in Public Venues, Creationism, School Vouchers, Faith-Based Services

To preserve the distinction between church and state, Boyd believes the church should not endorse candidates from the pulpit or support religious symbols in public venues. Just as he does not call the United States a "Christian nation," Boyd holds that "It might be helpful, from a kingdom perspective, if we didn't have those things [religious symbols in public places] because then we wouldn't have the confusion that the *civic* religion is actually the kingdom."[12]

On teaching creationism/intelligent design in public schools, Boyd begins with the belief that God "is responsible for the created order," but he notes that such a belief "is an assertion of faith, not a conclusion vindicated by scientific inquiry." Thus, it cannot be taught as science. Moreover, he says, "I wouldn't be trusting the education of my children, when it comes to religious matters, to the public school. That's the job of the parents."[13]

Boyd begins his assessment of faith-based social services by noting that the church is meant to serve the needy, and so it should partner with all who do. But he cautions: while Christians must follow their faith, the neutral government should follow no faith. "The trouble [with taking government funds] is all the strings that are attached.... Everything we do, we do in Jesus' name.... I'm really against

---

12. Interview with the author, May 4, 2009.
13. Interview with the author, May 4, 2009.

building a house to get someone to become a Christian. That's just manipulative. But as you build relationships with people, life questions come up and, out of integrity, we have to be able to talk that way [about our beliefs]. While there may be occasions where the church and government agencies can work together to accomplish positive things, like housing the homeless, I agree with keeping government funds and religious programming separate. That's why I don't take government funds for specifically Christian projects."

He applies the same principle to coreligionist hiring, holding that if one wants to hire only coreligionists, one cannot use public money: "If you're going to take their [state] money, you've given them authority to some degree to tell you what to do. . . . That's one more reason I think the church should not take government money." And he applies the separation principle again to conscience-based service refusal: "What is really inconsistent is for religious organizations to take money that comes with certain rules and then try to bend those rules. It's a no-brainer: if you take this [public] money, you have to perform abortions or you have to let gay couples adopt. If you don't want to do that, then don't take the money."[14]

Another voice in this cluster is Randall Balmer, professor of religion at Barnard College and an editor at *Christianity Today*. Balmer emphasizes the independence needed for the church's prophetic role: remain extrastate, free of government funds, so as to advise and critique the state. Echoing Boyd, he writes, "The early followers of Jesus were a counterculture because they stood apart from the prevailing order. A counterculture can provide a critique of the powerful because it is utterly disinterested — it has no investment in the power structure itself."[15]

Balmer, like Boyd, holds that conflating religious symbols with government trivializes God's kingdom by associating it with human, fallen institutions. He objects also to mixing religion and science education: "The problem with intelligent design," Balmer concludes, citing the journalist and writer George F. Will, "is not that it is false but that it is not falsifiable."[16] Balmer points up the inadvertent statism of

14. Interview with the author, May 4, 2009.

15. R. Balmer, *Thy Kingdom Come: How the Religious Right Distorts the Faith and Threatens America — an Evangelical's Lament* (New York: Basic Books, 2006), p. 189.

16. Balmer, *Thy Kingdom Come*, p. 139; G. Will, "A Debate That Does Not End," *Newsweek*, July 4, 2005.

those who disagree: on one hand, they value self-reliance but, on the other, they seek state support for religious beliefs. "Through the teaching of creationism in the schools, no less than through school vouchers or tax-supported religious schools, the religious right wants the state to propagate religious beliefs — more particularly the beliefs of one religious tradition to the exclusion of all others."[17] He repeats Boyd's point about parental responsibility for church-state separation: "Why would evangelical parents want to entrust catechetical instruction to public school officials?"[18] Creationism/intelligent design, on his view, should be taught at home or in church schools[19] to ensure church-state separation, which in turn allows church schools to teach the creation story of their choice without interference from the state.

School vouchers and homeschooling also cause Balmer concern. Over two million children are homeschooled in America. Yet, Balmer writes, it expresses a "fortress mentality," undermining the integration and toleration learned in public schools. Public schools "have provided a venue of common ground for students of different religious, ethnic, and socioeconomic backgrounds. . . . In short, they learned the rudiments of democracy."[20] Lose them, and one loses a bit of one's aptitude for political negotiation. Vouchers, Balmer holds, do little good. As they make religious institutions more dependent on state money, they vitiate church independence and the church's ability to critique the state. They are also a wedge to state influence over religious education: as parents, through vouchers, bring state funds into religious schools, schools must follow state, not church, mandates. Pedagogically, on Balmer's view, vouchers Balkanize education[21] as they segregate children into schools with homogeneous profiles, and they siphon funds away from already troubled public schools.

In sum, those in and around this cluster do not feel that government is exempt from advancing the well-being of its citizens but that the church does so best when it is extrastate. This allows programs to develop according to each church's religious beliefs, prevents preferential treatment of any faith by the state, and preserves the church's independent perch from which to criticize government when it is unjust.

17. Balmer, *Thy Kingdom Come,* p. 134.
18. Balmer, *Thy Kingdom Come,* p. 89.
19. Balmer, *Thy Kingdom Come,* pp. 188-89.
20. Balmer, *Thy Kingdom Come,* p. 107.
21. Balmer, *Thy Kingdom Come,* p. 94.

GREG BOYD, MINNESOTA

Greg Boyd is pastor at Woodland Hills Church on the outskirts of St. Paul, Minnesota.

GB There is still a fairly strong identification between conservative Christians and right-wing politics, but there has also been a pronounced shift. Conservative Christians are starting to realize that there's a lot more that God cares about than two particular things that you identify as sin [abortion and gay marriage]. The rationale behind electing Bush was the promise that if we get this godly man in office then we can put conservative people on the Supreme Court; we can start reversing *Roe v. Wade*. None of it has happened. On top of that, the harm done by the Religious Right under Bush is that they have given the general populace reasons to hate them. I'm trying to invite people to enter into the joy and life of Jesus Christ, and that is being destroyed when Christ is identified with questionable — at best — political views, sometimes with stunningly bad political views.

MP Are Christians reassessing their politics now because the Bush presidency made them reconsider their goals, or do they have the same goals as always but became annoyed that the Bush government didn't achieve them?

GB Both. Some are mad that government hasn't been effective. But others are reassessing the appropriateness of people of faith leveraging the credibility of the gospel on a particular political program.

MP So why did the Religious Right grow so over the last thirty-five years?

GB As long as evangelicalism was marginal, it did what it was supposed to do. But around the 1950s and 1960s, the evangelical movement grew rapidly and in the 1970s, someone got the idea that we had a voting base. If we started flexing our muscle, we could "take the country back for God." But the way of the church is Calvary, not Caesar.

MP So how did the "Caesar" way get going?

GB There's a long tradition in America of the church being close to the state, of supporting the military. I reviewed a new Bible called *The American Patriot's Bible* [Thomas Nelson, May 2009]. It is astounding — the most disturbing thing I've ever seen from a Christian publisher. Sprinkled throughout the Bible they have a revisionist reading of American history to make it seem that U.S. history parallels the narrative of God working with his people. It's the most idolatrous thing in the world, celebrating national violence on almost every page. You'll find pictures of bombers, soldiers, flags all over the place.

But to live a Christlike life, you have to crucify your natural fallen proclivities to have it your way and to be in charge. It's our inbuilt hubris; we think that we should rule the world. Nothing has caused more bloodshed in history than that. To be a follower of Jesus is to crucify that fallen instinct.

MP Are you saying that your coreligionists, like those at Thomas Nelson, should crucify their fallen temptations?

GB It's not my place to judge, but I do feel it's my place to say: this is the kingdom and nothing else is. Here's one quote [from *The American Patriot's Bible*]: "The soldier on the field represents the noblest development of mankind." I know the author means only American soldiers. Someone who kills for his country — you would have thought that, from a Christian perspective, this is the most demonic development of humankind! It's just Christianized American-empire thinking.

If that were the only version of Christianity available, I would be a Buddhist. Honestly.

MP In the years when the Religious Right was growing, how did you find your very different direction?

GB It evolved. In the mid-1980s in grad school, I identified as an evangelical Christian. But there was something about the Moral Majority movement that did not look or feel like Jesus. That's what began this ongoing theological program of assessing everything in the light of Christ. He never seemed to do that kind of stuff. As I learned about church history, I began to see a pattern where, whenever the church got into bed with a political regime and relied on power over people rather than on power under people, it's been disastrous to society and to the reputation it gave Christ. The Inquisition, the holy wars, and all the rest. At the same time, I had a growing awareness of how fundamental aspects of American culture are inconsistent with the values of the kingdom that Jesus brought.

MP An example?

GB Jesus' emphatic, unequivocal teachings against violence. And yet, it just came out in the Pew research that evangelicals are the most supportive of torture. That's crazy. Or greed. The second most important sin in Scripture, aside from idolatry, is greed. Our culture runs on greed.

MP What should the church do?

GB The most fundamental job of the church is to have a context in which people learn the values of Jesus Christ — to live these values, to serve in community with one another. We have a certain responsibility toward government. The Bible talks about those: submit to authority, pay taxes, etc. We go along as much as possible, but insofar as what the government requires of us is inconsistent with our obligation to God, we have to revolt.

MP What does that mean?

GB It never means violent revolt. You just obey God and buck the system. Those who refused to go along with Jim Crow laws were manifesting the kingdom of God. And it may bring persecution on you. But we're called to expect that.

It has been hard in my environment to help people see the complexities of the situation. A person could vote for a candidate who is not "pro-life" but who will help the economy and the poor. Yet this may be the best way to curb the abortion rate. So precisely because a Christian is pro-life, he or she might vote for a candidate who is not pro-life.

MP Do you work with secular or other institutions to reduce abortions?

GB We don't have an official relationship with any institution which counsels women on abortion, though we have people in the congregation who work with such organizations. We have a significant adoption ministry here. One of our church overseers has adopted eight kids now. It's been their calling. My main task is to help install the value of living counterculturally and then to help people figure out how to live out their particular callings — what ministries, what projects, to get involved in.

MP I notice you have a support group for the GLBT [gay, lesbian, bisexual, and transgender] community.

GB Sure we do. If we were hiring a senior pastor, a transgender candidate would be a much harder sell to the community. But our view here is: we view the Bible as being inspired, and our reading of the Bible is that God's ideal was for heterosexual relationships. You have a few verses that seem to point to homosexual erotic relationships as sin. At the same time, compared to other issues like greed, gluttony, and idolatry, the teachings on homosexuality are very, very minor. With homosexual and transgender folks, we embrace you as you are. *If* you invite us into your life and we invite you into our lives, in the context of the small-group discussions, we will wrestle with these things together — not that there's an easy answer.

Racial and ethnic inclusiveness are also a high priority here but implementation is always the rub. You have to measure progress in inches. Though Minnesota has increasing diversity, we are one of the most segregated states because the groups aren't talking to each other. The question is whether people build relationships across racial and socioeconomic lines. We try to get everyone involved in small-group communities that include diversity. The racial issue hasn't been as difficult as the socioeconomic one. You can take a white person and a black person from middle-class suburbs, and they have a lot to talk about. But if you take a person from the suburbs and the inner city, they are in different worlds. My gut instinct is that younger people have less difficulty on the race issue. We have quite a number of interracial marriages here. Our worship leader is an African American man; he has a white wife. We are known for standing for that, so people don't feel uncomfortable coming here.

MP Can you address all of society's problems by loving people as they are?

GB I don't have any special wisdom on fixing the country's structural problems. I don't think any Christian does. A lot of them think they do, but following Jesus does not make you smarter politically. It may make you dumber because you sometimes lose the capacity to deal with ambiguity. Faith tends to deal with absolutes and you can't see the complexity of things. But our job is self-sacrificial love.

*   *   *

The church where Greg Boyd is pastor, Woodland Hills Church, is located in a renovated K-Mart "big box" store in the middle of an enormous parking lot in the outskirts of St. Paul, Minnesota. Since the 1990s, it has grown from a congregation of 300 to one serving over 3,000 in three English-language services each weekend. On the weekend I visited, the service for the Hmong immigrant community met at 2 p.m.; Latino worship, at 4 p.m., served Spanish speakers from many countries, from Puerto Rico and Peru. In the English-language services, songs about God's love and grace, rather than traditional hymns, were played by an eight-piece band on the theater-sized stage, though traditional hymns are sung in worship services as well. The lyrics, along with close-ups of the band, were projected onto large screens so that the congregation could sing along. Total church participation is about 10,000 each week, 3,000 in attendance and an additional 7,000 participating as individuals, groups, and "house churches," from as far away as Qatar, watching services through television and the Internet.

In the early 1990s Boyd was a professor at Bethel, a Christian university in St. Paul. He was persuaded to become a congregation minister by the promise that he would have no administrative duties — a promise that he humorously admits hasn't exactly worked out. His wife was more dubious about the change from academia to "pastor's wife." "Shelly doesn't look good in a bun," Boyd jokes, "and she does *not* play the organ."

Woodland Hills was started nominally under the Baptist General Conference. But at a May 2009 "Learn about Woodland Hills" introduction class, so many people of differing confessions attended that an explanation was needed. The wife of an interracial Catholic couple asked, "I've never heard anything about this church having a denomination — does it?" An associate pastor turned to another associate and asked, "Are we even still in the [Baptist] Convention's stuff? Uh . . .

that's not something we . . . uh, care a lot about. We're loosely affiliated with the Baptists but it comes as a shock to most people that we are."

In starting Woodland Hills, Boyd's vision was of a church that bridged socioeconomic classes, races, and ethnic groups. But he was a little surprised when one of the first people to join was a man who had just completed a sex change. "That is, he was now a man," Boyd explains. However new this may have been for parishioners, the man joined the church. This anecdote is included in the church's welcome video so that those considering joining the church have an idea of its inclusiveness.

While the transgender gentleman did not rattle the church, Boyd's 2004 series of sermons on the "kingdom of God/kingdom of the world" did. Written in response to the pressures placed on pastors to persuade parishioners to vote for Bush, it highlighted Boyd's opposition to confusing political wins with Jesus-like conduct. The series lost the church a thousand members, greatly straining its financial resources. But the loss "made us realize," Boyd notes, "how much we still were a *de facto* white church. It made us intensify our commitment to bridge across racial and socio-economic lines." Today, the themes of "acceptance" and "ministry" are repeated as reasons for parishioner involvement in Woodland Hills. Three women from Nigeria said, "We're here because it's good for the youth, for the kids, to be here without discrimination by the other kids — you know, like they might get somewhere else." One of the women added, "In my home in Nigeria, we had close relationship between the Muslims and the Christians. I was born a Christian. And so when I pray here, with all the different people, it reminds me of home."

Ji-hye and Hank, Wisconsin

Ji-hye is a tailored Korean woman in her early fifties with a real estate business in Wisconsin. Inclusiveness was her first reason for attending Woodland Hills. She was raised in the Korean Catholic Church and also attends a Korean Catholic church near her home. "In other churches, there are different kinds of people. But each group stays separate from others. Here, everyone mingles. When my daughter was in middle school, there was a group of boys who teased her about being Korean. The kids hear it from parents. She came home crying. She said, 'There is no God, and if there is, he hates me.'"

The second reason for Ji-hye's interest in Woodland Hills is Boyd's sermons and a concern about reading the Bible. "I was thinking today, I'm going to go home and write down all verses they [the Catholic church] read this year. I want to check if they read whole books. I think they choose the parts they like and put away others. I don't believe in that."

Hank, Ji-hye's American partner, age sixty-six, works in commercial real estate but pioneered a business in medical databases in the 1980s. He stresses the church's inclusive, nondenominational character as he believes that communication across multicultural lines is key to the future. In contrast to the Catholic church he grew up in, which he feels was a "business," "This church does mission work; they go out and do the foundational things that church was designed to do. . . . We have an opportunity to shape the next economic game so that it is more sustainable with less trickery, lying, cheating, and stealing. If you earn $47,500 a year, you are in the top 1 percent of world income earners. This raises the question: How much is enough? Look at those with $400 a year. Why wouldn't they be upset with us, think we're arrogant, think we're not doing enough to solve poverty? Why wouldn't there be conflict? Then add feuding over which God is the highest and you get most of the trouble we have. What will help people have an eternal life with God and a happier life on earth? We need more empathetic listening, and less about 'me' and 'my interest group.' What's a code of conduct or ethical standards that we can all live by? Try helping somebody else first."

That, in Ji-hye's view, is the role of the church — "to make better conduct in each of us, close to God. People come to church are agree what pastor teaching but some, when they go out, it's gone. Their excuse is like, 'business is business' — like business is supposed to be lying and cheating. And like 'business is not "me."' But it is."

Activism and Cooperation with Government

Church-State Basics

"No policy improvement or military force can replace our individual responsibility in solving society's ills, yet the voices and actions of people of faith should shape our government's proper role in serving people."[22] In this one sentence, Joel Hunter, senior pastor at Northland Church in Longwood, Florida, reveals his hybrid stance: political engagement for Jesus-like ends. While Hunter's church, like Boyd's, sponsors a humbling list of community and poverty relief programs, it also works with local and federal government. Hunter himself, in 2009-10, served in Obama's Office of Faith-Based and Neighborhood Partnerships.

Hunter insists on a high wall between state and church — "Merging the institutions of church and state is out"[23] — because the two entities are fundamentally unalike. The purpose of liberal democracy, he holds, is to maintain order and protect the nation so that the individual may flourish; force is sometimes appropriate. The purpose of the church is to change the heart of the individual such that Jesus' way flourishes; only faith and service are appropriate.

On this principle, Hunter was openly uncomfortable with evangelical involvement in the Republican Party. "A voice of Biblical values cannot be in the pocket of one party."[24] Hunter suggests that pastors guide their congregations to think as Jesus thought but not tell them how to vote. For their part, evangelical voters should eschew "groupthink" and be wary of the human readiness to believe that benefits to oneself are benefits for all. Evangelicals, on Hunter's view, should evaluate candidates not by religious affiliation: no Christian leader "has been the solution to flawed government."[25] Rather, criteria for office should be "whether or not they [candidates] are willing to undertake for those who Jesus described in Luke 4 — the oppressed, the poor, and the captive."[26] This may lead to a Democratic vote, as poverty relief, injustice, and environmental protection have been better addressed by that party. Though Hunter opposes abortion, he works on abortion reduction with Democrats and pro-choice activists.

Yet while Hunter stresses the wall between the institutions of church and state, he holds that this wall does not extend between the

---

22. J. Hunter, *A New Kind of Conservative* (Ventura, Calif.: Gospel Light Publishing, 2008), p. 22; many of the ideas in this book can also be found in J. Hunter, *Right Wing, Wrong Bird: Why the Tactics of the Religious Right Won't Fly with Most Conservative Christians* (Longwood, Fla.: Distributed Church Press, 2006).

23. Hunter, *New Kind of Conservative*, p. 59.

24. Hunter, *New Kind of Conservative*, p. 31.

25. Hunter, *New Kind of Conservative*, pp. 54, 55.

26. Hunter, *New Kind of Conservative*, p. 172.

state and individual Christians, who can enter public debate and, through democratic mechanisms, try to persuade government and nongovernmental groups to engage in Jesus-like conduct. To do this sort of political work, evangelicals should first know "why the other side is for the other side," consider alternatives to long-held beliefs, and distinguish between emotional and thought-through positions.[27] In dealings with the state, they should be loyal to government (Rom. 13:1-7), engage in nonviolent critique when needed and in nonviolent civil disobedience when necessary (Acts 4:18-20; Acts 5:29), and in extreme circumstances leave the country (Matt. 10:23).[28]

Hunter's hybrid stance echoes the 2004 position paper of the National Association of Evangelicals (NAE), *For the Health of the Nation*. On one hand, the NAE describes political involvement as part of man's stewardship over the earth (Gen. 1:27-28), and so it encourages Christians to help government "live up to the divine mandate to render justice (Romans 13:1-7; 1 Peter 2:13-17)." This includes addressing the structural, socioeconomic, and political patterns that create human suffering, such as family breakdown and the lack of education. On the other hand, the institutions of church and state remain separate spheres (Rom. 13:1-7; Mark 12:13-17; Eph. 4:15-16; 5:23-32). The boundary keeps government out of religious matters and preserves freedom of conscience for all — what the NAE calls "gospel pluralism" — including the freedom of conscience to critique the state.[29]

The efforts at political independence and issue-by-issue decision making of this cluster are worth noting, especially because of its substantial political engagement. They have been on the rise since 2005, when *Christianity Today*[30] wrote, "George W. Bush is not Lord. . . . The American flag is not the Cross. The Pledge of Allegiance is not the Creed. 'God

27. Hunter, *New Kind of Conservative*, pp. 84-85.

28. See also Hunter's podcasts, http://www.rightwingwrongbird.com/.

29. The NAE and others explain this through the parable of the wheat and tares (Matthew and the noncanonical *Gospel of Thomas*). The weeds (tares) that grow amid the good seeds are not uprooted or destroyed until harvest time, suggesting that Christians may not uproot or persecute heretics, dissenters, or nonbelievers. Between now and judgment day (harvest time), they might accept Jesus, but in any case, no human knows whether there is only one path to salvation or, if there is, what it might be. This is for God to judge.

30. *Christianity Today* was founded in 1956 by Billy Graham and L. Nelson Bell; it prints ten periodicals with a total subscription of over 1 million and its Web site attracts nearly 12 million viewers monthly.

Bless America' is not Doxology."[31] It went on to reject the conflation of biblical truths with American or Republican values, and of church with state. In 2006, Frank Page, president of the Southern Baptist Convention, warned, "I have cautioned our denomination to be very careful not to be seen as in lock step with any political party."[32] Rick Warren was bolder still: "I don't talk policy ever with politicians — never. Never. And let me just say it again: never."[33] And the 2008 *Evangelical Manifesto* was even bolder still. It called on evangelicals to distance themselves from party politics, lest "Christians become 'useful idiots' for one political party or another and . . . Christian beliefs are used as weapons for political interests." It reprised the call for church-state separation and for political engagement as extrastate activity: "We . . . see it our duty to engage with politics, but our equal duty never to be completely equated with any party, partisan ideology, economic system, or nationality."[34]

David Gushee, professor at Mercer University, explains why political independence has gotten such play of late. "One reason why Christians must retain their political independence," he writes, "is so that they can retain their moral compass when they do venture into the political arena."[35] Gushee's litmus test for Christian political engagement is "whether we have the capacity to say no to our favorite party or politician."[36] His rules for evangelical politics parallel Hunter's: Christian leaders should not endorse candidates or parties, advise them, fund them, or distribute partisan material. They should attend campaign events only if they attend those of all candidates, and they should invite candidates to speak only if they invite all contenders. Electoral vic-

---

31. Michael Lindsay's content analysis of the magazine over the last forty years shows a significant increase in what he calls "cosmopolitan" content in contrast to "populist" content; see D. M. Lindsay, *Faith in the Halls of Power: How Evangelicals Joined the American Elite* (New York: Oxford University Press, 2007); see also Pew Forum on Religion and Public Life, "American Evangelicalism: New Leaders, New Faces, New Issues," May 6, 2008.

32. D. Kirkpatrick, "The Evangelical Crackup," *New York Times Magazine,* October 28, 2007.

33. Pew Forum on Religion and Public Life, "The Future of Evangelicals: A Conversation with Pastor Rick Warren," November 13, 2009.

34. *Evangelical Manifesto: A Declaration of Evangelical Identity and Public Commitment* (Washington, D.C.: Evangelical Manifesto Steering Committee, 2008).

35. D. Gushee, *The Future of Faith in American Politics: The Public Witness of the Evangelical Center* (Waco, Tex.: Baylor University Press, 2008), pp. 49, 51.

36. Gushee, *The Future of Faith,* p. 50.

tory should not be linked to victory for God's kingdom. Religious leaders should discuss the scriptural view of a given political issue, distinct from the range of party positions. They should "model and encourage respectful and civil discourse" and "teach and model respect for the Constitutional relationship between religion and the state."

War and Militarism

Unlike Boyd and Balmer, Hunter appreciates the attempt by just war theory to identify where war is the responsible course of action. However, he rejects preemptive military action absent imminent attack,[37] a stance that led him to oppose Bush's invasion of Iraq in 2003. Hunter notes also that building peace means not only the absence of conflict but also substantial efforts to reconcile peoples. Underscoring the difference between a political view of war and a Christian one, Hunter notes that the symbol of Christian spirit is the dove, that of the United States, the bald eagle.

Most "new evangelicals," like Hunter, do not hold pacifist views. Their positions range from "strict just war theory," which holds higher standards for judging a war to be just, to "permissive just war theory," which more easily concedes entrance into conflict, both for self-defense and for redistributive justice (punishment of evil).[38] On the permissive view, occasional governmental abuse of force does not invalidate the state's authority to conduct war.[39] Nonetheless, even permissive just war theorists seek extensive diplomatic efforts to avoid violence. They show greater resistance to military operations and much greater to torture. *Christianity Today,* for instance, did not oppose the 2003 invasion of Iraq but later wondered, in print, whether evangelicals should repent their avid support for the war.

Within this cluster, Gushee tips toward strict just war views. He recognizes that this may weaken one's ability to fight truly just wars but suggests that America's position as military hegemon makes too-

37. Hunter, *New Kind of Conservative,* p. 180.
38. Gushee, *The Future of Faith,* pp. 206-9.
39. See K. Pavlischek, "Just War Theory and Terrorism: Applying the Ancient Doctrine to the Current Conundrum," Family Research Council, Witherspoon Lectures, November 21, 2001; J. Skillen and K. Pavlischek, "Political Responsibility and the Use of Force," *Philosophia Christi* 3, no. 2 (2001): 443.

quick militarism the greater danger.[40] His blog posting on the death of Osama bin Laden is worth quoting at length.

> A nation has a right to defend itself. From the perspective of the fundamental national security of the United States, this action is legitimately viewed as an expression of self-defense. But as Christians, we believe that there can be no celebrating, no dancing in the streets, no joy, in relation to the death of Osama bin Laden. In obedience to scripture, there can be no rejoicing when our enemies fall. . . . For those of us who embrace a version of the just war theory, honed carefully over the centuries of Christian tradition, our response is disciplined by belief that war itself is tragic and that all killing in war, even in self-defense, must be treated with sobriety and even mournfulness. War and all of its killing reflects the brokenness of our world. That is the proper spirit with which to greet this news. . . . There can never be any moral justification for terrorist attacks on innocent people, such as the terrible deeds of 9/11. But we must recognize that to the extent that our nation's policies routinely create enemies, we can kill a Bin Laden on May 1 and face ten more like him on May 2. Might it now be possible for us to have an honest national conversation about these issues? May we learn the right lessons from the news of this day. For Jesus' sake.[41]

In line with Hunter and Gushee, the NAE urges government to "use it [force] in the service of peace and not merely in their national interest. Military force must be guided by the classical just-war principles." The NAE not only supports the UN's Universal Declaration of Human Rights but also insists on firm mechanisms of enforcement: "Insofar a person has a human right, that person should be able to appeal to an executive, legislative, or judicial authority to enforce or adjudicate that right."[42] The NAE's 2007 *Evangelical Declaration against Torture* rejected "the use of torture and cruel, inhuman, and degrading

---

40. Gushee, *The Future of Faith,* pp. 211-13.

41. D. Gushee, "Do Not Rejoice When Your Enemies Fall," New Evangelical Partnership for the Common Good, at http://www.newevangelicalpartnership.org/?q =node%2F124.

42. See National Association of Evangelicals, *For the Health of the Nation: An Evangelical Call to Civic Responsibility* (Washington, D.C., 2004).

treatment by any branch of our government (or any other government) — even in the current circumstance of a war between the United States and various radical terrorist groups."[43]

Richard Cizik, head of the New Evangelical Partnership for the Common Good, along with R. Scott Appleby, chaired the Task Force on Religion and the Making of U.S. Foreign Policy (Chicago Council on Global Affairs), which in 2010 issued its report, *Engaging Religious Communities Abroad: A New Imperative for U.S. Foreign Policy*.[44] It furthers Hunter's idea that peace requires not just the absence of violence but active society-building and the development of cooperation among hostile parties. These goals, the report states, should be immediately incorporated into U.S. foreign policy. The report notes that although religion is used to stoke violence, religious groups often provide much of the solace, inspiration, and infrastructure in distressed areas, and thus "a focus on religion through the lens of terrorism and counter-terrorism strategy is too narrow." Instead, it recommends a multifaceted, indirect approach. Domestically, this would include training personnel in many government departments to work with religious groups overseas; coordinating these efforts with the National Security Council; appointing an American Muslim leader as ambassador to the Organization of the Islamic Conference; and creating an ambassadorship for international religious freedom. Internationally, the report suggests substantial U.S. engagement not only by the government but also by civil society groups and not only with foreign governments but also with NGOs and local religious civil society groups abroad — even those that oppose U.S. foreign policy. The task force established six criteria for working with such groups because "evidence from the past decade indicates that religious political parties often place pragmatism and problem solving over ideology. Indeed, no Islamist party elected to national parliament," once it became busy with the daily burdens of governance and service provision, "has sought to put great emphasis on Sharia laws as the source of legislation, despite preelection rhetoric." Finally, the report suggests clarification of the establishment clause of the First Amendment to note that religious freedom and

---

43. National Association of Evangelicals, *An Evangelical Declaration against Torture: Protecting Human Rights in an Age of Terror* (2007).

44. R. S. Appleby and R. Cizik, *Engaging Religious Communities Abroad: A New Imperative for U.S. Foreign Policy*, report of the Task Force on Religion and the Making of U.S. Foreign Policy (Chicago: Chicago Council on Foreign Relations, 2010).

church-state separation include the right of religious groups — stateside and abroad — to advance their ideas in the public arena.

Unresolved Issues: Candidate Endorsement, Prayer in Schools, Religious Symbols on Public Grounds, School Vouchers, Faith-Based Services, and the Doctrine of "Substantive Neutrality"

Perhaps more interesting than the particular positions taken by this cluster is its picture of the political and legal process. Though adherents of this viewpoint locate themselves extrastate, they do not feel external to political/legal developments but rather part of them, working on policy along with government and other civil society actors. "In a democracy, nobody wins all the time," Rick Warren notes. "I don't win all the time and neither do you."[45] When they don't prevail, "new evangelicals" have to date adjusted to the law. For instance, while this cluster argues for coreligionist hiring, when the courts hold that this is an unduly sectarian use of public money, their faith-based agencies follow legal guidelines or forgo public grants — while continuing public education about their views. They neither become lawbreakers — indeed, efforts to persuade the public aim at modifying the law so that they do not break it — nor do they withdraw from civic engagement if law doesn't follow their preferences. "How much money did the Roman Empire provide to the early church?" Gushee asks. "None. The church has proven capable of delivering love and care without taking government money. So from the side of the church, it just might be simpler to get out of the business [of taking public grants] altogether."[46]

Hunter's position on unresolved legal issues reflects his overall hybrid stance. He emphasizes political involvement more than do Boyd and Balmer but opposes direct politicking and candidate endorsement by religious institutions. He also opposes sectarian prayer in public schools, drawing on the pluralist corrective to special pleading. Hunter's copastor Dan Lacich reviews the rationale frequent among "new evangelicals": since all religious groups must have equal privileges under the law, public school prayer would mandate prayers in all religious traditions, which is inappropriate for the state to administer and

45. Pew Forum on Religion and Public Life, "The Future of Evangelicals."
46. Interview with the author, May 13, 2009.

organizationally daunting. Regarding religious symbols in public places, Hunter considers the debate an indictment against Christians. "If Christians were loving other people and really making a huge difference in society, nobody would mind our displaying the Ten Commandments or manger scenes at Christmas time . . . this is about our ineffectiveness and our poor witness."[47] Hunter favors pluralistic public expression: "We [Northland Church] don't spend a lot of time on this, but my inclination is, put it all out there. I love when people think through the variety of presentations and perspectives."[48]

Building on the recognition of religious variety, one recently persuasive argument among evangelicals is "substantive neutrality."[49] This requires that the state place no special burdens on sectarian or nonsectarian groups. "Our commitment," the *Evangelical Manifesto* holds, "is to a *civil public square — a vision of public life in which citizens of all faiths are free to enter and engage the public square on the basis of their faith, but within a framework of what is agreed to be just and free for other faiths too.*" In practice, substantive neutrality promotes religious pluralism, but in some cases it challenges the religious exceptionalism of the First Amendment, where government may advance many ideas but not religious ones. The challenge goes like this: though the prohibition against endorsing religious views is meant to prevent discrimination against faith groups, it may in practice put government in the very position of discriminating against religious but not secular ideas (by funding secular but not religious social service programs, for instance) — exactly the opposite of First Amendment aims.

The way substantive neutrality works in practice can be illustrated through the voucher question. This cluster tends to hold that vouchers may be used for religious education as long as recipients have secular choices as well — the substantively neutral position on their view. The alternative, withholding vouchers from religious but not secular schools, discriminates against religion, which liberal democracies may not do. If, as voucher opponents argue, most schools that are affordable through government vouchers turn out to be church-subsidized ones, this does not invalidate the program's legality. It is not, according to

47. Hunter, *New Kind of Conservative,* pp. 184-85.

48. Interview with the author, May 11, 2009.

49. The most thorough legal analysis in favor of substantive neutrality can be found in the work of the Center for Public Justice (CPJ), founded in 1981 by Jim Skillen.

substantive neutrality, de facto support for religious schools, for communities that want *secular* private schools that are low-cost and thus voucher-affordable may raise the money to subsidize them, as churches raise funds for religious schools.

Substantive neutrality has also been applied to the regulation of faith-based social services, raising similar complexities and dividing evangelical opinion. Some believe the substantively neutral position allows government to fund religious programming — religious approaches to counseling drug addicts, for instance — just as it funds secular approaches. On their view, the alternative — funding secular but not religious approaches — discriminates against religious agencies. The substantively neutral position would be this: just as secular agencies are not disqualified from public grants because of their approaches to counseling (Freudian, Rogerian), so too religious services should not be disqualified because of theirs. This view confronts the religious exceptionalism of the First Amendment — government may support and fund many views but not religious ones — with the discrimination *against* religion that may result from it, however unintentionally. Others in this cluster, however, hold that public funds may pay for social services at faith-based institutions but *not* for religious programming or counseling. In a sense, they uphold the religious exceptionalism of the First Amendment — government may pay for many things but not religion. This was the position taken by President Obama's 2009-10 Office of Faith-Based and Neighborhood Partnerships and by Obama in his 2010 Executive Order — Fundamental Principles and Policymaking Criteria for Partnerships with Faith-Based and Other Neighborhood Organizations.[50] It is also the position of John DiIulio, the first director of G. W. Bush's White House Office of Faith-Based and Community Initiatives, and of the NAE. "Getting a grant," Carl Esbeck, NAE counsel, notes, "should be a measure not of who you are but how well you do the job. But we need government monitoring to ensure that government grant dollars are not diverted to explicitly religious programming. . . . You don't have to take a government grant but if you do, the ability to monitor and audit comes with it."[51]

---

50. http://www.whitehouse.gov/the-press-office/2010/11/17/executive-order
-fundamental-principles-and-policymaking-criteria-partner.

51. Interview with the author, May 5, 2009.

The substantive neutrality argument has also become part of the debate about coreligionist hiring: just as government does not withhold funds from secular agencies that hire Gestalt therapists rather than Jungian ones, so government may not withhold funds from agencies that hire Baptist therapists rather than Gestalt or Buddhist ones. To the argument that the distinction between Jungian and Gestalt therapists concerns *professional* competence (not faith), some evangelicals hold that religious beliefs help their clientele and that mastering those beliefs is also a professional competence. For this reason and reasons of institutional integrity, coreligionist hiring is supported by most "new evangelicals," including Hunter and Tony Campolo, who worked with the Democrats on the 2008 party platform, and Ron Sider, founder of Evangelicals for Social Action and the Evangelical Environmental Network.[52] Hunter notes, "Our values are our identity. I would not think of saying to Planned Parenthood 'you've got to hire a certain percentage of pro-life people.'" Similarly, the Council for Christian Colleges and Universities (CCCU)[53] holds that Christian institutions should be allowed to "hire as full-time faculty and administrators only persons who profess belief in Jesus Christ." It notes, however, that this limitation pertains only to religious faith; in the arenas of race and gender, it emphasizes diversity and equity, and supports active recruitment of minorities and women.

The controversy about coreligionist hiring was sufficiently complex that Obama's 2010 executive order retained the policy of evaluating instances of coreligionist hiring on a case-by-case basis.

Hunter does not avoid discussing the disinclination of many faith-based agencies to hire homosexuals. "If you're going to be part of our organization," he notes, "we want you to be living out the values of our organization." But, like Gushee, Esbeck, and others, he repeats, "If an organization feels it would have to sacrifice its identity, don't participate in the government program and don't take their funds."[54] As a practical matter, Gushee notes, "change on the homosexuality issue is slowly working its way across the Christian landscape. It begins with a rejection

52. J. Kennedy, "Preach and Reach: Despite His Liberal Record, Obama Is Making a Lot of Evangelicals Think Twice," *Christianity Today,* October 6, 2008.

53. The CCCU has 105 member institutions in the United States and Canada, 75 affiliate organizations in 20 countries, 300,000 student members, and 1.55 million alumni; its budget is $11 million; among its members is the prestigious Wheaton College.

54. Interview with the author, May 11, 2009.

of all the hatefulness. Next is the question: What does love require in rela-
tion to the gay and lesbian people with whom we relate or who come to
our churches? Whatever we think about the morality of homosexual
acts, we must love gay and lesbian people. Eventually we will have to ask:
Are we really sure that it is a fundamental, nonnegotiable Christian belief
that all same-sex sexual activity is sin? That's where the conversation has
to happen within the faith community. Even if we decide we are sure,
should we ask the state to enforce our convictions on this matter?
Change will come a lot more easily if it happens organically within the
churches rather than forced by the state. If it's forced, there'll be a serious
backlash. Of course, if the civil rights era is the proper historical parallel,
it's really hard to hold back the forces that say, 'this is no different from
segregation in the 1960s.' We may indeed be forced to change."[55]

The analogy with the civil rights movement, however, is an argument made by the gay community and its supporters, not by many
evangelicals. To date, most "new evangelicals" lambaste violence
against gay people and oppose discrimination against them in secular
arenas (housing, education, employment in nonchurch jobs), but they
do not engage gay people for church employment or social service jobs
where employees must express church values (see chapter 9).

Joel Hunter, Florida

Joel Hunter is an ordained minister and has a doctorate in Culture and Per-
sonality in Pastoral Care. He is presently senior pastor at Northland Church
in Longwood, Florida, and in 2009-10 was a member of Obama's Office of
Faith-Based and Neighborhood Partnerships.

He recalls that he was the kind of kid whose formative religious experiences included getting caught stealing a "men's magazine" and whose first
church skill was coughing loudly enough to cover the sound of opening
candy wrappers. At Ohio University he became active in the civil rights
movement.

JH [I] assumed, as we all did, that if we just got the right power in office, we'd be all right. When Dr. King was assassinated, I was thrown
into a crisis. The volatility and polarization of that time — we didn't

55. Interview with the author, August 17, 2010.

have graduation ceremonies because we had eight hundred National Guardsmen on campus — could get you caught up in politics without your knowing why you were doing it. I wanted a more stable foundation for political reform, an eternal reason, a deep kind of equality where all God's children would be cared for because he cared for them. So I committed myself personally to follow Christ as a result of that search for foundational meaning. I thought I'd go to seminary — though I was sure they'd throw me out as soon as they found out about me. I wasn't exactly the religious type.

Dr. King is partially why I identify with Barack Obama. King integrated faith with social policy in a way that benefits the vulnerable — which is our job. That's Jesus' reading of his job description in Isaiah 61. My grandparents were always broke because they were always giving their money away. On the other hand, I lived in an all-white town. So my journey was religious and social; it was part of my faith to learn to understand the common good.

In the next ten years we're going to see more cooperation between those who form public policy from a secular perspective and those who come to it from a religious one. This is part of the maturation of the evangelical movement and in a way a going back to our roots. Christianity started out as a compassionate movement. It grew because we responded to epidemics and catastrophes. We were for abolition, women's suffrage, and child labor laws. In maturity, you define yourself by what you're for, by how you can cooperate with those who aren't like you. There's an emerging constituency that, while not leaving behind earlier concerns, is putting a major amount of energy into climate change, poverty, justice issues, health issues. You're seeing a new evangelical maturity.

The iteration of the 1970s was a political, alarmed reaction to the perceived decadence in our culture, like abortion and the extraction of prayer from the public schools. For a couple of decades, the evangelical movement got stuck in this combative — "we have to win" — stance. There were issues where I agreed with [Religious Right leader Jerry] Falwell, like being pro-life, but the tone was off-putting. There was a silent majority to the silent majority. There came a time when many people started cringing. The AIDS issue — shouldn't these people be receiving the most compassion and understanding? There are twenty-five thousand children dying every day from poverty. What are we doing about that?

MP Is this a generational change?

JH Younger people are less ideological, care less about Democrat and Republican. They just want to get things done. But there's a lot now that reminds me of the 1960s — inspirational, idealistic. I have lived a long time to see this come about again.

MP Is it a response to the Bush years?

JH Let's say the Bush-Cheney years. Bush went in a compassionate conservative — at least that's who some of us voted for. But I'm not sure he had the capacity to handle the issues. So he delegated to Cheney.

There is a sense now among evangelicals that we did not think independently; we did not examine or analyze. We went along with this self-protective mentality that says, "let's get them before they get us." September 11 [2001] reinforced this but there already was a good deal of fodder to shape into fear. We've developed a consumerist, self-centered culture. That feeds into preemptive war because we fear that "they're going to take away what I have." Or "Government programs are going to take away my hard-earned dollars." There are remnants of that now, in right-wing talk radio — Limbaugh, Hannity, Michael Savage — just awful.

Here's what I think the enemy is: the luxury of being simplistic, of not understanding how complex problems are and how much cooperation is required to solve them. Evangelicals went through a period where we formed homogeneous affinity groups. You cloister together and think everybody else is the enemy. One reason I'm thrilled with Obama's presidency is that he likes a broad spectrum of perspectives. Out of those he will glean a practical solution good for everyone. He's got the intellectual capacity to handle the job.

MP Is your congregation bipartisan?

JH We're nearly half and half.

MP If you want to contribute to society but not marry a political party, how does that work?

JH If you're a Christian and want to make a difference in the world, you ask: What is the biblical basis for what I do? What would Jesus do?

We can't bank on winning or losing political battles. That's not what the kingdom of God depends on.

We, being the humans we are, will always be tempted to make spiritual progress by political means — to use power in order to make others have our values. But Christians have to be careful to exemplify what we believe is right and then let it go. There are three hundred million people in this country. I am one voice.

What I saw on the religious right was a lot of religious arrogance. Those who are theocrats — the Reconstructionists who insist that biblical mandates be law for everybody — will always believe they're losing if they don't get their way. We believe we are winning if we have the freedom to give our opinion along with everybody else. We don't need to have our way. God doesn't call us to be "successful"; he calls us to be faithful.

MP If you are one voice, how do you work with other voices?

JH We have extensive partnerships in our work on poverty, medical clinics, AIDS, housing. We partner with governments all over the world. Locally, when we have convocations on torture, creation care, and poverty, I ask for broad leadership: the bishop of the Catholic church, the head of the Islamic society, a rabbi. I ask them to explain, from the perspective of their scriptures, why this issue is important. Everybody begins to understand that "they" have values like I do and that this issue is too big for any one group to solve.

I was on the board of Jobs Partnership of Central Florida. The state government offered the finances to train the unemployed, and individual church-people became volunteer sponsors for each unemployed person. The sponsors said, "If your kid gets sick, we'll take him or her to the doctor. If your car breaks down, we'll get you to work and fix the flat problem." Since the business community was getting trained employees with backup support systems, they committed to taking the trainees into jobs where they could move into higher-paying ranks. Business people got what they needed. Church people were able to love like they needed to love. Government got people off of welfare into jobs.

Of course, there are still a lot of barriers to working together — not willful ones but we've gotten used to operating on our own realms. Having said that, we specifically invite the African American church, other churches and faith communities into much of what we do. We have a few that are our longtime partners. Same is true for our missions in other countries. We want to form partnerships — long-term partnerships with people who are different from the way we are. Westerners have a view of the gospel that's very different from someone in South America, China, or Africa. We need that kind of cross-pollination.

MP In cooperative projects, how do you handle the finances?

JH A church cannot take government funds into the church's general budget. So for instance, in our partnership with the county to renovate houses in poor areas, they buy the supplies and the churches bring in the [volunteer] craftsmen. The county pays for the materials; the money never comes to us.

MP What could mess up this picture of intergroup and church-state cooperation?

JH Militancy from one powerful group. If any group gets too much power, there is a tendency to suppress others. But as we continue listening with respect to multiple perspectives, we will begin to trust each other. I've been in conversations with organizations our government can't even talk to — like Hezbollah. The enemy is never as scary or threatening up close.

What also can sabotage dialogue is a structure where voices present their case to the governing authority but never have to listen to others. If you have a president who says, "give me one group at a time," the group comes in, presents its case, and if things don't go down their way, they're furious. But if all the groups sit together and hear what other people are saying, then they begin to see where others are coming from.

MP How do you answer those who think churches don't belong in political discussion?

JH We could diffuse some of the alarm if we think in terms of cooperation rather than "religion against secularism." Think more in terms of cooperation on projects rather than compromise on beliefs. We need to get away from the zero-sum game that says, if we allow them their voice, it will take away from what I have.

MP What's your response to those who say, "We don't want to dialogue with certain religious groups, like those that commit honor killings."

JH You take care of destructive behavior by law. All law is codified values, of course. But every society must decide what protecting its citizens entails. Yet you don't disenfranchise an entire faith group because of some of the people in it. You know the saying, you keep your friends close and your enemies closer.

The counterintuitive wisdom here is that the very people you don't want to talk to are the people you need to talk to the most. You start out by saying that this is going to be tough. But you never make any progress until you engage in those conversations. At least you're building relationships, and that enhances the probability of reaching consensus.

There's a very important conversation to be had with secular authorities about Muslims not being able to wear certain types of dress or Christians not being able to wear a cross of a certain size. Dialogue is necessary no matter how tough it is. Boundaries are not just dividing points. They are connecting points. They are not where the conversation ends but where it begins.

DAVID GUSHEE, GEORGIA

David Gushee is professor of Christian ethics at Mercer University and director of the Center for Theology and Public Life in Atlanta, Georgia, as well as cofounder of the New Evangelical Partnership for the Common Good. Prior to his position at Mercer, Gushee served for eleven years as Graves Professor of Moral Philosophy at Union University in Jackson, Tennessee. In 2008, he was appointed by the United States Holocaust Memorial Museum to serve as a member of the Church Relations and the Holocaust Committee. He is a columnist for Associated Baptist Press, the *Huffington Post,* and the *Washington Post,* and a contributing editor for *Christianity Today.*

DG In the 1960s and 1970s, when the Democratic Party identified itself with the changes launched by the civil rights movement, the women's movement, the antiwar and gay rights movements, the Republican Party made a decision to identify itself as the party of resistance, the party of the aggrieved white Southerner. It was a strategy that attracted cultural conservatives, of whom religious conservatives are a big part. In some respects, the marriage between the Christian Right and the Republican Party was a marriage of conviction; they were united against the social changes of the 1960s. But eventually, it became a marriage of convenience. Republicans could win elections by playing the culture cards. Leaders of the Christian Right could gain dramatic national visibility, make money, and build ministries.

That narrative arc has ended. Anger repels. Bitterness is repugnant. The Christian Right developed a rhetorical strategy of polemical enemy-bashing. It worked beautifully for a while in mobilizing their base and raising money. Local and state elections were won. But the image of the angry, red-faced white man yelling was awful to listen to and it is not in keeping with the spirit of Jesus Christ. There is now a sense of embarrassment internal to the evangelical community, especially among the university-educated, the young, the more urban — a sense that the Religious Right is not speaking for me. They are hurting the mission of the church, making the name of Christ odious to others, and triggering a new atheism. But it's not only the young and urban; it is a broader cultural change than that. The conservatives of the 1970s have lost on every point: race, gender, divorce, abortion. Homosexuality is their last stand.

MP Evangelicals of this "broader cultural change" — can you describe the politics — aims, means?

DG The Christian Right has an exceptionalist vision of America's God-given freedoms and special religious foundations. It also believes that the role of Christianity in America was itself exceptional — that Christianity was the quasi-established religion of America. What the Religious Right feared, beginning with the Supreme Court decisions removing prayer from the public schools, was that they were no longer the culturally "established" religion. Today, many believe the state is hostile to them. Those fears are being stoked intentionally by the Right because that's all they have right now. At 12 to 13 percent of the population, the Religious Right feels increasingly angry and apocalyptic about America, increasingly likely to believe the most outlandish things about Obama. But that's a vast overreaction.

What I notice in the evangelical center and left is the willingness to accept the cultural disestablishment of Christianity and to see possible advantages in it. It is harder to confuse America and the church, and easier to recall a more biblical understanding of the church as a counterculture community gathered around Christ — an international, interracial community. Nobody of the first century would have said "we" meaning the Roman Empire. But "we" has meant the American empire, with the church as its kind of religious sanctioner. This is painfully obvious in the heavy participation of evangelicals in the military. And it has made it hard for us to have a prophetic distance from our country, government, and economy. It is very hard for us to hear what Jesus says about violence in a context in which we are deeply invested in America's military role around the world.

Moderate evangelicals help others come to terms with the world in which we find ourselves — a more pluralistic America in which we don't get to dominate. Moderate evangelicals are willing to say: we get one place at the table, like everyone else — if we're able to play well with others. I have witnessed this in dealing with the Obama administration. I was in a meeting with twenty-five people talking about abortion reduction: U.S. Catholic bishops, the National Organization of Women, National Abortion Rights Action League, a Hispanic evangelical leader, the head of the mainline National Council of Churches, etc. We [evangelicals] had places at the table; everybody gets a voice and you get as much influence as your capacity to articulate a persuasive position.

Our [Christian] job is to bear faithful witness to the values that we hold dear and do our homework to understand which are most important to project in the public arena, how to project them, how to deal with differences of opinion. Not everything that is taught in the Bible will ever be the law of the U.S., nor should it be. But there are grand themes and broad principles that are significant. And you have to cooperate where you can, even when you disagree profoundly on some things. The National Abortion Rights Action League and U.S. Catholics bishops don't agree on legal abortion but they agree that 1.2 million abortions per year is a bad thing. We would like to see if we can reduce it by addressing the needs that give rise to it. Among the things being discussed are adoption, health care, financial support, contraception, sex education. The presupposition of the conversation is that, when we're talking about what is done in the interest of society, you figure out what works. The White House people began by saying, "We want data-driven proposals that can actually make a dent in this problem. What do you have?"

MP What could mess this sort of conversation up?

DG If the Democrats overreach and appoint judges or pass legislation that is seen as fundamentally hostile to the existing role of Christianity. Or laws that go after us in our space — like "here's what you can't say in the pulpit" or "you're going to have to hire homosexuals to be ministers."

MP The government has no say over hiring ministers, but it might have a say over hiring at publicly funded social service agencies.

DG On confessional hiring I see a bright red line. Every religious community has to be able to hire people whose beliefs and behavior conform to its religious values. But it may prove impossible for a society which has come to accept sex outside marriage, cohabitation, and gay relationships to fund that still sizable minority religious community that dissents from those beliefs. I predict a financial disentanglement between churches and government, maybe just as often initiated by the religious side.

Traditional marriage — one man, one woman — is sadly fading as the paradigmatic way we do relationships. I'm doing what I can to strengthen it where I can, in the church. But we're losing that argument even within our churches. The homosexuality issue is just one piece of the change. We're going to have to get more refined in our thinking. There is a category called pastoral accommodation, where you don't change the structure of your beliefs but you accommodate realistically to the patterns around you, so you can actually be of some use to the people who are coming your way.

HEATHER GONZALES, WASHINGTON, D.C.

Heather Gonzales is association director of the National Association of Evangelicals (NAE) in Washington, D.C.

HG There have been some shifts in evangelical activism in the last few years, but evangelicalism has always had a commitment to a broad agenda, to poverty relief and development overseas. In the past, that may have been more connected to evangelism efforts, but not necessarily. From the 1970s to 1990s, the media focused on two or three leaders, Jerry Falwell, Pat Robertson, etc. But now the evangelicals who had been engaged in a broad agenda all along are becoming more prominent.

MP Why?

HG Because there are new leaders who care about those broader issues: Galen Carey, director of governmental affairs here at the NAE; Richard Cizik, head of the New Evangelical Partnership for the Common Good; Sam Rodriguez, with the National Hispanic Christian Leadership Conference; Joel Hunter. It has to do with dynamic leadership that cares about these issues. And the NAE's *For the Health of the Nation* document, which includes seven areas of engagement, has also helped to catalyze a conversation about a broad agenda.

MP Given that, what is the NAE's vision of how churches should work with other groups in America?

HG The NAE tagline is "cooperation without compromise," and staying true to that objective, we regularly work with a variety of partners in order to accomplish our shared goals. The church should be involved in public policy but shouldn't be given a preferred position. The NAE works hard to make sure that evangelicals have a voice that allows them to fully participate in important conversations, but we don't think that requires that other voices be excluded. What we suggest for the common good may not be what others suggest, so it's important that all voices be included, the church among them.

Admittedly, there's some disagreement on this. There are some evangelical groups which have "getting back to our Christian roots" as their mission. The NAE has never worked on that. The NAE has always been a big advocate of religious freedom for everyone. We've worked with Buddhists and across the religious spectrum on common goals. Our policy opinions are influenced biblically, but not just biblically. They should be for the public good. For instance, on immigration reform: there are biblical reasons why that's important but there are other, social reasons — families are separated and so on.

MP Will you work on abortion reduction with other groups?

HG With our "cooperation without compromise" tagline, we have our principles that don't change, but we have recognized over sixty years that the way to achieve things is to cooperate on shared concerns.

MP Many nonevangelicals were worried that evangelicals had aims towards a . . .

HG . . . a Christian government? I'm sure there are some evangelicals who would like that. But that is not an objective of the NAE. The media likes to point out leaders who say extreme things since that makes more interesting news stories. But we've always felt that church should engage and inform government action, not replace it.

MP Did those who "say extreme things" damage the ability of evangelicals to be taken seriously, to advocate for their priorities?

HG In the NAE spirit, I don't want to be overly critical of the Religious Right because they do some important work. But I wouldn't mind saying that the Religious Right has hurt some of their own chances with some potential partners. They build coalitions but theirs tend to be a little more narrow. Our tactics are more cooperative with partners that you wouldn't necessarily expect. I can't imagine that many in the Religious Right would form a partnership with Harvard, as we did. But we avoid public criticism of other believers.

There are times when we get attacked from both the left and the right. We generally just choose to turn the other cheek. Their criticisms are almost a compliment because if we were really as irrelevant and out of touch as they suggest, they wouldn't spend so much time criticizing us.

Frankly, we've purposely kept some distance from both the Religious Right and the Religious Left. We really fit best in the middle ground of evangelicalism. We're all brothers and sisters in Christ. But we don't agree on everything. The NAE has always had a lot of opportunities to build unique partnerships partly because we've stayed apart from those stereotypical streams. A lot is about tactics. The NAE has never spent time on inflammatory rhetoric; that's not the way we function. We don't believe in gay marriage as an institution and our position is clear, but we haven't gotten into the heated rhetoric. We don't support abortion, but protests [in front of family planning clinics or the offices of congressional representatives] are not what the NAE does. At the same time, we won't say that all we need to do is reduce abortion. That's important, but we'll try to carve out a middle ground that addresses both the legality question and reduction of the number of abortions.

MP What's your position on gay civil unions?

HG *For the Health of the Nation* (2004) says that we don't support it and we haven't changed our policy. The whole thing about Richard Cizik leaving us [for saying in an NPR interview that he is shifting his views toward supporting gay civil unions] made some people say the NAE is "going to the right." That's incorrect. The NAE remains committed to the principles found in *For the Health of the Nation*.

MP What is the NAE position on coreligionist hiring?

HG The NAE is a strong advocate of being able to hire on religious grounds for faith-based organizations. But we don't have a large project on it.

MP On conscience-based service refusal?

HG No, we haven't been heavily engaged, but we tend to err on the side of favoring conscience protections.

One issue we are engaged in is religious-worker visas [which allow religious organizations to bring people into the United States as religious teachers, ministers, etc.]. Regulations were going to be passed that would severely limit them. Honestly, I don't know that evangelicals use them widely. But Muslim and Buddhist groups bring in people who build sanctuaries or perform religious rites. We were involved in an interfaith group that supported these visas. It might help us a little but it'll be more help to other groups. The principle is important even if it's not necessarily to our benefit.

MP What's the NAE position on intelligent design or creationism?

HG We haven't been very engaged in that lately. There's a lot of theological diversity within our body generally, and specifically about how creation plays out with science.

MP The NAE position on religious symbols in public places?

HG We follow the general lines of being in favor of religious expression and we've signed on to some court cases, but we don't work on it much.

MP Moments of silence in public schools?

HG We're not really engaged.[56] The fact that we're not deeply involved on these [issues], you could argue portrays a shift. We're spending more time on immigration reform, creation care, new ways to think about abortion. Some evangelical organizations specialize in taking an issue and beating it till no one can handle talking about it again. That's not the NAE.

MP How much time do you spend working with other groups?

HG A lot of what we do is collaborative.

MP Do you work with nonevangelical groups and secular groups?

HG Definitely. For instance, the United Methodists have a group on criminal justice reform — that's an interfaith group we've been involved with. On creation care, we've worked with the Harvard Center for Health and Global Environment, and on abortion reduction we are working with the National Campaign to Prevent Teen and Unplanned Pregnancy. We're in a lot of coalitions, but of course we make our own decisions.

I'm a bit skeptical of this whole "shift" thing. I've had to read every single press story about the NAE shifting. . . . Some things change but our position now is consistent with what we've always done. In response to articles in *Newsweek* and the *Christian Science Monitor* about the collapse of evangelicalism, Leith [Anderson, NAE president] wrote that of course churches will die, as businesses and other

56. In a separate interview, Carl Esbeck, legal counsel to the Office of Governmental Affairs, NAE, confirmed that the organization was not working in the area of conscience-based service refusal. How about moments of silence? "Nothing, it's an old issue," he said. Coreligionist student admissions? "It hasn't come up, though we have friendly conversations with the CCCU, where we see the commonality with staff and faculty-hiring rights."

things die. But look at all the churches being planted. That's life. There's a life cycle.

NAE Resolution on Immigration

In October 2009 the NAE published a position paper on the immigration debate in the United States. As an example of "new evangelical" thinking on this controversial issue, we publish a large portion of this resolution.[57]

> The significant increase in immigration and the growing stridency of the national debate on immigration compel the National Association of Evangelicals to speak boldly and biblically to this challenging topic. The complexity of immigration issues provides an opportunity to mine Scripture for guidance. A biblically informed position provides a strong platform for the NAE to make a contribution in the public square that will be explicitly Christian. Out of commitment to Scripture and knowledge of national immigration realities comes a distinct call to action.

> ### Biblical Foundations

> Discussion of immigration and government immigration policy must begin with the truth that every human being is made in the image of God (Genesis 1:26-28). Immigrants are made in the image of God and have supreme value with the potential to contribute greatly to society. Jesus exemplifies respect toward others who are different in his treatment of the Samaritans (Luke 10:30-37; John 4:1-42).
>
> The Bible contains many accounts of God's people who were forced to migrate due to hunger, war, or personal circumstances. Abraham, Isaac, Jacob and the families of his sons turned to Egypt in search of food. Joseph, Naomi, Ruth, Daniel and his friends, Ezekiel, Ezra, Nehemiah, and Esther all lived in foreign lands. In the New Testament, Joseph and Mary fled with Jesus to

---

57. The position paper is available on the Web at http://www.nae.net/resolutions/347-immigration-2009.

escape Herod's anger and became refugees in Egypt. Peter referred to the recipients of his first letter as "aliens" and "strangers," perhaps suggesting that they were exiles within the Roman Empire. These examples from the Old and New Testaments reveal God's hand in the movement of people and are illustrations of faith in God in difficult circumstances.

Migration was common in the ancient world. Outsiders were particularly vulnerable. They stood outside the kinship system that regulated the inheritance of property. They did not have extended family to care for them in case of need. The Law recognized their helplessness and stipulated measures that served as a safety net. The motivations behind this generous spirit were that the people of God were not to forget that they had been strangers in Egypt (Exodus 22:21; Leviticus 19:33-34) and that God loved the foreigner (Deuteronomy 10:18-19). The New Testament adds that all believers are spiritual sojourners on earth (Phil. 3:20; 1 Peter 2:11). Christians should show compassion and hospitality to outsiders (Rom. 12:13; Heb. 13:2).

The Bible does not offer a blueprint for modern legislation, but it can serve as a moral compass and shape the attitudes of those who believe in God. An appreciation of the pervasiveness of migration in the Bible must temper the tendency to limit discussions on immigration to Romans 13 and a simplistic defense of "the rule of law." God has established the nations (Deut. 32:8; Acts 17:26), and their laws should be respected. Nevertheless, policies must be evaluated to reflect that immigrants are made in the image of God and demonstrate biblical grace to the foreigner.

National Realities

Immigration is a worldwide phenomenon. People migrate due to economic globalization, armed conflicts, and a desire to provide for their families. The United States of America is a country founded by immigrants, and its history has been characterized by waves of immigrants from different parts of the world. Immigrants will continue to be an essential part of who we are as a country. Our response to immigration must include an understanding of this immigrant history and an awareness of the positive impact of multiple cultures on national life over the last 250 years. The challenge today is to determine how to maintain the integrity of national borders, address the situation with millions of undocumented immigrants, devise a realistic program to respond to labor needs, and manifest the humanitarian spirit that has characterized this country since its founding. . . .

Due to the limited number of visas, millions have entered the United States without proper documentation or have overstayed temporary visas. While these actions violate existing laws, socioeconomic, political, and legal realities contribute to the problematic nature of immigration. Society has ignored the existence of an unauthorized work force due to the economic benefits of cheap immigrant labor. Without legal status and wary of reporting abuses, immigrants can be mistreated and underpaid by employers. Deportation of wage-earners has separated families and complicated the situation for many. Most undocumented immigrants desire to regularize their legal status, but avenues to assimilation and citizenship are blocked by local, state, and federal laws. This has generated an underground industry for false documentation and human smuggling.

These quandaries offer fresh opportunities for the church. Immigrant communities offer a new, vibrant field for evangelism, church planting, and ministry. Denominations have launched efforts to bring the gospel to these newcomers, establish churches, and train leaders for immigrant believers. Millions of immigrants also come from Christian backgrounds. These brothers and sisters in Christ are revitalizing churches across the country and are planting churches and evangelizing. Their presence is a blessing of God. These spiritual realities remind evangelicals that an evaluation of recent immigration cannot be reduced to economics and national security issues.

Call to Action

Motivated by the desire to offer a constructive word for the country's complicated immigration situation and guided by the Scripture, the National Association of Evangelicals calls for the reform of the immigration system. We believe that national immigration policy should be considerate of immigrants who are already here and who may arrive in the future and that its measures should promote national security and the general welfare in appropriate ways. Building upon biblical revelation concerning the migration of people and the values of justice and compassion championed in For the Health of the Nation: An Evangelical Call to Civic Responsibility, we urge:

- That immigrants be treated with respect and mercy by churches. Exemplary treatment of immigrants by Christians can serve as the moral basis to call for government attitudes and legislation to reflect the same virtues.
- That the government develop structures and mechanisms that safeguard and monitor the national borders with efficiency and respect for human dignity.
- That the government establish more functional legal mechanisms for the annual entry of a reasonable number of immigrant workers and families.
- That the government recognize the central importance of the family in society by reconsidering the number and categories of visas available for family reunification, by dedicating more resources to reducing the backlog of cases in process, and by reevaluating the impact of deportation on families.
- That the government establish a sound, equitable process toward earned legal status for currently undocumented immigrants, who desire to embrace the responsibilities and privileges that accompany citizenship.
- That the government legislate fair labor and civil laws for all residing within the United States that reflect the best of this country's heritage.
- That immigration enforcement be conducted in ways that recognize the importance of due process of law, the sanctity of the human person, and the incomparable value of family.

Activism without State Involvement:
A More Countercultural Emphasis

Church-State Basics

Shane Claiborne works in what are loosely known as "emergent churches," younger believers who meet in storefronts or homes to pray, study, and minister to the needy. Claiborne aims to radicalize the status quo rather than only work within it — to bring Jesus' "radical counterculture" into this world and offer Jesus' "invitation" to downward mobility, to become the least.[58] He called his first book *The Irresistible Revolution: Living as an Ordinary Radical* because he believes Jesus' followers always do.

As Claiborne describes it, he is moving away from "the health and wealth gospel" by "following the Homeless Rabbi."[59] Social and economic change will come not through government but "when people fall in love with each other across class lines."[60] The issue with faith-based social services, Claiborne says, is not so much the regulations governing the use of public money but that faith-based social services, like secular ones, keep donors and the poor separated by layers of agency professionals. By contrast, Claiborne tries to follow Jesus more directly, having worked with Mother Teresa and in a leper colony in Calcutta. His Simple Way community, founded in 1997 in one of Philadelphia's poorest quarters, offers food, used clothes, furniture, and a place to hang out to people in the neighborhood. They plant gardens in abandoned lots, renovate abandoned houses, and organize barter economies, all part of what Claiborne calls "the Christian underground" — massage therapists who tend to the feet of the homeless, engineers who build unofficial generators or water-purification systems in poor areas, and doctors who set up free clinics. Claiborne himself belongs to a group of over 200,000 Christians who pool money to cover each other's medical needs — a Christian alternative to state or private insurance that handles $12 million in medical expenses a year. "One reason we can do it is that we're not paying for anyone's yacht. Over 90

---

58. S. Claiborne, *The Irresistible Revolution: Living as an Ordinary Radical* (Grand Rapids: Zondervan, 2006), pp. 41, 127.

59. Claiborne, *The Irresistible Revolution*, p. 169.

60. Claiborne, *The Irresistible Revolution*, pp. 163, 329.

percent of contributions go directly to medical bills. We also negotiate our hospital bills. We have charts that show, historically, what we paid for a procedure, and if a new one is higher, we negotiate it down."[61]

In this and in his generally spunky approach, Claiborne recalls the 1960s counterculture. To emphasize his "Jubilee economics" of wealth distribution, he staged a Jubilee festival on Wall Street in which thousands of dollars in coins were strewn across the pavement for anyone to pick up. He helped organize homeless families who were being evicted from an abandoned church, for which he got arrested. The Simple Way distributes food without proper authorization, for which they got arrested. He went to Iraq with the Iraq Peace Team,[62] for which he got in trouble with Homeland Security. He and friends served communion to the homeless, for which they were arrested. At trial, they gave out "Jesus Was Homeless" T-shirts. The judge ruled in their favor.

War and Militarism

Claiborne and many emergent churches fall close to "new evangelical" pacifist positions. Claiborne begins with a broad critique of military hegemony and is loud on the topic of U.S. violence: America is "the greatest purveyor of violence in the world today," teaching "the myth of redemptive violence." But there is, on Claiborne's view, no such redemption. The Gospels teach, "all who draw the sword will die by the sword (Matthew 26:52)." Claiborne updates the passage: "A shock-and-awe bombing leads to a shock-and-awe beheading. A Pearl Harbor leads to a Hiroshima."[63]

There are, Claiborne writes, "extremists, both Muslim and Christian, who kill in the name of their gods." But he does not see that their evil mitigates the violence of retaliation. He advocates Martin Luther King's vision of "worldwide fellowship" and recalls those American churches that, grasping the universalism of Jesus' compassion, placed Afghan flags next to the U.S. ones already in their churches after the invasion of Afghanistan in 2001. On his trip to Iraq, Claiborne was most moved by the Iraqi Christians who could not grasp why American Chris-

---

61. Interview with the author, May 6, 2009.
62. Veterans, doctors, journalists, and ordinary citizens constituted the team.
63. Claiborne, *The Irresistible Revolution,* pp. 206, 263.

tians supported the 2003 war. One bishop told Claiborne, "We Christians do not believe this. We believe, 'Blessed are the peacemakers. . . .'" The bishop said he'd pray "for the church in the US . . . to be the church."[64]

Being the church, on Claiborne's view, does not mean passivity but faith in the power of returning anger with love and humor. "When someone tries to sue you for the coat on your back," Claiborne writes, "in court take all of your clothes off and hand them over."[65]

Unresolved Issues: Religious Symbols in Public Venues,
Creationism, Faith-Based Services

In keeping with his person-to-person emphasis, Claiborne hopes we can finesse the issue of religious symbols in public places by finding consensus on beautiful ones — like the one on his computer that shows a gun whose barrel is knotted so that it cannot shoot. He concedes that not all would find that image equally pleasing, but the public-symbols issue is not a high priority for his community. On creationism/intelligent design, Claiborne holds that both the biblical creation story and evolution can be respectfully taught in public schools, with students and teachers being honest about their beliefs and open to other views: "Some of the problem about this seems so fearful. We don't trust the spirit at work in people so we don't allow them to see other options. . . . I'd love it if a kid asked me what I think about evolution. I'd tell him, but I'd also say, 'you know Amber disagrees with me and you should talk to her because she might be right.'"[66]

Consistent with his extrastate approach, Claiborne does not take government funds. "Not a chance," as he put it. So the issue of coreligionist hiring doesn't arise at the Simple Way. Yet he sees the need for it in some social services. While he works with city agencies to build affordable housing, where the plumbers and electricians hold various beliefs, in programs that mentor children "we want people that are growing into the kids the values and practices that we find in Scripture. It has to do with who's best suited to do that work."[67] Echoing

64. Claiborne, *The Irresistible Revolution,* pp. 213, 215.
65. Claiborne, *The Irresistible Revolution,* p. 282.
66. Interview with the author, May 6, 2009.
67. Interview with the author, May 6, 2009.

many "new evangelicals," Claiborne holds that if religious programming or coreligionist hiring is important, an agency can, as the Simple Way does, raise its funds privately.

In considering conscience-based service refusal, Claiborne distinguishes among four situations: one, jobs that directly conflict with Christlike practices, like running a brothel; two, situations where one works within the system to change it, like the tax collector Zacchaeus who stayed in tax collection but "did business differently" (Luke 19:1-9); three, situations where one must hold to Christian values though they conflict with one's job ("It may mean that we withdraw or get fired. I have a lot of respect for those who have left the military though they may face a court-martial"); four, situations where individuals can find creative ways out. The first group of jobs is not consistent for Christians to hold, but in the latter three, Christians must search for the most productive solution according to their consciences. Claiborne offers an example: though a friend of his does not perform gay commitment ceremonies, he directed a gay couple to another pastor who was comfortable performing them, thus holding to his beliefs but respecting the beliefs of the other pastor.[68]

SHANE CLAIBORNE, PENNSYLVANIA

SC Without a doubt there's a reshaping of evangelicalism in post-Religious Right America. They haven't reproduced a new generation of charismatic leaders, and younger evangelicals are aware that the world is fragile. God cares about the way we live in it. People are asking: Should CEOs be making 500 times as much as their workers? It doesn't mean that people aren't concerned about abortion or homosexuality, but people are more suspicious of the arrogance on both the left and right. We see Christians who are hungry for a consistent ethics of life.

It's not just a generational shift. A good example is the Two Futures project to abolish nuclear weapons. While people under forty were leading, like Rob Bell and myself, the other voices were George Schultz, Reagan's secretary of state, Lynn and Bill Hybels from Willow Creek, and Chuck Colson [Prison Ministries founder]. Many evangeli-

68. Interview with the author, May 6, 2009.

cals — of any age — see that bad theology gets people killed. The theology prevalent today is that Jesus preached, lived, and taught the kingdom of heaven come on earth. Lots of folks are thinking missionally: As a doctor, nurse, lawyer, how do I live into Jesus' lesson in my life?

MP Why do you think this shift happened?

SC For many Religious Right strategists, it was about voting blocs. So people started to see in Scripture whatever they wanted to, in order to justify their politics. What's happening now is that dangerous thing when people read the Bible. It puts them at odds with many things that had come to characterize evangelical Christianity. They see that, when Jesus is asked to support the death penalty by stoning a woman, he says, "Let the person who's without sin cast the first stone."

Also, some of the older folks bought into a pattern of living that hasn't brought them life. It's been consumer-driven, radical individualism that has robbed them of community and vitality. It's no coincidence that the U.S. is one of the wealthiest countries in the world and yet has one of the highest rates of depression, loneliness, and medication use. Maybe God's dream doesn't look like the American dream. I was in L.A. in one of the wealthiest areas of the country, where a group of suburban families said, not all of us need a washer and dryer. The Taylors can have one and we'll create a schedule so all of us can use it. We'll share. The Cunninghams will have the lawn equipment. . . .

MP What's the role of the church in this shift?

SC A lot of my ecclesiology comes from the Anabaptist tradition. In the earliest days of Christianity there was the sense of being a contrast society. We're to Jubilee, dismantle inequality, give special care to the alien and stranger. We have a prophetic role — to speak to government, to go to jail when things are wrong, to work together on interrupting things that destroy life — like getting guns out of our neighborhoods.

While the church is God's primary instrument for bringing God's reign on earth, we also need to be really good collaborators. Jesus challenges us to see where God is at work — in all kinds of places, like in the Good Samaritan example.

MP What kind of collaborations do you do?

SC When I went to Iraq with the Peace Team, it was a multifaith and no-faith group. The Christian peacemaker teams that we work with also work with Muslim peace teams. Locally, we have connections across religions and with nonreligious people. We're very careful to form communities that are growing similar values but that allow us to work with others. It's part of the language of the "new monasticism," where within our group, values are closely shared, but we work on projects with others even when we don't agree on everything.

MP Do you collaborate with the state?

SC I have very modest expectations of what kings and presidents can do. Scripture calls for everything in the world to align with God's kingdom. That means speaking truth to those [governmental] places. But we're not pretending God's kingdom will be embodied in any person or party. That's where the Religious Right went wrong. The framework through which they saw Jesus was political. I'm the first to critique a banner that has Obama's picture and the word "Hope" on it. Appropriate hope is okay — hope that some things he does get us closer to what God wants. But our ultimate hope does not rest in a person or a party. Tony Campolo says, "When we marry it [the church to government], it's like mixing ice cream with horse manure. It may not do much damage to the horse manure but it really messes up the ice cream." I don't see, especially in young Christian circles, any idea of wedding ourselves to a party or platform. Jesus is the framework we use. [Lawyer and theologian William] Stringfellow said, "I'm not trying to read the Bible Americanly but America Biblically."

We cooperate with government without taking money from it. We're critiqued by even more anarchist groups who say that our tax-exempt status is a form of support from the state. But we feel there are things the city does well, like building affordable housing. One of the most creative projects we're connected to is Urban Homeworks. They create faith-based, affordable housing where church congregants subsidize the new units, meet with the residents, and pastor them as well. The church's vocation is the redemptive work of healing relationships and hearts as well as buildings and streets.

MP What could mess up this cooperation?

SC [laughs] Probably us. Allowing ourselves to fall into the same temptations that Jesus had. The temptation to astound people with our effectiveness, to turn stones into bread, or use the power of this world. We've made deliberate moves to try to protect ourselves from ourselves. For one thing, being connected to elders — Tony Campolo, John Perkins, and Sister Margaret, people who are seventy, eighty years old. Also, being good collaborators with projects that are already out there. The movement now is more communal, based not so much on charismatic leaders, which means more checks on what happens.

One of the critiques of the [1970s] Jesus movement is that it had a pretension to say, "We don't need the rest of the church." I'm careful with the "emerging church" language because it sounds like we're doing this on our own. We're not. Our discontent is the very reason we engage. As Gandhi said, "Be the change you want to see." Be the change you want to see by being *within* the church — heal hearts, heal streets, heal addiction, the environment, homelessness, the emptiness and loneliness of affluence and individualism, heal the world, make peace. That means gardening, planting flowers with kids, helping neighborhood kids with homework, teaching kids not to hit each other and connecting that lesson to a world that continues a pattern of violence. On a larger scale, writing and speaking, connecting people. We have a Web site, Community of Communities. We put out a new magazine for people to tell their stories. I'm writing a liturgy book now that will cross different ways people have prayed together, psalms, old spirituals, freedom songs, hymns, new things as well.

MP How do you get the time to do all this?

SC Community. I just do my little bit.

NATIONAL COMMUNITY CHURCH, WASHINGTON, D.C.

In 1996, National Community Church (NCC) began meeting in a school so dilapidated it had been closed for fire code violations. Today the NCC has four locations in the D.C. area, one with Spanish-language worship and one near Capitol Hill, with many young government staffers as members. In addition, NCC has over seventy-five small groups that minister to the community and the needy, in the United States and abroad. Its podcast is at theaterchurch.com. Seventy percent of its parishioners come from "un-churched" or "dechurched" backgrounds.

One church venue is a coffeehouse that the church constructed in an abandoned crack house. Funds from the lattes and biscotti go to the church's ministry projects. I met with two thirtysomething women staffers, Stephanie Modder (SM in the following discussion), a lay program adminis-trator, and Heather Zempel (HZ), a pastor "ordained," as she put it, "but not with a traditional church." Zempel began her career as an environmen-tal engineer and came to NCC after five years as a legislative assistant on environment and energy policy in the Senate. David Schmidgall (DS in the discussion), in the church's Protégé discipleship program, also attended our talk, having just returned to the United States after getting his master's degree in international policy at the University of Edinburgh, Scotland.

Local programs at NCC run from helping Little League baseball teams to feeding the homeless. Additionally, overseas mission teams within the last year were sent to India, Kenya (well digging, orphans, microfinance), Thai-land (helping women in the sex industry), Malawi (working with orphanages and non-Christian tribal leaders), Dominican Republic (construction), Leb-anon (Muslim-Christian dialogue), Northern Ireland (Catholic-Protestant reconciliation), Ethiopia (working in Toto Mountain, where over 3,000 peo-ple with AIDS live, ostracized by much of society), and Uganda (orphanage construction).

MP Is there direct financial assistance from the church to these [parishioner-led] missions overseas?

SM No. We give suggestions about how we've done it in the past, give samples, etc. But the parishioners do it.

HZ When we went to Kenya, the church put in two thousand dollars but the project cost way more than that. We raised the rest on our own. When we built an orphanage in Uganda, the church put a cou-ple thousand dollars in the pot but it took forty thousand to build the orphanage.

SM One trip this year was to this amazing ministry in Calcutta that has existed for over fifty years, called Calcutta Mercy Ministries, run by a couple, friends of Mother Teresa, who built a hospital for the poor. They needed [architectural] measurements and a fire escape plan. It's not what you might think of a mission trip. We did not stand on the corner and pass out Bibles. To serve Jesus, we have to love people, including in practical ways. If we end up talking about Jesus, that may come about, but maybe architectural fire plans or building a hut for that grandmother is what's needed most.

DS Some of the trips do have a little bit of it [evangelizing], but there are many Christians who are sensitive and don't want to be part of perpetuating the stereotype of the proselytizing missionary.

MP Is that change recent?

SM When I went to the University of Minnesota in the 1990s, there was an ever-present, hellfire and brimstone, Bible-thumping preacher on campus who made me cringe. I grew up in a church that was prototypical, aggressive evangelizing. . . . But being a Christian is *so* not about that. It's about relationships; it's grace-based. It's about, "Love the Lord your God with all your heart, soul, and might and love your neighbor as yourself."

DS We might talk about some of these recent political shifts. Christianity is not a political party. It transcends politics. In our church, we have people on both sides of the [political] aisle. The Religious Right thing — we tend to expose that as not always truthful. Oftentimes, evangelicals or the Religious Right have taken the subversive out of the gospel. They trusted the political process as a space for social change more than it should be trusted. They took responsibility off of ourselves as a body of believers to do it ourselves. That's a huge mistake. Homosexuality, abortion — we wedged the issue through politics where we could be taking a very different approach.

HZ I was involved in politics. We should be involved in politics. For some it's a noble calling, but when we have relied on politics to do our faith for us, we've missed it. It's laziness. Our responsibility as a church is not to take a stand on a political issue but to equip the people in our community in living like Jesus.

DS It would be a dream for government to come to us and say, "You guys are doing something awesome. How do you do it?"

MP As a kind of modeling?

DS As not always being reactive.

SM Think what it would be like if each church loved the people in each community that it's in. We wouldn't need many of the social programs that exist. We wouldn't need the government to step in because we would be doing it.

MP To be "doing it," does your church partner with other organizations or with government in helping the needy?

HZ We partnered with Convoy of Hope and through that, there may have been some contact with the mayor's office. But not much with government.

MP If it's important to be part of political process but not partisan, how do you work?

HZ I want to make disciples of people who are working on Capitol Hill so that when they go to work every day, they have the mind and heart of Christ — and so that informs the decisions that they make. They can be on either side of the aisle, in either party.

MP "Having the heart and mind of Christ" would move them to do more of or less of what?

SM If you're totally bashing someone because they have a different political view from you, that's not being a Christian.

MP And politically, what would "having the mind and heart of Christ" mean?

HZ I'm trying to get people to be people of integrity, which would be a *huge* thing on Capitol Hill. People who are honest, full of love, joy, peace, patience, gentleness.

SM People with self-control.

DS Homosexuality is a perfect example of where Christians have tried to use politics to separate people out. Eighty-six percent of the GLBT [gay, lesbian, bisexual, transgender] community has come out of churches — that's from *Love Is an Orientation*, by Andrew Marin. But the church hasn't cultivated a space of safety where they can discuss these issues.

SM Whether or not you attribute "sin" to that orientation, if we believe what Scripture says, we've all sinned and fallen short of the glory of God. If they [homosexuals] need to be ostracized, then most pastors would need to be ostracized. Who knows what's going on in their brains.

HZ There has been growing frustration among younger people about what happened with the Religious Right. The solution is not a religious left. It's keeping the gospel central. It's about a God who created and lost his creation, and came to earth on the most daring rescue mission in history to redeem it. Does that mean saying that "Jesus is the truth and the light, and there is a real heaven and a real hell." Sometimes, that could be the most loving thing we say. Could it mean shutting up and loving and serving people — yes.

EMILY, ILLINOIS/MICHIGAN

At the time of this interview in April 2009, Emily was a junior at Trinity Christian College in Palos Heights, Illinois, majoring in education. She works with Acting on AIDS, a campus project of World Vision, among the largest Christian aid organizations. Acting on AIDS raises awareness about AIDS on campuses and in local communities, but Emily has also worked directly with AIDS orphans and infected children in Zambia. In addition, she has worked with children in Jamaica and with deaf children in Guatemala, for which she is studying American Sign Language. For her summer break, she had a choice to return to Zambia or work with children with AIDS in Tanzania. She already had two work offers for 2010, after she completes her university degree, one, to continue working with orphans in Zambia, and the other, to work with a new orphanage in Angola.

MP Do you work with children who are not Christian?

EMILY They come from every background. We've had children who believe in witchcraft — the so-called possessed children. Their communities believe they are invaded by the devil. When they hear about Jesus and the love they can have — some of them have never heard they are loved before. I work in a Christian organization, so religion is just part of daily life. With older children, teenagers, I teach English. It's the most important thing for getting ahead. Even though they've never been to any kind of school before, they just soak it up.

MP Does your organization work in cooperation with others?

EMILY Our church is sponsoring ten missionaries who work with other churches in Nigeria, Liberia, Ecuador, and in the U.S.

MP How did you become involved in this work?

EMILY Since I was seven, my parents have taken us on mission trips, with Friendship Christian Reformed Church in Michigan. Within the U.S., we went to Virginia and West Virginia, building houses and working on other aid programs for the poor. My family still goes; they did flood work this past spring. When I was in junior high school, I went to Guatemala for the first time with my youth group. I fell in love with it. That was the starting point: I knew this is what I want to do. I found my heart, my passion. I realize that was something God was calling me to do. My heart has always been with the kids.

The Evangelical Left: Activism Since the 1960s

The Evangelical Left emerged in protest against the Vietnam War and in support of the civil rights movement, and it remained a small if passionate voice until a resurgence in 2005. In its approach to the state, it shares a good deal with the cluster here represented by Hunter and Gushee, as all work with government. But its issue-by-issue positions tend to be closer to Claiborne's. Two representative figures are Jim Wallis and Tony Campolo.

In 1971, Wallis was among the students at Trinity Evangelical Divinity School who protested against the Vietnam War and the evangelical church establishment — and was nearly expelled for his efforts. All told, he has been arrested twenty-two times for civil disobedience. He is a founder of the progressive evangelical Sojourners Community, which publishes *Sojourners* magazine, and he participated in Obama's advisory Office of Faith-Based and Neighborhood Partnerships in 2009-10. Today, he says, the Evangelical Left provides a middle ground, sharing biblical values with the evangelical right and progressive politics with the secular left. For Wallis, this religio-political middle is the church's "revolutionary posture," "calling us all to higher ground and challenging political and economic power when it becomes abusive of the religious values of compassion and justice."[69]

On Wallis's view, the role of the church in the political sphere is to talk to government when it does not execute its responsibilities well. And this requires the church to be extrastate. "Only through its independence and separation from any party and state can religion exercise its vital prophetic role in every society."[70] Wallis described how the prophetic role worked in the bipartisan Poverty Forum, comprised of leaders and policy experts from across the political and Christian spectra.[71] Rather than following the economic policies of the political parties, "We started every meeting with prayer, saying we are followers of Jesus first and Republicans, Democrats, and independents second. It freed us to talk about what actually works."

In addition to speaking to government, Christians may change society, Wallis holds, by being a pilot community (or contrast society) within the civil sphere. "Majorities normally don't change things," Wallis points out, "creative minorities do."[72] Pilot communities, for instance, might forge inventive syntheses between conservative and progressive approaches to reducing poverty — both reducing out-of-wedlock births and raising public investment in education, health care, and affordable housing. Nonprofit agencies, private individuals, businesses, and government all share responsibility in achieving these goals — though much of the old left falls on the greater-government-involvement end of the evangelical range. For instance, in the area of race relations, Wallis goes beyond "reconciliation" (where people of all races work together for a better future unmarred by prejudice) to-

---

69. J. Wallis, *The Great Awakening: Reviving Faith and Politics in a Post–Religious Right America* (New York: HarperOne, 2008), p. 181.

70. Wallis, *The Great Awakening*, p. 181.

71. http://www.thepovertyforum.org/about-the-poverty-forum.php.

72. Wallis, *The Great Awakening*, p. 65.

ward social justice and government compensation for past wrong-doings. He quotes Scott Garber, pastor of Washington Community Fellowship: "Racism does not disappear just because of the passage of time. Racism does not disappear just because we are sorry . . . [racism] will disappear when, and only when, it is replaced by its opposite."[73]

In the global arena, Wallis emphasizes fair trade policies. He criticized G. W. Bush's foreign policy as "perhaps the *least* likely to result in genuine democracy" abroad.[74] He did not support the 2003 Iraq war nor does he unreservedly support the present war in Afghanistan. He advocates "nonviolent realism," which begins with a presumption against violence but, like "strict just war" theory, concedes its use to avoid greater violence.[75]

Though church-state separation is a given for the Evangelical Left, Wallis supports coreligionist hiring to preserve the institutional integrity of faith-based agencies. On religious symbols, he — like Hunter — applauds the "cultural visibility of religious language and symbols" in public "if all the pluralistic faith traditions of the nation can enjoy public displays." Here is an echo of the "substantively neutral" approach: If government allows all manner of symbols in public save religious ones, does that discriminate against religion? But Wallis adds, "Does anybody really want to say that America has behaved in the world as a 'Christian nation'? For the sake of Christian integrity, I hope not."[76]

Wallis's colleague Tony Campolo, a Baptist minister and professor of sociology, has for many years taken a hybrid stance similar to Wallis's but also to Hunter's: political engagement for Jesus-like ends. We "should have no problem," Campolo says, "viewing the government as a possible instrument of God" when the government follows gospel teachings.[77] To assess state conduct, Campolo, like Wallis, stresses the church's prophetic role — to talk to government, not be government. While churches do advocate for legislation, churches do so nonpartisanly, advancing the policy, case by case, that best realizes Jesus' teachings. "There are more than two thousand verses of Scripture,"

73. Wallis, *The Great Awakening*, pp. 185-86.
74. Wallis, *The Great Awakening*, p. 253.
75. Wallis, *The Great Awakening*, p. 255.
76. Wallis, *The Great Awakening*, p. 181.
77. T. Campolo, *Red Letter Christians: A Citizen's Guide to Faith and Politics* (Ventura, Calif.: Regal, 2008), p. 24.

Campolo notes, "that call us to express love and justice for those who are poor and oppressed; we promote legislation that turns biblical imperatives into social policy."[78]

In thinking through the church's political role, Campolo considers the distinction between power and authority, made by the German sociologist Max Weber at the turn of the twentieth century. Power achieves its aims by imposing sanctions or force (or by threatening either of these); authority moves by moral suasion. Campolo sees evangelical influence emerging from the authority and moral gravitas of Jesus' teachings. He thus rejects the politics of putting "our own people" into power, as (human) evangelicals may err has much as anyone else. "A non-Christian candidate," Campolo writes, may "espouse political commitments on crucial social issues that are more in line with what the Bible teaches than a deeply religious born-again opponent may."[79] Because of this political reality, Campolo advises against pigeonholing or any uncritical embrace of a party or politician. "[T]here are millions of us who espouse an evangelical theology," he writes, "but who reject being classified as part of the religious right."[80] They may also reject being classified as the Democratic Left. Though he worked with the Democrats to develop their program of abortion reduction, Campolo finds merit in both political parties and expects that evangelicals, guided by the gospel, will vote for one or the other, depending on the issue.

To "promote justice for the poor and oppressed," Campolo founded the Evangelical Association for the Promotion of Education (EAPE), which sends young people to live and serve in poor neighborhoods and which supports projects to improve inner-city schools. Both Campolo and Wallis have worked with Call to Renewal,[81] an interdenominational Christian organization dedicated to ending racial discrimination and to improving the incomes, health care, housing, and education of America's poor. On matters of war and peace, Campolo is a "troubled pacifist," owing to his uncomfortable support for military intervention for humanitarian aims. Though he does not believe that Bush deliberately misled America to gain support for the 2003 Iraq war, he holds that the war failed just war criteria. "We could make a lot of

---

78. Campolo, *Red Letter Christians,* p. 24.
79. Campolo, *Red Letter Christians,* p. 207.
80. Campolo, *Red Letter Christians,* p. 17.
81. In 2006, Call to Renewal merged with Sojourners.

friends by meeting the needs of the poor and oppressed people of the world with the billions of dollars we continue to waste on this war."[82]

Campolo opposes sectarian prayer in public schools, relying on the pluralistic corrective to special pleading: if one has Christian prayers, one must also have all others, which most Americans feel is inappropriate and organizationally impractical. He supports coreligionist hiring but, unlike many "new evangelicals," not school vouchers. Campolo fears that vouchers will hobble an institution of integration and tolerance. "Will children from differing religious backgrounds," he asks, "be encouraged in religious and ethnic prejudices if they never interact in public schools with children from other backgrounds?"[83]

The table on page 208 summarizes "new evangelical" positions on the unresolved issues described in chapter 4 and above.

JIM WALLIS

The article below is excerpted from the August 13, 2009, edition of *Sojourners* online newsletter, which focused on the U.S. health care debate. Its author, Jim Wallis, stresses three points: public education about all positions on the issue, the importance of contacting one's representatives in Congress, and the destructiveness of silencing tactics by both the Right and the Left. "We have a democracy crisis," Wallis writes. "Left-right shouting matches and confrontational tactics will not create the civil discourse we need."

> The health-care system in the U.S. is sick and broken, forty-six million of God's children are left out with no health insurance coverage. . . .
>
> We have a democracy crisis, with right-wing forces trying to prevent and destroy a civil debate with their "mob rule" campaigns. . . . The campaign tactics include lies, intimidation, character assassination, verbal abuse, and even mob behavior against members of Congress trying to conduct town hall meetings on the issues. In some places violence has broken out. . . .
>
> There are also now some stories of left-wing groups organizing to confront these disruptions. Left-right shouting matches

82. Campolo, *Red Letter Christians,* p. 63.
83. Campolo, *Red Letter Christians,* p. 114.

	Positions associated with the Religious Right	Extrastate emphasis (Boyd et al.)	Greater focus on conventional politics and co-operation with government (Hunter et al.)	Extrastate emphasis with a more counter-cultural approach (Claiborne et al.)	Evangelical Left
Candidate endorsement by churches	Tend to support	Reject	Reject	Reject	Reject
Religious symbols in public places	Support	Mixed, not a focus of activism	Support if equal conditions are granted to all faiths; not a focus of activism	Mixed; not a focus of activism	Tend to support if equal conditions are granted to all
U.S. as a Christian Nation	Support	Reject	Reject	Reject	Reject
Moments of silence in public schools	Support school prayer	Reject school prayer; mixed on moments of silence; not a focus of activism	Reject school prayer; tend to support moments of silence; not a focus of activism	Reject school prayer; mixed on moments of silence; not a focus of activism	Reject school prayer; mixed on moments of silence; not a focus of activism
Teaching creationism in public schools	Support	Mixed; not a focus of activism	Mixed; allow if all views are taught; not a focus of activism	Mixed; allow if all views are taught; not a focus of activism	Mixed; allow if all views are taught; not a focus of activism
School vouchers	Support	Mixed; more support from historically black churches	Support	Mixed; not a focus of activism	Tend to reject; not a focus of activism
Regulation of publicly funded faith-based social service agencies:					
• coreligionist hiring	support	mixed; not a focus of activism	support	tend to support; not a focus of activism	support
• public funding of religious approaches to care delivery	support	tend to reject; not a focus of activism	mixed	tend to reject; not a focus of activism	tend to reject; not a focus of activism
• religious/ conscience-based service refusal	support	mixed; tend to support; not a focus of activism	support	support; not a focus of activism	support

support   mixed   reject

and confrontational tactics will not create the civil discourse we need, and could finally sabotage health-care reform. . . .

It's time for the faith community to practice nonviolent tactics of reconciliation and resistance against those on either side who would threaten the public debate with intimidation, fear, and even the threat of violence. . . .

So I am personally asking each of you to do some very important things:

1. Make it a point this August to talk to your representatives in Congress and your senators (or their staff). Tell them that as a person of faith you want serious and comprehensive health-care reform that covers everybody. . . .
2. Write letters of support for health-care reform to the editor of your daily newspaper, or write an opinion-page commentary yourself.
3. Plan study, prayer, or Bible study groups on health care in your congregation for September. Use the new resource for congregations that we have helped to create.
4. Encourage your pastor, rabbi, or imam to preach a sermon related to healing and health care on the last Sunday of August. There are resources on our health-care reform Web page.
5. Pray without ceasing that the nation will not lose its soul at this critical moment.

Tony Campolo, Pennsylvania

Tony Campolo is professor emeritus of sociology at Eastern University, a Christian school in Pennsylvania; he also served for a decade as professor of sociology at the University of Pennsylvania. He is also a Baptist minister, serving as associate pastor of the Mount Carmel Baptist Church, and he founded the Evangelical Association for the Promotion of Education (EAPE), which helps educate at-risk youth in the United States and abroad. He was a spiritual adviser to Bill Clinton and worked with the Obama campaign on its 2008 election platform.

I met Tony Campolo at the Grand Hyatt Hotel in Manhattan, between a performance of *Rigoletto,* which he and his wife had attended at the

Metropolitan Opera, and a visit to his daughter Lisa, an environmental-protection lawyer, and son-in-law, Marc Goodheart, assistant to the president of Harvard University. Tony Campolo's son, Bart Campolo, heads the Walnut Hills Fellowship, which works with the disadvantaged in inner-city Cincinnati, and is founder of Mission Year, a Christian ministry that recruits young adults to live and work among the poor in inner-city neighborhoods across the country.

TC What's happened overall in the last few years is that a younger generation is emerging with different values. Consider the homosexual issue. Recent studies indicate that older people tend to be opposed to gay marriage and younger people, while still conservative on the issue, do not consider it a defining issue for Christians. While conservative in their thinking, they put it in emphasis alongside of their concerns about the environment, their opposition to war, their concerns about human trafficking, and, most of all, their concerns about poverty.

I'm in the middle, closer to the younger. Of all the things to be upset about, this is not a big one. I put homosexuality in the same category as divorce and remarriage. Do I approve? Of course not. Do I accept people who are divorced and remarried and receive them into the church? Of course. If they want to become clergy, will I stand in opposition? Of course not. I'm a Baptist. That means I believe in sole conscience, which is to say that each individual has a right to interpret Scripture for himself or herself. My wife is not in agreement with me in my conservative view on gay marriage. She supports gay marriage. But we have no problem because we recognize that we are not infallible interpreters of Scripture.

After Proposition 8 passed [the California referendum prohibiting gay marriage], conservatives said, we won. But tens of thousands of gays and lesbians marched in San Francisco, Los Angeles, New York, Atlanta, and Chicago looking at the Bible as an instrument of oppression and at Jesus as their enemy. If you call this winning, we are not on the same page.

If you talk to young people on these divisive issues [abortion, gay marriage], they say, it's not that we've changed our minds but that they're not as important to us anymore. George Santayana once said, "On such concerns, we do not reject; we simply bid them a fond farewell." So, as to the broadening of the evangelical agenda, there has been a shift. What appeals to young people is a call to do something heroic with their lives — they respond to our challenge when we say to them, "Through you Christ wants to help the poor, save the environment, end war, end oppression, bring justice."

MP What does that mean politically?

TC On these poverty and war issues, the shift of young people toward the Democratic Party looks inevitable. Many say, if it wasn't for the abortion issue, there would be no question how the vote would go. The idea is that war is the major cause of poverty. When you're spending $250,000/minute in Iraq, you don't have money to take care of the poor in our country or in Iraq.

The argument that has cut into the support of the Republican Party is the reality that 73 percent of all abortions are economically driven. Are the Republicans willing to address these issues? In the 2008 election, the Republican platform originally had a proposal that would have addressed the economic forces that are driving so many women to have abortions. It was deleted because the Republicans, at their national convention, contended it would cost the taxpayers too much money to do that. Tell that to young people, and they are not sure they want to be Republicans anymore.

MP What could frustrate this move among evangelicals toward the Democrats?

TC President Obama, during the election period, made a strong pronouncement that the U.S. government would not fund any faith-based social program that exercised any form of discrimination. I disagree, as do most young evangelicals, with that position. There are some legitimate forms of discrimination that can be exercised by evangelicals. For instance, a Christian organization should be allowed to discriminate in hiring when it comes to considering non-Christians or even anti-Christians for employment.

Furthermore, if the convictions of a Christian group (let's say a church) call for discrimination against people because of their sexual orientation, most evangelical young people would say that should be allowed. Certainly, that was the case during the Clinton administration. Clinton allowed certain forms of discrimination to preserve the integrity of faith-based organizations. Sometimes discrimination is necessary.

In discussions that I had with leaders on the platform committee of the Democratic Party, I asked whether or not those in the national offices of the Democratic Party, when hiring secretaries and other workers for their office work, should be allowed to discriminate against some deeply committed Republicans. Would they really want Republicans involved in the inner workings of the national office? The answer I got was no. So it is that I believe certain forms of discrimination seem to be legitimate, and I use that as an example.

The real problem could be the conscience clause on abortion [which allows doctors to refuse, on religious grounds, to perform them]. That's going to lose Obama ground among the young who say people should be allowed their conscience. Young people believe that conscientious objectors should not have to go to war, and what they believe about war is what they believe about abortion. Doctors and nurses who are opposed to abortion should not be forced to perform an abortion if they work in a hospital that is receiving government funding. I'm going to stand for the conscience clause.

MP At the end of his presidency, Bush issued a policy that allowed not just doctors but janitors or accountants to refuse to perform their jobs if they disagreed with services — like abortion — offered by their employer.

TC Certainly, conscience objections apply to doctors and nurses — those who are directly involved in performing abortions. But I think that's where I'd draw that line.

MP During the heyday of the Bush administration, many people were concerned that evangelicals would interfere with church-state separation, so today . . .

TC We are pressing for greater church-state separation, not less. Take marriage: what the state should do is guarantee people's rights. We should follow a model such as that employed in Holland where, if you want to get married, you go to the city hall and register there as a couple, entitled to all the legal rights of a civil union. If you want to call it a marriage, you then go to a church and the church blesses the union. I think that churches should determine who is married and who is not. If marriage is a sacred institution, which President Bush said it is, then it should remain within the domain of the church to define who is to be married and who is not. The state's only responsibility is to guarantee the legal rights of couples who want to live together in a committed union.

This idea is picking up so much momentum that a petition is circulating in California to make that state policy. I have gotten no opposition to this idea even among older evangelicals. It looks like a solution where nobody is imposing on anyone else. *This is the big principle: we don't have the right to impose what we believe in religious matters, such as who is married and who is not, on other people.*

We're moving to an enhanced understanding of separation of church and state. If we're going to "speak truth to power," we can't be the power. We can be a prophetic church only if we are not in bed with the state.

MP Where are "new evangelicals" on foreign policy?

TC Religious legitimization of the war in Iraq raises serious questions, and these questions are raised not only among younger evangelicals. And today, Religious Right rhetoric is increasingly anti-Muslim. They are creating Islamo-phobia. The coming Armageddon for Christian Zionists is now being defined as a conflict between the Islamic and Christian worlds. Older Christian Zionists see that the only solution to the Mideast crisis is a Lieberman solution [Israel's minister of foreign affairs at the time of the interview], where all Arabs leave Israel because God promised the land to the seed of Abraham. But Christian Zionists often fail to realize that the Arabs are also of the seed of Abraham via Ishmael.

This could influence the relationship between evangelicals and Obama. He has put out the olive leaf to the Muslim community. If there is another terrorist attack, it could shift people back in the direction of the Religious Right.

MP With another terrorist attack, will evangelicals return to a more theocratic vision of church-state relations?

TC I don't think so. The influx of immigrants has been huge, and the Religious Right has alienated Hispanics with its anti-immigrant mentality. White Protestant Christianity is still a gigantic plurality, but it is no longer a majority. The new majority is very concerned to keep the older plurality from imposing itself on the rest.

MP They don't want to give the white evangelical majority the help of the state to impose itself?

TC Right, they don't.

MP Let me ask you where evangelicals are on a few high-profile issues, like evolution.

TC Evangelicals are moving more toward biological evolution. Creationism is a dying issue. You have Ph.D.s teaching evolution and biology courses at Christian academic institutions. But young people say that intelligent design should be taught simply because, if we're going to have liberal education, we should be open to all points of view. Here we come back to the problem of imposing: Do you impose one set of views on all people — about homosexuality or about evolution? If we are really going to affirm open minds and avoid bigoted responses to questions, then young people want all points of view expressed. Creationism and intelligent design cannot simply be dismissed out of court as being unscientific without an honest discussion on these subjects.

MP Your stand on religious symbols in public places?

TC We'll win the argument on the liberal side. Take religious symbols in courts of law. What right have we, in a pluralistic society, to say *in a court of law* that our God takes precedence over your God?

MP Moments of silence in the public schools?

TC I am opposed to silent prayer being ordered. I'm in favor of students taking the initiative and saying, "I'd like to share some of my beliefs with the class about how we should live out our lives." But no employee of the school system should impose that because everyone in society is paying this guy's salary, including atheists.

The schoolroom should be open to Christians expressing their beliefs openly. Freedom of speech in the Bill of Rights should guarantee that for the student. I hasten to add, however, that the door should be open for Muslim students and for Jewish students, as well as those of other religions, to do the same. We would have a better situation if everyone had an opportunity to share beliefs and convictions in the classroom. Even atheists and agnostics should have that same right. I believe that the Bill of Rights does not exclude religion from the classroom. What it does do is exclude the propagation of any one single religion at the expense of others. I would not be opposed to a time of silent meditation, but to call it prayer has religious overtones. If someone, during that time of silent meditation, wants to pray, this is something that each person has to decide for him or herself.

MP School vouchers?

TC I'm opposed to vouchers because of my experience in Northern Ireland. Because of the voucher system, Protestants have become increasingly disconnected from Catholics. Everyone in Ireland agrees: if we're going to solve the problem, we've got to do something to get these kids to know each other. To be a pluralistic society where people get along, the voucher system must be opposed. Also, the minute I ask, "Are we going to allow the black Muslims to have their own schools?" evangelicals who are in favor of vouchers suddenly say, "Oh, I hadn't thought about that."

MP Is this the view that most evangelicals hold?

TC Centrists are still very much for vouchers and will continue to be because the public school system is so lousy.

MP The future of "new evangelical" politics?

TC I expect that progressive evangelicalism will win. I am not sure that this means that they will be Democrats, nor do I care. But I do know that their positions on social issues will be progressive. When anybody asks me if I am a Democrat or a Republican, my response is always: name the issue. McCain's daughter represents them. She's evangelical; she's where we are; she's a Republican, so what?

"New Evangelicals" Look Back at 1970-2004

"New evangelicals" overall hold much respect for the energy of this period — the commitment to social activism; the willingness to look at the long-term implications of cloning, euthanasia, and abortion; and the protest against the use of people in pornography, prostitution, and slavery. But they also find that the activism of this time exhibited an un-Jesus-like list of descriptors: judgmental, militaristic, in bed with money and power, aggressive in tactics, enmeshed in the Republican Party, obsessed with homosexuality, and insensitive to the long evangelical tradition of church-state separation and pluralistic freedom of conscience. To follow their theology and ethics, some, such as David Gushee, Helene Slessarov-Jamir, and Chris Boesel, have left conservative institutions. In a particularly pointed piece of self-criticism, the 2008 *Evangelical Manifesto* declared, "We have become known for commercial, diluted, and feel-good gospels of health, wealth, human potential, and religious happy talk."

Not all "new evangelicals" are as critical as this. Though Claiborne's work in emergent churches is among the furthest from the vision and tactics of the 1970-2004 era, he sees the latter as yet another effort by the fallen human family, one "built around isolating ourselves from evil doers and sinners, creating a community of religious piety and moral purity. That's the Christianity I grew up with. Christianity can also be built around joining with the broken sinners. . . . That's the Christianity I have fallen in love with."[84] Recalling Augustine, he notes that "'The Church is a whore but she's my mother.' She is a mess and has many illegitimate children. But she is also our mama and managed to give birth to us and to give us enough of the truth."[85]

Joel Hunter, in looking over evangelical history, distinguishes between nominal Christianity and Christlike conduct. Some evangelicals, he believes, have lost Christlike conduct in their search for political wins and have been too "limited to the Republican Party."[86] He sees evangelicals today as "looking for new leadership," but "no WACKOs need apply." "Wackos" are those who **W**ant only what is good for their own group; are **A**ngry; are oriented toward hot-button issues; are **C**hristian in name but not Christlike in nature; **K**nock others who are different; and are interested **O**nly in winning, not in growing spiritually.[87]

---

84. Claiborne, *The Irresistible Revolution,* pp. 159, 246.

85. Claiborne, *The Irresistible Revolution,* p. 354.

86. Hunter, *New Kind of Conservative,* pp. 30-32.

87. Hunter, *New Kind of Conservative,* p. 10.

Both Hunter and Gushee note the nostalgia running through certain conservative evangelical positions — nostalgia for a supposedly more moral time when societal conventions made evangelicals feel safe perhaps because those conventions conformed to their own. "In our personal need for security and certainty," Hunter writes, "we are tempted to assume that what elevates our group is best for the entire nation."[88]

As John Franke has noted, "evangelicalism has generally failed to appreciate the ways in which the practice of biblical interpretation and the construction of theology is always a contextual enterprise. . . . Evangelical theology has been thoroughly shaped by its participation in the dominant North American cultural trends. This has meant that in both the church and the academy evangelicalism is largely a white, middle class movement that has been dominated by males."[89] But, Gushee notes, this "mood of angry nostalgia"[90] will have to come to terms with the "pluralism in our land," and evangelicals will have to "develop a far more sophisticated response than the current reactionary pining for homogeneous community."[91] The coalition with the Republicans — in an effort to revive or enforce such homogeneity — was, on Gushee's view, politically and religiously unethical, mixing church and state and not furthering Jesus' ways. "When [Religious Right] Websites and spokespersons are clearly working from talking points that every Republican is using at a given time . . . it is clear that Christian conservative activists are being employed as agents of a party's agenda rather than as independent actors seeking to advance a particularly Christian agenda."[92]

David Kinnaman and Gabe Lyons, two younger evangelicals, devote their book *Unchristian* to questioning the Religious Right. Their chapter titles suggest some of their accusations: "Hypocritical," "Get Saved!" (an overemphasis on evangelizing), "Antihomosexual," "Sheltered," "Too Political," and "Judgmental." The book begins with survey data from the Barna Group, which provides statistical and other research for Christian organizations.[93] Barna finds that young adults

---

88. Hunter, *New Kind of Conservative*, p. 40.

89. J. Franke, "Church," in *Prophetic Evangelicals*, ed. Peter Goodwin Heltzel, Bruce Ellis Benson, and Malinda Elizabeth Berry (Grand Rapids: Eerdmans, forthcoming).

90. Gushee, *The Future of Faith*, p. 52.

91. Gushee, *The Future of Faith*, p. 54; J. Skillen, *Recharging the American Experiment* (Grand Rapids: Center for Public Justice, 1994).

92. Gushee, *The Future of Faith*, p. 48.

93. http://www.barna.org/.

consider evangelicals to be antihomosexual (91 percent), judgmental (87 percent), and hypocritical (85 percent), as well as old-fashioned, too involved in politics, out of touch, insensitive, boring, and unaccepting of other faiths. Kinnaman and Lyons ask, "What if young outsiders are right about us?"[94] "The truth is we have invited the hypocritical image,"[95] the authors continue, by living in a Christian "bubble," by attempting to legislate morality, and by failing to serve.

Greg Boyd is too a critic. On one hand, he finds some on the Religious Right guilty of "irresponsible escapism" born of an apocalyptic eschatology that allows Christians to neglect social justice, peacemaking, and the environment.[96] On the other hand, he finds them guilty not of escapism but of zealotry, recruiting Christianity to justify violence and using state mechanisms to impose their view of Christianity on others. Boyd writes, "when Jerry Falwell [Baptist televangelist and cofounder of the Moral Majority in 1979], reflecting a widespread sentiment among conservative Christians, says America should hunt terrorists down and 'blow them all away *in the name of the Lord,*' he is expressing the Constantinian mindset."[97] Boyd notes that this belligerence was especially loud under G. W. Bush, but he holds that "American Christianity has tended in this direction from the start" as slaveholders and during 250 years of fighting Amerindians.[98] Boyd's perspective finds substantial echo in the writings of Latino pastor, educator, and activist Gabriel Salguero: "What I found profoundly inconsistent with the cross of Christ was that superimposed on the cross was a waving United States flag. While I have deep respect and admiration for the U.S. flag, and the flags of any country, the flag and the cross should never be confused. Patriotism has its place, but any confusion of national pride (that means any nation) with the cross of Christ is a clarion call to revisit the cross and its interpretations for our time and place."[99]

94. D. Kinnaman and G. Lyons, *Unchristian: What a New Generation Really Thinks about Christianity and Why It Matters* (Grand Rapids: Baker, 2007), p. 37.

95. Kinnaman and Lyons, *Unchristian,* pp. 52, 191.

96. Boyd, *The Myth,* pp. 65, 72.

97. Boyd, *The Myth,* p. 80.

98. Boyd, *The Myth,* p. 210 n. 5; see also R. Jewett and J. Lawrence, *Captain America and the Crusade against Evil: The Dilemma of Zealous Nationalism* (Grand Rapids: Eerdmans, 2004); E. Tuveson, *Redeemer Nation* (Chicago: University of Chicago Press, 1968).

99. G. Salguero, "The Cross," in *Prophetic Evangelicals.*

Randall Balmer despairs not because American Christianity has always been aggressive but because, on his view, it has not. The Religious Right since the 1970s, he feels, betrayed the long-standing evangelical tradition of service and toleration. "The evangelical faith that nurtured me as a child and sustains me as an adult," he writes, "has been hijacked by right-wing zealots who have distorted the gospel of Jesus Christ, defaulted on the noble legacy of nineteenth-century evangelical activism, and failed to appreciate the genius of the First Amendment."[100]

Balmer accuses the Religious Right first of fundamentalist "selective literalism" — emphasizing, for instance, the injunctions against homosexuality in Leviticus while following few other laws in that book. This "allows them to locate sin [such as homosexuality] *outside* of the evangelical subculture (or so they think) . . . a favorite tactic of fundamentalists everywhere."[101] Second, he indicts them for blasphemy: identifying Republican wins with Christ's way "is blasphemy, pure and simple."[102] Third, he charges them with failure to serve: the Religious Right "support tax cuts for the wealthiest Americans . . . and a rejigging of Social Security . . . to fray the social safety net for the poorest among us."[103] Fourth, he castigates their militarism. Not only did the Iraq war fail "even the barest of just-war criteria," but pastors who glorify violence desecrate the Christian core. "Ron Parsley, pastor of World Harvest Church in Ohio, issues swords to those who join his religious right organization, the Center for Moral Clarity, and calls on his followers to 'lock and load' for a 'Holy Ghost invasion.' The Traditional Values Coalition advertises its 'Battle Plan' to take over the federal judiciary. . . . I wonder how this sounds to the Prince of Peace."[104]

100. Balmer, *Thy Kingdom Come*, p. ix.
101. Balmer, *Thy Kingdom Come*, pp. 8-10.
102. Balmer, *Thy Kingdom Come*, p. 180.
103. Balmer, *Thy Kingdom Come*, pp. 170, 171.
104. Balmer, *Thy Kingdom Come*, p. 175.

chapter 9

"New Evangelicalism" in Practice

....

The Environment, Abortion, Gay Unions

"New evangelical" activism in these high-profile arenas reflects not only their views on these issues but also their views about their role in civil society and politics more generally. In working toward environmental protection, for instance, how do they engage other civil society groups and government; how do they balance constitutional and biblical law? Two notable features run through "new evangelical" practices here: the ethical and political importance of understanding opposing views and of developing structures that attract consensus and coalition. As in the previous chapter, the positions sketched below are signposts along a continuum; "new evangelicals" move among them and take positions between them.

Environmental Protection: From Dominion to Creation Care

In the period following the Civil War, during the society-transforming jolts of industrialization, John Nelson Darby's dispensational premillennialism became persuasive to many evangelicals. Dispensationalism holds that Jesus' return will inaugurate a thousand years of peace, but until his arrival, conditions on earth will degrade into chaos. To his followers, the rapid changes of modernity were just the sort of bedlam Darby was talking about. So, given the inevitable unraveling of this-worldly life, concern with the environment seemed somewhat beside the point. Many twentieth-century premillennialists found the dominion view of creation more convincing. Developed by E. Calvin Beisner and others in the 1970s (not all of them dispensationalists or premillenialists), it holds that the earth was made for the use of man, who is "lifting it out of unfruitful bondage and into productive liberty. . . . All of our acquisitive activities should be undertaken with the purpose of extending godly rule, or dominion."[1] On this view, the planet's natural resources are intended for man to use while he is on the earth.

Yet a number of evangelicals, influenced less by dispensationalism, felt that man's relationship to the planet was not one of dominion but one of "stewardship." Informed by other interpretations of the Bible and by the nation's growing sensitivity to environmental degradation, Calvin DeWitt founded the Au Sable Institute of Environmental Studies in 1979, which aims at "bringing Christians and non-Christians to a better stewardship of God's creation."[2] The central campus in Michigan holds classes on environmental protection and environmental ethics. Sister programs are found in Florida, India, Africa, and the Pacific Rim. In the 1980s, as the idea of stewardship gained sway among evangelicals, the term "creation care" was coined. In 1993, Ron Sider launched the Evangelical Environmental Network to draw attention to pollution's effects and to work toward environmental protection policies. In 2004 the National Association of Evangelicals (NAE) published *For the Health of the Nation*, which declared, "We are not the owners of creation, but its stewards summoned by God to 'watch over and care for it' (Genesis 2:15). This implies the principle of sustainability: our uses of the Earth must be designed to conserve and renew the Earth rather than to deplete or destroy it. . . . Because clean air, pure water, and adequate resources are crucial to public health and civic order, government has an obligation to protect its citizens from the effects of environmental degradation."[3] The NAE advocates recycling, fuel efficiency, natural resources and energy conservation, and the care of wildlife and natural habitats.

Also that year, the cheekily titled "What Would Jesus Drive?"[4] was

1. E. C. Beisner, *Prospects for Growth: A Biblical View of Population, Resources, and the Future* (Wheaton, Ill.: Crossway, 1990), pp. 22, 30.

2. http://www.ausable.org/au.main.cfm.

3. National Association of Evangelicals, *For the Health of the Nation: An Evangelical Call to Civic Responsibility* (Washington, D.C., 2004).

4. Evangelical Environmental Network and Creation Care Magazine, "What Would Jesus Drive?" (2004).

issued by the Evangelical Environmental Network to build evangelical support for a key environmental bill in Congress. It became a national slogan. The 2006 *Environmental Climate Initiative/Evangelical Call to Action on Climate Change* further expanded evangelical efforts. With David Gushee as principal author, it identifies ending global warming as a Christian imperative. It was signed by over one hundred evangelical leaders and was supported by *Christianity Today*,[5] by World Vision (the world's largest Christian relief organization), and by presidents of thirty-nine Christian colleges. And it provoked avid opposition. Though Richard Cizik (then vice president at the NAE) was a contributor to the document, he could not get full endorsement from his organization. Challenging his opponents, Cizik told the *New York Times*, "I don't think God is going to ask us how he created the earth, but he will ask us what we did with what he created."[6] Cizik organized a joint conference with the NAE and the Center for Health and the Global Environment at Harvard Medical School. It ended with a statement of commitment to biodiversity and ending climate change. That in turn led two dozen evangelical leaders to call for Cizik's resignation. The NAE did not follow their suggestion.

Since 2008, environmental protection has become a widespread concern among evangelicals, finding support among conservative Baptists, dispensationalists like Charles Ryrie (of the *Ryrie Study Bible*, the premier dispensationalist Bible), and dispensationalist institutions like Dallas Theological Seminary. The annual National Day of Prayer for Creation Care, which hosts prayer, workshops, and festive events around the country, is sponsored by the Evangelical Environmental Network, National Hispanic Christian Leadership Conference, the National Association of Evangelicals, Eden Vigil, Care of Creation, Inc., and Blessed Earth, among many others.[7] In its environmental protection resolution in July 2010, the Southern Baptist Convention set the very notion of dominion in a new framework: "God-given dominion over the creation is not unlimited, as though we were gods and not

5. Editor David Neff played key roles in the writing of *For the Health of the Nation* and *An Evangelical Declaration against Torture*, and is central in evangelical environmental activism.

6. L. Goodstein, "Evangelical Leaders Swing Influence behind Effort to Combat Global Warming," *New York Times*, March 10, 2005.

7. See the resource guide for the National Day of Prayer for Creation Care, http://prayerforcreationcare.creationcare.org.

creatures." It called for "energy policies based on prudence, conservation, accountability and safety." By 2010, 47 percent of Americans who attend worship services regularly heard teachings about the environment from their clergy, almost all pro-environment. Ten percent heard explicit messages about creation care or stewardship of the earth — which became evangelical rallying cries during the Gulf oil spill that year. "Caring for creation," Russell Moore, dean of Southern Baptist Seminary, wrote, "is an extension of loving your neighbor as yourself."[8]

In putting their views into practice, "new evangelicals" take a number of approaches, in keeping with their ideas about church activism overall. Claiborne and others of a countercultural stripe run their cars on vegetable oil that they get from restaurants in return for improvised theater performances or other barter. They set up environment-friendly generator systems outside official electrical grids. Many more evangelicals look to market systems and civil society activism, donating to renewable-energy research, running church programs to insulate homes in poor neighborhoods or outfit them with solar panels, and reforesting land and purifying water supplies overseas. Evangelicals who work with governmental agencies unsurprisingly give greater importance to government's role in protecting the environment, both through legislation and incentives for environment-friendly construction and other programs. They have also made substantial lobbying efforts to raise fuel efficiency standards. Ben Lowe, an Illinois evangelical and Democrat who ran for Congress in the 2010 midterm elections, listed "green jobs/clean energy economy" first among the "key issues" of his campaign. He cofounded Renewal, which encourages students at Christian colleges to work toward environmental protection. His book *Green Revolution: Coming Together to Care for Creation* addresses the wider evangelical community.[9]

Like other Americans, evangelicals are divided about signing on to international environmental protection treaties. Some are wary of hobbling the U.S. economy with restrictions that America's economic competitors do not follow, and they are thus cautious about signing agreements that tie America's hands. Others find this hesitation unchristian. Gushee notes, "the United States cannot (or at least will not)

8. http://news.yahoo.com/s/ap/20100707/ap_on_re/us_rel_religion_today.

9. http://features.pewforum.org/politics/news-briefs/the-environment-religion-and-the-2010-elections.html; see also B. Lowe, *Green Revolution: Coming Together to Care for Creation* (Downers Grove, Ill.: InterVarsity, 2009).

sign on to programs that would do more harm to the U.S. economy than to the economies of other countries. It is an unfortunate stance in light of the seriousness of the [environmental] problem."[10] Similarly, Greg Boyd and Randall Balmer hold that national self-protection may be appropriate to governments but that the work of Christians is not in national interests but transnational, to preserve God's creation.

Abortion: "Adopting Some Babies and Caring for Some Mothers"

Overwhelmingly, "new evangelicals" oppose abortion on religious and ethical grounds. Indeed, the idealism of young evangelicals, which leads them to work in poverty relief and environmental protection, leads them also to strong opposition against abortion. Seventy-three percent of evangelicals under the age of thirty believe abortion should be illegal in all or most cases; 71 percent of older evangelicals do.[11]

Yet "new evangelicals" have changed the way they approach the issue, away from the sort of activism that garnered so much publicity from the 1980s to G. W. Bush's first term. This activism — from harassing women at family-planning clinics to threatening or killing doctors who perform abortion — is seen as contravening the most basic of Jesus' teachings and ethics. Instead, "new evangelicals" hold that the Christlike relationship to pregnant women is one of service, requiring that evangelicals provide financial, medical, and emotional support for pregnant women pre- and postpartum. On this view, if one wishes to reduce abortion, one must remove the central financial and emotional reasons to abort. Many "new evangelicals" believe also that a consistent pro-life ethics demands what Joseph Cardinal Bernardin in 1984 called "the seamless garment of life." If one is pro-life, one must care for the poor, champion human rights, and oppose not only abortion but also capital punishment.[12]

10. Interview with author, October 30, 2009.

11. Religion & Ethics Newsweekly/United Nations Foundation, "Religion & Ethics Newsweekly/UN Foundation Survey Explores Religion and America's Role in the World," October 22, 2008; see also Pew Forum for Religion and Public Life, "A Post-election Look at Religious Voters in the 2008 Election," December 8, 2008.

12. R. Balmer, *Thy Kingdom Come: How the Religious Right Distorts the Faith and Threatens America — an Evangelical's Lament* (New York: Basic Books, 2006), p. 187.

Among the few evangelicals who feel that legal abortion at least prevents the grim realities of back-alley operations are Jim Wallis; Leah Daughtry, the Pentecostal minister who ran the 2008 Democratic nominating convention; and Randall Balmer, professor of religion at Barnard University. Balmer's aim is not to make abortion illegal but "to make it unthinkable"[13] by providing significant support for pregnant women and children. He has also written critically of those evangelicals who, he believes, instrumentalized abortion for political gain. Noting that the biblical passages most cited against abortion all have other glosses (Deut. 30:19; Ps. 139:13-16; Luke 1:14-42), Balmer holds that squeezing anti-abortion interpretations out of them is a case of "selective literalism." The Deuteronomic verse that encourages us to "choose life," for instance, has become an evangelical bumper sticker, but in its original context the passage means "choose the way of life, God's path." Why do those who say they read Scripture literally, Balmer asks, not devote their energies also to oppose divorce, which the Bible explicitly condemns?

In his historical review of evangelical activism, Balmer notes that the anti-abortion movement gained momentum not in spontaneous outrage against legalization in 1973 but nearly a decade later, in the 1980s. Its purpose, on his view, was to unite evangelicals as a political bloc and win votes for the Republican Party. At the time of legalization, abortion had evangelical support. The official Southern Baptist position, expressed in its 1971 resolution, was to allow abortion under a wide range of conditions, including the emotional state of the pregnant woman: "we call upon Southern Baptists to work for legislation that will allow the possibility of abortion under such conditions as rape, incest, clear evidence of the likelihood of severe fetal deformity, and carefully ascertained evidence of the likelihood of damage to the emotional, mental and physical health of the mother." Commenting on *Roe v. Wade* in 1973, the *Baptist Press* wrote, "Religious liberty, human equality, and justice are advanced by the Supreme Court abortion decision." W. A. Criswell, pastor at the First Baptist Church in Dallas and former president of the Southern Baptist Convention, also had no complaint: "I have always felt that it was only after a child was born and had a life separate from its mother that it became an individual person and it has always, there-

13. Balmer, *Thy Kingdom Come*, p. 188.

fore, seemed to me that what is best for the mother and for the future should be allowed."[14]

Those who disagree with Balmer's analysis hold that evangelical opposition to abortion indeed began in the 1970s, as a religious and moral protest against legalization. The Hyde amendment, banning the use of federal funds for abortion, was passed in 1976 with considerable evangelical support. Balmer does not disagree, but holds that opposition to abortion became a *mass* movement only in the next decade. On his account it was not abortion that politicized evangelicals in the 1970s but government's threat to withdraw tax exemption from religious schools (or any nonprofit) that remained racially segregated. Paul Weyrich, a key architect of evangelical politics in the 1970s and 1980s, confirmed, "What caused the [Religious Right] movement to surface was the federal government's moves against Christian schools. It was not the other things."[15] After the tax-exemption battle subsided, Weyrich recalls, evangelical leaders held a conference call to identify a new cause that would keep evangelicals united as a Republican bloc. Several possibilities were discussed, and abortion was selected. "And that is how abortion was cobbled into the political agenda of the religious right." Balmer confirms this account with evangelical leaders of the time, including Christian Coalition leader Ralph Reed and Tim LaHaye, author of the best-selling Left Behind series of evangelical, apocalyptic thrillers.[16]

Balmer finds it inconsistent that abortion was chosen as the evangelical banner issue, given evangelical distrust of government meddling in private matters and given evangelical support for capital punishment. Balmer asks why the Republican–Religious Right coalition didn't outlaw abortion when it had the majority in Congress between 1994 and 2006 and when it controlled both the Congress and the presidency from 2000 to 2006. "Could it be," Balmer writes, "that they are less interested in actually reducing the incidence of abortion . . . than they are in continuing to use abortion as a very potent political weapon, one guaranteed to mobilize their political base and get out the vote?"[17]

---

14. Balmer, *Thy Kingdom Come*, pp. 12-13, and *Annals of the Southern Baptist Convention* (Nashville: Executive Committee, 1971).

15. W. Martin, *With God on Our Side: The Rise of the Religious Right in America* (New York: Broadway Books, 1996), p. 173.

16. Balmer, *Thy Kingdom Come*, p. 16; R. Reed, *Active Faith: How Christians Are Changing the Soul of American Politics* (New York: Free Press, 1996), p. 216.

17. Balmer, *Thy Kingdom Come*, p. 174.

Most evangelicals, however, share neither Balmer's support for legal abortion nor his historical-political critique. They spend their resources instead on developing service programs for women in crisis pregnancies. "New evangelicals" like Boyd and Claiborne focus on individual, voluntary action, following their overall extrastate stance. "The distinctly kingdom question," Boyd writes, "is not, How should we *vote?* The distinctly kingdom question is, How should we *live?* . . . How can we who are worse sinners than any woman with an unwanted pregnancy — and thus have no right to stand over them in judgment — sacrifice our time, energy, and resources to ascribe unsurpassable worth to them and their unborn children?"[18]

Boyd and Claiborne tell parallel stories. Boyd describes a middle-aged woman in his parish who, on learning that a teenager in the neighborhood was pregnant, took the girl into her home when her angry parents threw her out, and gave the girl financial and emotional support so that she could finish school. Claiborne tells of his friend Brooke, who not only helps out a young woman who first became a mother when she was a teenager but also has two of the woman's four children living with her. Claiborne writes, "I just have a more holistic sense of what it means to be for life, knowing that life does not just begin at conception and end at birth, and that if I am going to discourage abortion, I had better be ready to adopt some babies and care for some mothers."[19]

Joel Hunter and many "new evangelicals" who are active in politics and work with government have much the same ethics. "I am decidedly pro-life," Hunter writes. "But by working together instead of arguing, both sides [those for and against legal abortion] can get what they want."[20] Beginning from the obligation to protect those who cannot protect themselves, Hunter opposes both abortion and capital punishment. Yet he works on abortion reduction with Democrats and progressives — as does the New Evangelical Partnership for the Common Good — and he helped write abortion reduction into the 2008 Democratic Party platform. Hunter supported Obama's legislation to help pregnant

18. G. Boyd, *The Myth of a Christian Nation: How the Quest for Power Is Destroying the Church* (Grand Rapids: Zondervan, 2006), p. 143.

19. S. Claiborne, *The Irresistible Revolution: Living as an Ordinary Radical* (Grand Rapids: Zondervan, 2006), p. 44.

20. J. Hunter, *A New Kind of Conservative* (Ventura, Calif.: Gospel Light Publishing, 2008), p. 176.

girls finish their education and to help poor women obtain contraception, pre- and postnatal medical care, and financial support.

Representing many in this cluster, the NAE's *For the Health of the Nation* holds to similar ethics: "We believe that abortion, euthanasia, and unethical human experimentation violate the God-given dignity of human beings. . . . A threat to the aged, to the very young, to the unborn, to those with disabilities, or to those with genetic diseases is a threat to all." But it spends more of its energies advocating restrictions on abortion. In 2009 the NAE asked Congress to continue prohibitions against using public funds for abortions.[21] Most NAE members also oppose using government grants to support stem cell research and facilities offering abortion in developing nations. Obama reversed G. W. Bush's policies and allowed government funds to go to both, raising tensions between himself and "new evangelicals."[22]

Tony Campolo and Jim Wallis, of the Evangelical Left, characteristically call for both governmental and private efforts to reduce abortion. Both support contraceptive use, as does the New Evangelical Partnership for the Common Good, with Campolo noting that if government health plans for the poor included contraceptives, 500,000 abortions could be prevented each year.[23] "We should be *consistently* pro-life," Campolo writes, "which means that life is sacred and should be protected not only for the unborn *but also for the born.* This requires commitments to stop wars, end capital punishment and provide universal healthcare for all our citizens — in addition to stopping abortions."[24] Wallis echoes this sentiment: "It will be a great day when both poverty reduction *and* abortion reduction become non-partisan issues and bipartisan causes."[25] Wallis, like Balmer, is one of the few evangeli-

21. http://www.nae.net/news/365=letter=to=senators=on=abortion.

22. See David Gushee's comments on Obama policy: "Mr. President, We Need More Than Lip Service," *Right Democrat: A Mainstream Populist Voice* (blog), March 16, 2009, http://rightdemocrat.blogspot.com/2009/03/david-gushee-mr-president-we-need -more.html.

23. J. Dreweke and R. Wind, "Expanding Access to Contraception through Medicaid Could Prevent Nearly 500,000 Unwanted Pregnancies, Save $1.5 Billion," Guttmacher Institute, August 16, 2006; see also J. Frost, A. Sonfield, and R. Gold, *Estimating the Impact of Expanding Medicaid Eligibility for Family Planning Services.* Occasional Report of the Guttmacher Institute, no. 28 (2006), pp. 23-25.

24. T. Campolo, *Red Letter Christians: A Citizen's Guide to Faith and Politics* (Ventura, Calif.: Regal, 2008), p. 121.

25. J. Wallis, "A New Conversation on Abortion," *God's Politics* (blog), October 16, 2008, http://blog.sojo.net/2008/10/16/a-new-conversation-on-abortion/.

cals who would retain legal abortion.[26] He also makes a point of discussing male sexual responsibility, which "is essential to finding solutions to the abortion dilemma and should be a primary message that men are speaking to other men."[27]

In sum, by 2008, a consensus appears to have developed among "new evangelicals" that opposition to abortion is essential but coherent and Christlike when enmeshed in "seamless garment of life" advocacy on behalf of poor families and against other forms of killing such as capital punishment. The differences between Boyd and Claiborne on one hand and Hunter, the NAE, and the Evangelical Left on the other hand concern the degree of engagement with government, with greater engagement being the course that the latter three generally pursue.

Gay Unions: Other People's Sins

On one hand, David Kinnaman and Gabe Lyons devote a chapter of their book *Unchristian* to what they see as un-Christlike homophobia among evangelicals. Moreover, Billy Graham, father of postwar evangelicalism, noted, "it [homosexuality] is wrong, it's a sin. But there are other sins. Why do we jump on that sin as though it's the greatest sin? The greatest sin in the Bible is idolatry."[28] On the other hand, Richard Cizik was asked to resign his position as vice president for governmental affairs at the NAE when, in a December 2008 National Public Radio interview, he noted his "shifting feelings" about gay civil unions.[29] "I'm shifting I have to admit. In other words I would willingly say I believe in civil unions. I don't officially support redefining marriage from its traditional definition, I don't think."[30] Cizik noted that 40 percent of young evangelicals have a gay friend or family member, and that over 50

26. J. Wallis, *The Great Awakening: Reviving Faith and Politics in a Post–Religious Right America* (New York: HarperOne, 2008), p. 195.

27. Wallis, *The Great Awakening*, p. 197.

28. D. Kinnaman and G. Lyons, *Unchristian: What a New Generation Really Thinks about Christianity and Why It Matters* (Grand Rapids: Baker, 2007), p. 96.

29. NAE president Leith Anderson felt "there is a loss of trust in his credibility as a spokesperson among leaders and constituents"; see J. Wallis, *SojoMail* (e-zine), December 18, 2008, at SojoMail@sojo.net.

30. T. Gross, "Rev. Richard Cizik on God and Global Warming," National Public Radio, December 2, 2008.

percent favor same-sex civil unions or marriages. Moreover, only 29 percent of evangelicals under thirty hold that the "homosexual lifestyle" is a "major" problem. But Cizik's problems came from the 58 percent of elderly evangelicals and 46 percent of baby boomers who do think homosexuality is a serious problem. Eighty percent of theological conservatives report strong discomfort with homosexuality; 40 percent of evangelicals say schools should have the right to fire gay teachers, and some are wary of donating to HIV/AIDS relief agencies.[31]

(There were other matters in Cizik's interview that raised eyebrows. Cizik said he would work with Obama on abortion reduction and that he voted for Obama in the primaries and possibly in the election as well. On contraception, Cizik held, "We are not Catholics who oppose contraception per se. And let's face it, what do you want? Do you want an unintended pregnancy that results in abortion or do you want to meet a woman's needs in crisis, which frankly, would [be] better contraception [to] avoid that choice, avoid that abortion that we all recognize is morally repugnant — at least it is to me.")

At present, most Christian denominations (evangelical and otherwise) do not support same-sex marriage, with some exceptions: the Episcopal Church[32] and the Evangelical Lutheran Church in America support gay men and lesbians and allow individual congregations to bless monogamous same-sex unions. The Presbyterian Church (U.S.A.) similarly allows individual ministers to bless same-sex unions though not to equate them with marriage, and it urges states to give same-sex civil unions legal status. In May 2011, it allowed the ordination of gay people in committed same-sex relationships.[33] Both the Unitarian Universalist Association of Congregations and the United Church of Christ recognize same-sex marriage, with United Church of Christ ministers free to bless them or not.[34]

One approach that is gaining ground among "new evangelicals" is the distinction between homosexuality as sin and homosexuality as a crime or condition for diminished rights. "We should calm down," Hunter says, "and think about what the religious issue is and what the

---

31. Kinnaman and Lyons, *Unchristian,* pp. 92, 102 chart.

32. See Resolution A095 and C056.

33. L. Goodstein, "Presbyterians Approve Ordination of Gay People," *New York Times,* May 10, 2011.

34. http://pewforum.org/Gay-Marriage-and-Homosexuality/Religious-Groups-Official-Positions-on-Same-Sex-Marriage.aspx.

legal issue is."[35] With this church-state distinction, one may hold that homosexuality is a sin but that the neutral state may not criminalize it, as the neutral state may not enforce religious belief. The state does not, for instance, take away civil rights because people commit other sins, such as adultery or greed. Evangelicals who hold this view believe that heterosexual marriage is God's way, but they oppose discrimination against gay people in all civil rights arenas (housing, education, and employment outside of church agencies), and they strive to "walk with" gay people and serve them, as they walk with all people.

Another approach gaining ground concerns the state's role in marriage more broadly. Campolo and others suggest that government should grant only civil unions to hetero- and homosexual couples, as that is the state's legitimate purview. Such unions would grant rights and responsibilities that promote the common good (such as parental responsibility for child support). Indeed, divorce is already civil, and religious divorce procedures have no bearing on legal status or rights.

On this view, faith traditions may have many regulations regarding marriage: Catholics may not marry those who have been divorced, for instance, while Protestants and Jews can. But the neutral state should not enforce religious views of marriage — not religious views of gay marriage anymore than religious views of heterosexual marriage. The religious institution of marriage should be left to the churches, with each congregation deciding whether to bless gay ones. "The bonding of state and church in the recognition of marriages," Gushee notes, "is a vestige of an earlier day. . . . I don't support gay marriage partly because of hesitations about furthering a system that is incoherent, but we need some sort of legal recognition for heterosexual and homosexual long-term co-habitation and domestic partnerships as well" because "it is not good for society to have relationships in legal limbo. When the state is not leveling the playing field and providing procedural justice, then the most powerful interests prevail."[36]

Perhaps because views about homosexuality are changing most rapidly among young evangelicals, gay unions have been a visible issue on campus. The Council for Christian Colleges and Universities and most member universities oppose homosexual conduct and unions. The council itself supports coreligionist hiring, including the right of

---

35. Interview with the author, May 11, 2009.
36. Interview with the author, May 13, 2009.

faith-based institutions not to hire homosexuals, as their way of living does not conform to Christian values. Yet the council, as former president Robert Andringa said, is "trying to figure out how to sit down with leaders of the gay rights movements so we can relate to people, not just to fears and threats."[37]

Figuring just how to do this has become a challenge as students come out and press college administrations for recognition. SoulForce's aim, as a national organization of gay religious-college alumni, is to open up campus discussion on the subject. After years of debate, Nashville's Belmont University, with Baptist origins, has cautiously allowed on-campus gay student groups. United Theological Seminary of the Twin Cities is also more accepting of gay students. Yet most Christian campuses are not. The most common practice is to distinguish between same-sex attraction, which usually warrants no university action, and open gay conduct, which often does. North Central University, a Minneapolis Pentecostal Bible college, has suspended students after they came out, one of whom calls the atmosphere at the university "spiritually violent." Abilene, affiliated with the Churches of Christ, did not permit formation of a campus Gay-Straight Alliance, though some students are openly gay and others work for acceptance more discreetly. A spokeswoman for Baylor noted, "Baylor expects students not to participate in advocacy groups promoting an understanding of sexuality that is contrary to biblical teaching." Yet over fifty students hold weekly gatherings of their Sexual Identity Forum and continue efforts to obtain formal campus status. Saralyn Salisbury, a student and girlfriend of the forum's (female) president, underscores the generation gap that characterizes this debate: "The student body at large is ready for this but not the administration and the Regents."

Echoing Salisbury's point, events at Harding University (also affiliated with the Churches of Christ) illustrate the increasing complexities facing older evangelicals in positions of responsibility at universities. When the administration tried to block access to a student online magazine about the trials of being gay on campus, the site went viral across religious universities.[38]

37. R. Andringa, *President's Self-Evaluation for the Council for Christian Colleges & Universities Board,* July 12, 2005; see also D. Gushee, *The Future of Faith in American Politics: The Public Witness of the Evangelical Center* (Waco, Tex.: Baylor University Press, 2008), p. 99.

38. E. Eckholm, "Even on Religious Campuses, Students Fight for Gay Identity," *New York Times,* April 18, 2011.

Among our clusters, Randall Balmer's look at gay unions parallels his historical research on abortion. He finds that gay unions were instrumentalized by Religious Right leaders during and after the 1990s much as abortion was instrumentalized a decade earlier. After the demise of the Soviet Union, he writes, "The religious right desperately searched for a new enemy.... I won't dispute that the leaders of the religious right were acting, at some level, out of conviction, but they, along with leaders of the Republican Party, sensed a political opportunity as well." Balmer finds this opportunism odious, as he finds judging the sins of others, including homosexuals.[39] He is concerned to establish legal rights for gays. "Is the denial of equal rights to anyone — women or Muslims or immigrants or gays," he writes, "consistent with the example of the man who healed lepers and paralytics and who spent much of his time with the cultural outcasts of his day?"[40]

Both Balmer and Boyd ask whether homosexuality is a frontburner issue among evangelicals because they think it is one sin from which they are free. (Kinnaman and Lyons note that a third of gays and lesbians regularly attend church and nearly 17 percent are evangelical.)[41] Evangelicals, Boyd writes, think we "may be divorced and remarried several times. We may be as greedy and as unconcerned about the poor and as gluttonous as others in our culture; we may be as prone to gossip and slander and as blindly prejudiced as others. . . . These sins are among the most frequently mentioned sins in the Bible. But at least we're not *gay!*"[42]

Boyd's approach, characteristically, focuses on private, voluntary initiative. "What if, instead of trying to legally make life more difficult for gays, we worried only about how we could affirm their unsurpassable worth in service to them?"[43] His idea is not "that the church should publicly take a stand *for* gay marriage . . . but that in our role as public representatives of the kingdom of God, Christians should stick to replicating Calvary toward gay people (as toward all people), and trust that their loving service will do more to transform people than laws ever could."[44] Kinnaman and Lyons echo this point: "gays and les-

39. Matt. 7:1-5; Rom. 2:1-3; 14:2-3, 10-13; James 4:10-12.
40. Balmer, *Thy Kingdom Come*, p. 191.
41. Kinnaman and Lyons, *Unchristian*, pp. 97-98.
42. Boyd, *The Myth*, pp. 137-38.
43. Boyd, *The Myth*, p. 116.
44. Boyd, *The Myth*, pp. 138-39.

bians should not be surprised to find us working side by side with them to address HIV/AIDS and to end workplace discrimination in nonreligious settings."[45]

Hunter, like many evangelicals who are active in political advocacy and work with government, does not propose legal status for gay unions. He defines the "ideal marriage" as between a man and a woman (Matt. 19). But "I just don't put a lot of energy into this issue. With 25,000 kids dying of starvation each day, this is not an issue I'm going to spend time on."[46] Making a similar point about evangelical priorities, Tony Evans, founder of the Urban Alternative, notes, "If the church would have treated racism like it did the sins of adultery, homosexuality, and abortion, racism would have been addressed a long time ago."[47] Hunter believes much of the focus on gays is based on the fear that a gay-tolerant climate will prevent Christians from preaching their religious beliefs. "People fear that, if you say from the pulpit that homosexuality is a sin, you'll go to jail, and the state will take away the church's tax exempt status. It's all hysteria." (Legally, the neutral state may not comment on religious doctrines of sin expressed from the pulpit or elsewhere.) Echoing Balmer's thoughts on the instrumentalization of gay unions for political and other purposes, Hunter continues, "The prophets — maybe I should say 'profits' — of polarization promote these views to increase their audience and income from that kind of misinformation. There's a market for fear."[48]

Finally in this cluster, the NAE characteristically comes down in the evangelical center. On one hand, it supports neither gay marriage nor civil unions. "We also oppose innovations such as same-sex 'marriage.'"[49] On the other, the NAE does not support discrimination: "homosexuals as individuals are entitled to civil rights, including equal protection of the law"; yet, "the NAE opposes legislation which would extend special consideration to such individuals based on their 'sexual orientation.'"[50] Carl Esbeck, NAE's legal counsel, gives an example of how this balance might work out: "We would *not* support a law that forbade including the names of gay and lesbian soldiers on the Viet-

---

45. Kinnaman and Lyons, *Unchristian,* p. 106.
46. Interview with the author, May 11, 2009.
47. T. Evans, *What a Way to Live!* (Nashville: Nelsonword Publishing, 1997), p. 26.
48. Interview with the author, May 11, 2009.
49. National Association of Evangelicals, *For the Health of the Nation.*
50. National Association of Evangelicals, *Homosexuality* (2004).

nam War memorial. That's capricious and violates the equal protection clause of the Fourteenth Amendment to the Constitution."[51]

In the emergent churches, Shane Claiborne, following his countercultural approach, writes, "My studies taught me that the higher a person's frequency of church attendance, the more likely they are to be sexist, racist, anti-gay, pro-military, and committed to their local church."[52] In response, he extends this challenge: "We need to call out the terrible theology that 'God hates fags.' The starting point is that we love gay people and God loves gay people." But Claiborne is aware of the range of views on the issue, and he finds that even evangelicals who support gay marriage do not feel that "anything goes" in sex. When holding public discussions, his Simple Way community presents four perspectives, "four people talking about how they worked out their salvation and how they think God feels about the way they live." The audience thus gets a sense of the range of evangelical views. His community's position on gay civil unions reflects its overall spunky style: "If you think it's a sin to be gay," Claiborne says, "you can live here as long as you love gay people. And if you think it's a sin to say that, you can live here as long as you love the person who said that."[53]

Campolo, Wallis, and Ron Sider, on the evangelical left, seek to separate the religious from the legal issues — the question of sin on one hand and, on the other, the matter of diminished rights. Wallis supports gay civil unions and equal legal protection for homosexuals (in housing, employment, etc.). Campolo notes that the U.S. government grants 1,138 rights to heterosexual but not to homosexual couples, and finds no justification for this in Jesus' teachings. With some irony, he points out the fallacy in the claim that gay marriages would undermine heterosexual ones. "Heterosexuals are the ones getting divorces — gays want to get married!" Thus, gay marriage "may do just the opposite, strengthening traditional marriages." Returning to Jesus' teachings as a guide, Campolo writes, "Justice for gays and lesbians should be on the political front burner . . . because it is impossible to tell people we love them if we deny them the basic rights we enjoy. And loving people — *all* people — is clearly preached in the red letters [Jesus' words] of the Bible."[54]

51. Interview with the author, May 5, 2009.
52. Claiborne, *The Irresistible Revolution,* p. 269.
53. Interview with the author, May 6, 2009.
54. Campolo, *Red Letter Christians,* p. 98.

*   *   *

The following table summarizes "new evangelical" views on environmental protection, abortion, and homosexuality, in comparison with the traditional Religious Right.

	Positions associated with the Religious Right	Extrastate emphasis (Boyd et al.)	Greater focus on conventional politics and co-operation with government (Hunter et al.)	Extrastate emphasis with a more counter-cultural approach (Claiborne et al.)	Evangelical Left
Environmental protection	Tend to be skeptical and not to support	Support	Support	Support	Support
Abortion	Firmly oppose; have employed a range of tactics from persuasion to harassment of pregnant women, doctors, and clinics	Most oppose; seek to reduce abortion by personal service to mothers and children	Oppose; seek to reduce abortion by personal service to mothers and children and by working with the state and progressive institutions	Most oppose; seek to reduce by personal service to mothers and children	Most oppose; seek to reduce abortion by personal service to mothers and children and by working with the state and progressive institutions
Gay unions	Oppose gay marriage and civil unions	Oppose gay marriage; mixed on unions; oppose discrimination and violence	Oppose gay marriage; mixed on gay unions; oppose discrimination and violence	Oppose gay marriage; mixed on gay unions; oppose discrimination and violence	Oppose gay marriage; mixed on gay unions; oppose discrimination and violence

 support   mixed   reject

Concluding Remarks

Against Sectarian and Secular Fundamentalism

What are the doctrinal beliefs and political practices that advance religious life, liberal democracy, and economic justice? This has been the question of the present book. As a case study, it has described one nexus of beliefs and political practices that advances these goals, those of the "new evangelicals" — devout believers whose socioeconomic priorities focus on poverty relief, environmental protection, and immigration reform and whose political methods emphasize pluralistic freedom of conscience and church-state separation.

I am keenly aware that, in looking at how faith groups position themselves in society, no one template — no one nexus of goals and means — will speak to all circumstances. Each model emerges from a specific cultural, historical, and political context. The Indian constitution, for instance, allows the secular, democratic state explicitly to assist minority faith groups in ways impermissible under the church-state separation in the United States. Yet each model may offer something to those who are thinking through this issue, in mature democracies and developing ones. As we consider a variety of examples, we will hopefully come to better syntheses. This is especially pressing as the global movement of migrants, ideologies, and goods brings people with varying worldviews into close contact, potentially provoking religio-political conflict. Tossed into this mix, "new evangelical" ideas may be debated, modified, and possibly made useful to people as they consider their future. Because "new evangelicals" take both Scripture and the U.S. Constitution seriously, both secularists and believers may find something fruitful in their proposals.

Should "new evangelicals" at some future point work less well with the liberal, democratic state, the practices of this period will nonetheless remain important for those concerned to preserve liberal democracy and the richness of religious life and thought, in forms productive to the local context.

*   *   *

Throughout this book I have followed Richard Cizik, head of the New Evangelical Partnership for the Common Good, in using the term "new evangelicals." But as Cizik would quickly note, this efficient term is a misnomer. "New evangelicals" are not new; they are people returning to the political visions and social activism that characterized evangelicals from the seventeenth century through the early twentieth. "New evangelicals" maintain and update the political visions of toleration and church-state separation developed by the sixteenth-, seventeenth-, and eighteenth-century devout (chapter 2). These ideas of church-state separation and respect for the way others see things have led "new evangelicals" to issue-by-issue policy assessment rather than aligning the Christian way with the way of a political party or government. The 2008 *Evangelical Manifesto* holds that "We see it our duty to engage with politics, but our equal duty never to be completely equated with any party, partisan ideology, economic system, or nationality."[1] Frank Page, president of the more conservative Southern Baptist Convention, has warned, "I have cautioned our denomination to be very careful not to be seen as in lock step with any political party."[2] In the socioeconomic sphere, "new evangelical" programs — the National Association of Evangelicals' *For the Health of the Nation*[3] and the programs at Willow Creek, the New Evangelical Partnership, Sojourners, and the many churches in this study — are too not new but draw on the antebellum activism that earned Tocqueville's praise and on the postbellum Social Gospel.

1. *Evangelical Manifesto: A Declaration of Evangelical Identity and Public Commitment* (Washington, D.C.: Evangelical Manifesto Steering Committee, 2008).

2. D. Kirkpatrick, "The Evangelical Crackup," *New York Times Magazine*, October 28, 2007.

3. National Association of Evangelicals, *For the Health of the Nation: An Evangelical Call to Civic Responsibility* (Washington, D.C., 2004).

Indeed, so thoroughly did evangelicals link faith and poverty relief that some in the nineteenth century were not only devout but also socialist. Edward Bellamy, whose cousin Francis wrote the original version of the American Pledge of Allegiance, was one such person: a socialist and Baptist preacher. Arguing for a more just world, his utopic novel, *Looking Backward,* was a best seller in 1887, outstripped only by the 1896 publishing hit, *In His Steps: What Would Jesus Do?* Written by the Congregationalist minister Charles Sheldon, *In His Steps* suggests that true followers of Jesus serve the needy as Jesus had: "What would Jesus do in the matter of wealth? How would he spend it? What principle would regulate his use of money? . . . What would Jesus do about the great army of unemployed and desperate? . . . Would Jesus care nothing for them?"[4]

Even the *Fundamentals* pamphlets — written in 1910-15 as a conservative call to evangelism over the Social Gospel — included a chapter, "The Church and Socialism," that acknowledged "the wisdom of many Socialistic proposals." Its author, Charles Erdman (Princeton Theological Seminary), suggested that "government ownership might be extended to the railroads, mines, public utilities, factories" — that is, an evangelical theologian of the *Fundamentals* series proposed an idea many Americans today would find disturbingly socialist and unacceptable. In his criticism of socialism, Erdman objected not to government poverty-relief efforts or state ownership of public utilities but to those who conflate Jesus' teachings with a particular political ideology — socialist or otherwise. Erdman writes, "As to Jesus Christ, it is impossible to identify Him with any social theory or political party. His teachings are of universal application and eternal validity."[5]

The evangelical focus on poverty relief remained strong — and *In His Steps* remained a best seller — into the middle of the twentieth century, when the Federal Council of Churches (today the National Council of Churches) wrote its 1947 *Report on the National Study Conference on the Church and Economic Life.* That work stated, "Property represents a trusteeship under God, and should be held subject to the needs of the community. . . . Christians must be actuated more largely by a service motive than a profit motive."[6]

4. C. Sheldon, *In His Steps: What Would Jesus Do?* (1896; reprint, Ada, Mich.: Revell/Baker, 2004), p. 207.

5. C. Erdman, "The Church and Socialism," *The Fundamentals,* vol. 4, 1917, pp. 100, 99.

6. *Report of the National Study Conference on the Church and Economic Life* (New York:

These evangelical calls for more service than profit were endorsement of neither state-planned economies nor undemocratic government. Rather, they emerged from a concern for each individual, the common man and woman — the same concern undergirding liberal freedom of conscience. This sort of individualism aligns liberty, self-reliance, freedom of conscience, anti-elitism, and anti-authoritarianism with freedom from controlling governments, to be sure, but also with freedom from controlling economic powers. Government's job, on this view, is to protect the common man from the tyrannies of wealth, corporations, and cartels. Government should be not small — with light market regulation — but large enough to ameliorate labor abuses and give the little guy a leg up (guy in the contemporary, gender-neutral sense). The economic, fiscal, and monetary policies emerging from this view contributed to the "Great Compression" of income and wealth — the narrowing of the gap between the nation's rich and poor, first in the Progressive Era under Teddy Roosevelt, then during the Depression and World War II under his nephew Franklin, and through to the 1960s.

This leg-up type of individualism was eclipsed in the 1970s, when the Democrats in government seemed to be protecting neither the little guy from big money nor the nation from foreign enemies (chapter 3). Domestically, they failed to protect the working and middle classes as U.S. firms moved to low-wage countries and as developing countries undersold U.S. products with cheaper ones. Abroad, they failed in Vietnam, in OPEC negotiations, and in the Iran hostage crisis, all of which Americans of the Greatest Generation saw as a failure of nerve and responsibility to preserve liberty worldwide.

Given this poor record, it seemed to many Americans — evangelicals among them — that a different sort of individualism was needed, one which had thrived between the Roosevelts and before them through most of American history. In this individualist tradition, liberty, self-reliance, and anti-authoritarianism mean absence of constraint — most of all, constraint by government. Their finest flowering is in relatively unregulated markets. Government is not best when it is big enough to give the common man a leg up but when it is small, so that it cannot overregulate or constrain his opportunity and rights. In the 1960s, when "special" civil rights for minorities and expanded government programs

Religious Publicity Service of the Federal Council of the Churches of Christ in America, 1947), pp. 14, 15.

for the poor became associated with hippy self-indulgence, the anti-constraint, small-government type of individualism found wide audience. It felt to many Americans — and perhaps more so to disciplined, self-responsible evangelicals — that the nation needed sober redirection back to the self-reliant values that had built the country. Starting in the 1980s, the anticonstraint, small-government view became even more attractive, as the middle classes, labor unions, and pension programs began investing their assets in stocks, giving millions an interest in the opportunities of relatively unregulated markets.

It may appear from shifts in evangelical politics that there are two evangelical political traditions. In the leg-up approach, there is greater reliance on government, which steps in to protect the little guy from controlling and monied elites so that he has a chance in the open market. In the anticonstraint approach, government gets out of the way — so that the little guy can take his chances in the market. For much of American history, these two traditions have existed side by side, with one or the other gaining persuasiveness for a time. In the anticonstraint, small-government approach, evangelicals may be as deeply or more embedded in government than they are in the leg-up approach, but they aim at making that government small (except for the military) and the market expansive. This has been much the situation in the evangelical-Republican cooperation since the late 1960s.

Yet, however much they appear different or even contradictory, both traditions are rooted in the same principle: the anti-authoritarian, self-reliant individualism shared by Protestant dissenters and American settlers. From a concern for the individual, people may see government's job as limiting the powerful — the dominant churches, the wealthy, and corporations — or they may see government's job as limiting itself.

This common root may be one reason why, historically, the nation has shifted from one perspective to the other, and evangelicals along with it. Holding one underlying worldview, evangelicals have embraced antebellum, civil-society entrepreneurialism (to free the individual from the controlling state), and within a generation the Social Gospel (to free the individual from controlling wealth), and within a generation and a half the postsixties Republican Party (to free the individual from the controlling state). And in the next generation, the vision and priorities of "new evangelicals." All societies sustain tensions. This one, regarding the desire for individual freedom and the need for government, is one of America's most fundamental.

But what prompts these religio-political shifts? The generational factor is somewhat predictable, given the modern era's affection for change. Young people tend to want to distinguish themselves from their parents. Yet the change in evangelical political ethics is more complex. What prompts evangelicals to think, for centuries, that the individual is treated most ethically when the church is outside the state — and then when the church works through the state? What prompts evangelicals to think that the individual is treated most ethically by a government that stands up for the little guy against banks and corporations — and then by a government that stands down and deregulates them?

The economic and political conditions surrounding each shift may offer some guidance. Perhaps it's not surprising that the persecution facing sixteenth- and seventeenth-century dissenters prodded evangelicals toward church-state separation, so that states could neither judge nor punish in cases of conscience. Religion was safest left alone, out of government's reach, in the civil sphere. The rough conditions of American settlement reinforced this antistatist, anticonstraint stance, as there was relatively little state to rely on, and what state there was — the British — was resented as a constraint on the new frontiersman. Best to keep whatever one could, including religion, out of its control.

It is also not surprising that, postbellum, this antistatism gave way a bit to greater reliance on government. The appalling poverty and labor conditions of laissez-faire industrialization led many ethically minded people — evangelicals and others — to feel that the little guy needed government help against the greedy and powerful. Though advocates of small government continued to be a strong voice, advocates of leg-up government were persuasive. Precisely because the arm of the state had always been relatively light in the United States (far lighter than in many European countries), the absence of a helpful government was keenly felt. The absence was seen by many as a greater problem than overly present state regulation — a view sustained through the Depression, World War II, and the early postwar era.

But as the Cold War progressed and threats to political and economic liberty came not from business run amok but from the overarching Soviet state, evangelicals, like much of the nation, turned again to the ethics of anticonstraint small government. It leaves the individual free by reducing the very governmental regulations that the Social

Gospel and the Federal Council of Churches had earlier advocated. Moreover, the postwar economic boom dimmed the memory of the robber baron and Depression eras, and as they dimmed so did the idea that government should help the little guy out. While the problem of the 1890s had been a government that was small compared to other industrialized nations (and relatively ineffective in curbing labor abuses), the evangelicals of the 1960s and 1970s faced a much expanded state, the result of Depression-era economic policies and World War II/Cold War military ones.

As government set out to expand further, with its civil rights and Great Society aid programs, evangelicals felt pressed to protect the individual from it — especially under the shadow of the Soviet example. Indeed, they felt so pressed that, to limit the state, they made the statist move of hooking up with a political party that wanted to get into government to limit government.

Since 2005, many evangelicals have considered the consequences of this political move. First, difficult conditions in the Iraq and Afghanistan wars and the 2008 economic crash — born of market deregulation by the party most white evangelicals voted for — led to disillusionment with political wins per se as a way to serve God and his children. More importantly, this disillusionment with political wins comes not only lately but also from the long history of political shifts just described. Moving from anticonstraint small government to leg-up government and even socialism and then again to small government has highlighted what's wrong with identifying Jesus with an economic theory or political party. As we've seen Charles Erdman say in the *Fundamentals* series and Greg Boyd say more recently, when you hook your gospel to a political regime, "when the regime tanks, you've just tanked your Gospel."[7]

In sum, these shifts have left "new evangelicals" with a new political synthesis. The *content* or goals of "new evangelical" activism follow the long-standing mandates of religious freedom, state neutrality, church-state separation, and service to the needy. The *form* or means of "new evangelical" politics — how these goals are reached — span the historical alternatives described above. While "new evangelicals" reject the idea of the church as a governmental power, some engage the state more and act more often as its "prophetic" advisers. Others take a

---

7. Interview with Greg Boyd, May 4, 2009.

more resolutely extrastate role, leaving the government to its interests and the church to the kingdom's.

*   *   *

What do religio-political shifts suggest about religion? Possibly that it is a pawn, an institution that follows the fashion of the day or is recruited for economic and political interests. Perhaps, but these historical shifts may also point to something else — religion's unremarkable humanness. The Divine may be omniscient and infallible, but religion as practiced in this world is a human institution. Like other such institutions, churches respond to circumstances and change in their perspectives and conduct. Though each faith tradition maintains core tenets, these tenets rarely fully determine religious praxis. Religion, as it is practiced, is both adaptable and corruptible, as are all (human) social, political, and economic systems. Any history of religion makes it trite to say that practices today differ from those of yesterday; they differ from country to country, at times from street corner to street corner.

Though this variability may at first appear as a weakness, it argues against fundamentalism of both the secular and sectarian kind. Those who hold that religion is at bottom fundamentalist — that it does not change, is premodern and thus incompatible with liberal democracy — themselves hold to an unchanging view of religion. They hold to a secular fundamentalism, which religious variability belies. On the other hand, those who, from a religious perspective, hold that religion truly is unchanging and incompatible with modern democracy, espouse a sectarian fundamentalism — which religious variability also confounds. Both fundamentalisms deify a human institution, to make of it devil or savior. Yet both argue against history and the case study presented here.

A look at "new evangelicals" might be twice useful to discussions on religion, democracy, and economic justice: first, for their model of robust religion as a contributor to both; second, for highlighting the antifundamentalist fact of religious variation. Indeed, ignoring this variety is what so dismays "new evangelicals" when their brothers and sisters fail to listen not only to secularists but also to coreligionists — when Christians lack engagement with the views of other believers and with their own history. If "new evangelical" experience has anything to offer, it has this antifundamentalism to offer as well.

Bibliography

Alfonso, F., III. "Religious Left, Disillusioned with Obama, Coming to D.C." Religion News Service, June 9, 2010. http://pewforum.org/Religion-News/Religious-left,-disillusioned-with-Obama,-coming-to-D-C-.asp.

American Jewish Committee and the Feinstein Center for American Jewish History at Temple University. "In Good Faith: Government Funding of Faith-Based Social Services." In *Sacred Places: Civic Purposes; Should Government Help Faith-Based Charity?* edited by E. J. Dionne and M. H. Chen. Washington, D.C.: Brookings Institution Press, 2001.

"America's Religious Right: You Ain't Seen Nothing Yet." *Economist,* June 23, 2005. http://www.economist.com/displayStory.cfm?Story_ID=E1_QTDNNTN.

Andringa, R. *President's Self-Evaluation for the Council for Christian Colleges & Universities Board.* July 12, 2005.

Annals of the Southern Baptist Convention. Nashville: Executive Committee, 1971.

Appleby, R. S., and R. Cizik. *Engaging Religious Communities Abroad: A New Imperative for U.S. Foreign Policy.* Report of the Task Force on Religion and the Making of U.S. Foreign Policy. Chicago: Chicago Council on Foreign Relations, 2010.

Austin, J. *Constitutional Republicanism in Opposition to Fallacious Federalism.* Boston, 1803.

Austin, S. "Faith Matters: George and Providence." Political Research Associates, 2003. www.publiceye.org/apocalyptic/bush-2003/austin-providence.html.

Bacevich, A. *The New American Militarism.* New York: Oxford University Press, 2005.

Backus, I. *An Appeal to the Public for Religious Liberty.* 1773. http://oll.libertyfund.org/?option=com_staticxt&staticfile=show.php%3Ftitle=816&chapter=69242&layout=html&Itemid=27.

Balmer, R. *Mine Eyes Have Seen the Glory: A Journey into the Evangelical Subculture in America.* New York: Oxford University Press, 1998.

———. *Blessed Assurance: A History of Evangelicalism in America.* Boston: Beacon Press, 2000.

———. *Thy Kingdom Come: How the Religious Right Distorts the Faith and Threatens America — an Evangelical's Lament.* New York: Basic Books, 2006.

———. *God in the White House: A History; How Faith Shaped the Presidency from John F. Kennedy to George W. Bush.* New York: HarperOne, 2009.

Banks, A. M. "Evangelicals Find New Unity on Immigration." *Huffington Post,* July 13, 2010. http://www.huffingtonpost.com/2010/05/13/evangelicals-find-new -uni_n_575585.html.

Barna, G. *Revolution: Finding Vibrant Faith beyond the Walls of the Sanctuary.* Wheaton, Ill.: Tyndale House, 2006.

Bebbington, D. *Evangelicalism in Modern Britain: A History from the 1730s to the 1980s.* New York: Routledge, 1989.

———. *The Dominance of Evangelicalism: The Age of Spurgeon and Moody.* Downers Grove, Ill.: InterVarsity, 2005.

Beisner, E. C. *Prospects for Growth: A Biblical View of Population, Resources, and the Future.* Wheaton, Ill.: Crossway, 1990.

Bell, D. *Silent Covenants: Brown v. Board of Education and the Unfulfilled Hopes for Racial Reform.* New York: Oxford University Press, 2004.

Berger, M. "New Health Regulation Permits 'Conscience' Exceptions." Religion News Service, December 18, 2008.

Berger, P., ed. *The Desecularization of the World: Resurgent Religion and World Politics.* Washington, D.C.: Ethics and Public Policy Center; Grand Rapids: Eerdmans, 1999.

Berkhof, H. *Christ and the Powers.* Scottdale, Pa.: Herald, 1962.

Black, E., and M. Black. *The Rise of Southern Republicans.* Cambridge: Harvard University Press, 2002.

Blumhofer, E. *Restoring the Faith: The Assemblies of God, Pentecostalism, and American Culture.* Urbana: University of Illinois Press, 1993.

Boles, J. *The Great Revival: Beginnings of the Bible Belt.* Lexington: University of Kentucky Press, 1996.

Boyd, G. *God at War: The Bible and Spiritual Conflict.* Downers Grove, Ill.: InterVarsity, 1997.

———. *Repenting of Religion: Turning from Judgment to the Love of God.* Grand Rapids: Baker, 2004.

———. *The Myth of a Christian Nation: How the Quest for Power Is Destroying the Church.* Grand Rapids: Zondervan, 2006.

———. "Don't Weep for the Demise of American Christianity." *Christus Victor Ministries* (blog). April 8, 2009. http://www.gregboyd.org/blog/dont-weep-for-the-demise-of-american-christianity/.

———. *The Myth of a Christian Religion: Losing Your Religion for the Beauty of a Revolution.* Grand Rapids: Zondervan, 2009.

Boyd, G., and P. Eddy. *Across the Spectrum: Understanding Issues in Evangelical Theology.* Grand Rapids: Baker Academic, 2009.

Boyd, R. "Evolution War Still Rages 200 Years after Darwin's Birth." McClatchy Newspapers, January 26, 2009. http://www.mcclatchydc.com/244/story/60746.html.

Braml, J. "The Religious Right in the United States: The Base of the Bush Administration." Stiftung Wissenschaft und Politik [German Institute for International and Security Affairs]. Nr. S 35. Berlin, 2004.

―――. *Amerikas Gott und die Welt. George Bushs Außenpolitik auf Christlich-rechter Basis* (America's God and the world: George Bush's foreign policy and its Christian-right basis). Berlin: Matthes & Seitz, 2005.

Brekus, C. *Strangers and Pilgrims, 1740-1845: Female Preaching in America.* Chapel Hill: University of North Carolina Press, 1998.

Brocker, M. *God Bless America: Politik und Religion in den USA.* Darmstadt: Primus Verlag, 2005.

Burgess, S., and E. Van der Maas, eds. *The New International Dictionary of Pentecostal and Charismatic Movements.* Rev. ed. Grand Rapids: Zondervan, 2002.

Butz, H. "Conditions of Authentic Biblical Criticism." *Methodist Review,* March 1896.

Campolo, T. *Twenty Hot Potatoes Christians Are Afraid to Touch.* Nashville: Nelson, 1993.

―――. *Speaking My Mind: The Radical Evangelical Prophet Tackles the Tough Issues Christians Are Afraid to Face.* Nashville: Nelson, 2005.

―――. *Letters to a Young Evangelical.* New York: Basic Books, 2008.

―――. *Red Letter Christians: A Citizen's Guide to Faith and Politics.* Ventura, Calif.: Regal, 2008.

Campolo, T., and G. Aeschliman. *Everybody Wants to Change the World: Practical Ideas for Social Justice.* Ventura, Calif.: Regal, 2006.

Capitol Square Review Board v. Pinette. 1995. http://www.oyez.org/cases/1990-1999/1994/1994_94_780/.

Carney, J. "The Rise and Fall of Ralph Reed." *Time,* July 23, 2006. http://www.time.com/time/magazine/article/0,9171,1218060,00.html.

Caron, C. "Evangelicals Go Green — Will Conservative Candidates Follow Suit? Some Christians Lead the Charge in Environmenal Policy." *ABC News,* August 23, 2007. http://abcnews.go.com/Technology/GlobalWarming/story?id=3511781&page=1.

Carpenter, J. "From Fundamentalism to the New Evangelical Coalition." In *Evangelicalism in Modern America,* edited by G. Marsden. Grand Rapids: Eerdmans, 1984.

―――. *Revive Us Again: The Reawakening of American Fundamentalism.* New York: Oxford University Press, 1997.

Carwardine, R. "Methodist Ministers and the Second Party System." In *Rethinking Methodist History: A Bicentennial Historical Consultation,* edited by R. Richey and K. Rowe. Nashville: Kingswood Books, 1985.

Casanova, J. *Public Religions in the Modern World.* Chicago: University of Chicago Press, 1994.

―――. "The Problem of Religion and the Anxieties of European Secular Democracy." Paper presented at the 25th Jubilee Conference on Religion and European Democracy, September 1-3. Jerusalem: Van Leer Institute, 2007.

———. *Europas Angst vor der Religion.* Berlin and Cologne: Berlin University Press, 2009.

Castellio, S. *Concerning Heretics and Whether They Should Be Persecuted, and How They Should Be Treated.* 1554. Edited and translated by R. Bainton. New York: Octagon Books, 1965.

Center for Religion, Ethics, and Social Policy. "The Rise of the Religious Right in the Republican Party." Theocracy Watch Web site, February 2005. Ithaca, N.Y.: Cornell University. http://www.theocracywatch.org/taking_over.htm.

Church, F., ed. *The Separation of Church and State: Writings on a Fundamental Freedom by America's Founders.* Boston: Beacon Press, 2004.

Claiborne, S. *The Irresistible Revolution: Living as an Ordinary Radical.* Grand Rapids: Zondervan, 2006.

Clinton, H. "Remarks by Senator Hillary Rodham Clinton to the Ten Point National Leadership Foundation." On Hillary Clinton's Senate Web site. January 19, 2005. http://clinton.senate.gov/speeches/2005125C01.html.

Cnaan, R., S. Boddie, C. McGrew, and J. Kang. *The Other Philadelphia Story: How Local Congregations Support Quality of Life in Urban America.* Philadelphia: University of Pennsylvania Press, 2006.

County of Allegheny v. ACLU. 1989. http://www.oyez.org/cases/1980-1989/1988/1988_87_2050/.

Cox, D. "Young White Evangelicals: Less Republican, Still Conservative." Pew Forum on Religion and Public Life. September 28, 2007. http://pewforum.org/docs/?DocID=250.

Crevecoeur, J. Hector St. John de. *Letters of an American Farmer.* 1782. New York, 1981.

Croft v. Perry. 2008. http://www.nsba.org/cosa2/clips/docs/croft_v_perry.pdf.

Cunningham, S. *Dear Church: Letters from a Disillusioned Generation.* Grand Rapids: Zondervan, 2006.

Cutler, W., and J. Cutler. *Life, Journals, and Correspondence of Rev. Manasseh Cutler.* 2 vols. Cincinnati: Ohio University Press, 1888.

Davie, G. "Europe — the Exception That Proves the Rule." In *The Desecularization of the World: Resurgent Religion and World Politics,* edited by P. Berger, 65-84. Washington, D.C.: Ethics and Public Policy Center; Grand Rapids: Eerdmans, 1999.

Dayton, D. *The Theological Roots of Pentecostalism.* Metuchen, N.J.: Scarecrow, 1987.

Dayton, D., and R. Johnston. *The Variety of American Evangelicalism.* Knoxville: University of Tennessee Press, 2001.

De Young, C. P., M. Emerson, G. Yancey, and K. C. Kim. *United by Faith: The Multiracial Congregation as an Answer to the Problem of Race.* New York: Oxford University Press, 2004.

DiIulio, J. *Godly Republic: A Centrist Blueprint for America's Faith-Based Future.* Berkeley and Los Angeles: University of California Press, 2007.

Dionne, E. J., and M. H. Chen, eds. *Sacred Places: Civic Purposes; Should Government*

Help Faith-Based Charity? Washington, D.C.: Brookings Institution Press, 2001.

Dreweke, J., and R. Wind. "Expanding Access to Contraception through Medicaid Could Prevent Nearly 500,000 Unwanted Pregnancies, Save $1.5 Billion." Guttmacher Institute, August 16, 2006. http://guttmacher.org/media/nr/ 2006/08/16/index.html.

Early, J. *Readings in Baptist History: Four Centuries of Selected Documents.* Nashville: B&H Publishing, 2008.

Echegaray, C. "Baptist Leader Richard Land Backs Citizenship for Illegal Immigrants." *Tennessean,* June 8, 2010. http://www.tennessean.com/article/ 20100608/NEWS01/6080339/2066/news03.

Edgar, B. *Middle Church: Reclaiming the Moral Values of the Faithful Majority from the Religious Right.* New York: Simon and Schuster, 2007.

Edgell, P., G. Joseph, and H. Douglas. "Atheists as 'Other': Moral Boundaries and Cultural Membership in American Society." *American Sociological Review* 71, no. 2 (2006): 211-34. http://www.soc.umn.edu/pdf/atheistAsOther.pdf.

El-Faizy, M. *God and Country: How Evangelicals Have Become America's Mainstream.* New York: Bloomsbury, 2006.

Ellingsen, M. *When Did Jesus Become Republican? Rescuing Christianity from the Right.* Lanham, Md.: Rowman and Littlefield, 2007.

Emerson, M., and C. Smith. *Divided by Race: Evangelical Religion and the Problem of Race in America.* New York: Oxford University Press, 2000.

Environmental Climate Initiative/Evangelical Call to Action on Climate Change. 2006. http://www.npr.org/documents/2006/feb/evangelical/calltoaction.pdf.

Epperson v. Arkansas. 1968. http://www.oyez.org/cases/1960-1969/1968/1968_7/.

Erdman, C. "The Church and Socialism." *The Fundamentals.* Vol. 4. 1917.

Evangelical Environmental Network and Creation Care Magazine. "What Would Jesus Drive?" 2004. http://www.whatwouldjesusdrive.org/.

Evangelical Manifesto: A Declaration of Evangelical Identity and Public Commitment. Washington, D.C.: Evangelical Manifesto Steering Committee, 2008. http:// www.anevangelicalmanifesto.com/docs/Evangelical_Manifesto.pdf.

Evans, T. *What a Way to Live!* Nashville: Nelsonword Publishing, 1997.

Everson v. Board of Education. 1947. http://www.oyez.org/cases/1940-1949/1946/ 1946_52/.

Falwell, J. *Listen, America!* New York: Bantam Books, 1980.

Farkas, S., J. Johnson, and T. Foleno. *For Goodness Sake: Why So Many Americans Want Religion to Play a Greater Role in American Life.* New York: Public Agenda Foundation, 2001.

Feldman, G., ed. *Politics and Religion in the White South.* Lexington: University Press of Kentucky, 2005.

Feldman, M. *Divided by God: America's Church-State Problem — and What We Should Do about It.* New York: Farrar, Straus and Giroux, 2005.

Finke, R., and R. Stark. "How the Upstart Sects Won America: 1776-1850." *Journal for the Scientific Study of Religion* (March 1989).

Finney, C. *Lectures on Systematic Theology*. Edited by G. Redford. London: William Tegg and Co., 1851.

Flast v. Cohen. 1968. http://www.oyez.org/cases/1960-1969/1967/1967_416/.

Flesher, J. "Green Religion Movement Hopes Gulf Oil Spill Wins Converts." *Huffington Post*, July 7, 2010. http://www.huffingtonpost.com/2010/07/07/green-religion-movement-h_n_638054.html.

Ford, N. *We the Purple: Faith, Politics, and the Independent Voter*. Carol Stream, Ill.: Tyndale House, 2008.

Frost, J., A. Sonfield, and R. Gold. *Estimating the Impact of Expanding Medicaid Eligibility for Family Planning Services*. Occasional Report of the Guttmacher Institute, no. 28 (2006).

Gardiner, F. "Darwinism." *Bibliotheca Sacra* (April 1872).

———. "The Bearing of Recent Scientific Thought upon Theology." *Bibliotheca Sacra* (1878).

Gaustad, E. *Historical Atlas of Religion in America*. New York: Harper and Row, 1962.

Gaustad, E., and P. Barlow. *New Historical Atlas of Religion in America*. New York: Oxford University Press, 2001.

Gehrke-White, D., H. Sampson, and A. Veciana-Suarez. "Coral Ridge Presbyterian Puts Politics Aside for Now." *Miami Herald*, August 28, 2007. http://www.nacdweb.org/files/2007/Coral%20Ridge%20Presbyterian%20puts%20politics%20aside%20for%20now%20-%2008.pdf.

Gerson, Michael J. *Heroic Conservatism: Why Republicans Need to Embrace America's Ideals (and Why They Deserve to Fail If They Don't)*. New York: HarperOne, 2007.

Gilgoff, D. "Ralph Reed Launches New Values Group: 'Not Your Daddy's Christian Coalition.'" *U.S. News & World Report*, June 23, 2009. http://www.usnews.com/blogs/god-and-country/2009/06/23/exclusive-ralph-reed-launches-new-values-group-not-your-daddys-christian-coalition.html.

Glaser, J. *Race, Campaign Politics, and the Re-alignment of the South*. New Haven: Yale University Press, 1996.

———. *The Hand of the Past in Contemporary Southern Politics*. New Haven: Yale University Press, 2005.

Goldberg, M. *Kingdom Coming: The Rise of Christian Nationalism*. New York: Norton, 2006.

Gomes, P. *The Good Book: Reading the Bible with Mind and Heart*. New York: Harper Perennial, 1998.

———. *The Scandalous Gospel of Jesus: What's So Good about the Good News?* New York: HarperOne, 2008.

Goodstein, L. "Evangelical Leaders Swing Influence behind Effort to Combat Global Warming." *New York Times*, March 10, 2005. http://www.nytimes.com/2005/03/10/national/10evangelical.html?_r=1&oref=slogin.

———. "Without a Pastor of His Own, Obama Turns to Five." *New York Times*, March 15, 2009. http://www.nytimes.com/2009/03/15/us/politics/15pastor.html?scp=2&sq=obama%20wright&st=cse.

Goodstein, L., and D. Kirkpatrick. "On a Christian Mission to the Top." *New York*

Times, May 22, 2005. http://www.nytimes.com/learning/teachers/featured _articles/20050523monday.html.

Goss, C. *Statistical History of the First Century of American Methodism.* New York: Carlton and Porter, 1866.

Graf, F. W. *Die Wiederkehr der Goetter: Religionen in der modernen Kultur.* Munich: Beck Verlag, 2004.

Grant, G. *The Changing of the Guard: Biblical Principles for Political Action.* Fort Worth, Tex.: Dominion Press, 1987.

Graves, R. "A Passion for Mixing Religion and Politics." *Houston Chronicle,* May 20, 2005. http://www.chron.com/.

Green, J. *The American Religious Landscape and Political Attitudes: A Baseline for 2004.* Washington, D.C.: Pew Forum on Religion and Public Life, 2004. http:// pewforum.org/publications/surveys/green-full.pdf.

Griffin, D., et al. *American Empire and the Commonwealth of God: A Political, Economic, Religious Statement.* Louisville: Westminster John Knox, 2006.

Grimm, D. "Conflicts between General Laws and Religious Norms." *Cardozo Law Review* 30 (2009).

Griswold v. Connecticut. 1965. http://www.oyez.org/cases/1960-1969/1964/1964_496/.

Gross, T. "Rev. Richard Cizik on God and Global Warming." National Public Radio, December 2, 2008. http://www.npr.org/templates/story/story.php?story Id=97690760.

Gushee, D. *Toward a Just and Caring Society: Christian Responses to Poverty in America.* Grand Rapids: Baker, 1999.

———. *Christians and Politics beyond the Culture Wars: An Agenda for Engagement.* Grand Rapids: Baker, 2000.

———. *Righteous Gentiles of the Holocaust: Genocide and Moral Obligation.* St. Paul, Minn.: Paragon House, 2003.

———. *The Future of Faith in American Politics: The Public Witness of the Evangelical Center.* Waco, Tex.: Baylor University Press, 2008.

———. "The Shameful Mosque Controversy." *Huffington Post,* August 11, 2010. http://www.huffingtonpost.com/dr-david-p-gushee/the-shameful-mosque -contr_b_678419.html.

Hammond, S., K. Hardwick, and H. Lubert. *Classics of American Political and Constitutional Thought: Origins through the Civil War.* Indianapolis: Hackett, 2007.

Harris, S. *Letter to a Christian Nation.* New York: Knopf, 2006.

Hatch, N. *The Democratization of American Christianity.* New Haven: Yale University Press, 1989.

Hein v. Freedom from Religion Foundation. 2007. http://www.oyez.org/cases/2000 -2009/2006/2006_06_157/.

Heineck, G. *The Determinants of Church Attendance and Religious Human Capital in Germany.* Discussion paper no. 263 (October). Berlin: Deutsches Institut fuer Wirtschaftsforschung, 2001.

Heltzel, Peter Goodwin, Bruce Ellis Benson, and Malinda Elizabeth Berry. *Prophetic Evangelicals.* Grand Rapids: Eerdmans, forthcoming.

Hertzke, A. *Freeing God's Children: The Unlikely Alliance for Global Human Rights.* Lanham, Md.: Rowman and Littlefield, 2004.

Holmes, D. *The Faiths of the Founding Fathers.* New York: Oxford University Press, 2006.

Hoskyns, E., and N. Davey. *The Riddle of the New Testament.* 1947. London: Faber and Faber, 1957.

Hout, M., and A. Greeley. "A Hidden Swing Vote: Evangelicals." *New York Times,* September 4, 2004, A17.

Hunter, A. *Evangelicalism: The Coming Generation.* Chicago: University of Chicago Press, 1987.

Hunter, G., III. *Christian, Evangelical, and . . . Democrat?* Nashville: Abingdon, 2006.

Hunter, J. *Prayer, Politics, and Power: What Really Happens When Religion and Politics Mix?* Carol Stream, Ill.: Tyndale House, 1988.

————. *Right Wing, Wrong Bird: Why the Tactics of the Religious Right Won't Fly with Most Conservative Christians.* Longwood, Fla.: Distributed Church Press, 2006.

————. *A New Kind of Conservative.* Ventura, Calif.: Gospel Light Publishing, 2008.

Israel, J. *Radical Enlightenment: Philosophy and the Making of Modernity, 1650-1750.* New York: Oxford University Press, 2002.

Jefferson, T. *Writings.* Library of America. New York: Literary Classics of the United States, 1984.

————. *The Political Writings of Thomas Jefferson.* Edited by M. Peterson. Chapel Hill: University of North Carolina Press, 1993.

Jensen, Merrill, ed. *The Documentary History of the Ratification of the Constitution.* Vol. 18. Edited by J. Kaminski and G. Saladino. Commentaries on the Constitution, Public and Private: 10 May to 13 September 1788. Madison: Wisconsin Historical Society Press, 1997.

Jewett, R., and J. Lawrence. *Captain America and the Crusade against Evil: The Dilemma of Zealous Nationalism.* Grand Rapids: Eerdmans, 2004.

Johnson, B. *Objective Hope: Assessing the Effectiveness of Faith-Based Organizations: A Review of the Literature.* Center for Research on Religion and Urban Civil Society, Manhattan Institute and University of Pennsylvania, 2001.

Kennedy, J. "Preach and Reach: Despite His Liberal Record, Obama Is Making a Lot of Evangelicals Think Twice." *Christianity Today,* October 6, 2008. http://www.christianitytoday.com/ct/2008/october/18.26.html.

Kindy, K. "In Rebuking Minister, McCain May Have Alienated Evangelicals." *Washington Post,* May 29, 2008, A08. http://www.washingtonpost.com/wp-dyn/content/article/2008/05/28/AR2008052803037.html.

King, M. L., Jr. *Remaining Awake through a Great Revolution.* Washington, D.C.: Washington National Cathedral Archives, 1968.

Kinnaman, D., and G. Lyons. *Unchristian: What a New Generation Really Thinks about Christianity and Why It Matters.* Grand Rapids: Baker, 2007.

Kirkpatrick, D. "The Evangelical Crackup." *New York Times Magazine,* October 28, 2007. http://www.nytimes.com/2007/10/28/magazine/28Evangelicals-t.html?th=&emc=th&pagewanted=print.

Kitzmiller v. Dover Area School District. 2005. http://www.pamd.uscourts.gov/kitzmiller_342.pdf.

Kohut, A., et al. *The Diminishing Divide: Religion's Changing Role in American Politics.* Washington, D.C.: Brookings Institution Press, 2000.

Kosmin, B., and A. Keysar. *American Religious Identification Survey.* Hartford, Conn.: Trinity College, 2009. http://livinginliminality.files.wordpress.com/2009/03/aris_report_2008.pdf.

Kramnick, I., and R. L. Moore. *The Godless Constitution: A Moral Defense of the Secular State.* 2nd ed. New York: Norton, 2005.

Kuo, D. *Tempting Faith: An Inside Story of Political Seduction.* New York: Free Press, 2006.

Kyle, R. *Evangelicalism: An Americanized Christianity.* New Brunswick, N.J.: Transaction Books, 2006.

Lambsdorff, O. "Three Corners of the World Try to Find Their Bearings." *International Herald Tribune,* June 22, 2005. http://www.iht.com/articles/2005/06/21/opinion/edlambs.php.

Lampman, J. "Obama Weighs Patient Rights vs. Doctor's Conscience." *Christian Science Monitor,* March 26, 2008. http://www.csmonitor.com/2009/0326/p01s03-ussc.html.

Larson, E. *Summer for the Gods: The Scopes Trial and America's Continuing Debate over Science and Religion.* Cambridge: Harvard University Press, 1998.

Lecler, J. *Toleration and the Reformation.* London: Longmans, Green, 1960.

Lemon v. Kurtzman. 1971. http://www.oyez.org/cases/1970-1979/1970/1970_89/.

Lerner, M. *The Left Hand of God: Taking Back Our Country from the Religious Right.* New York: HarperOne, 2007.

Levin, J., and H. Koenig, eds. *Faith, Medicine, and Science: A Festschrift in Honor of Dr. David B. Larson.* Binghamton, N.Y.: Haworth Pastoral Press, 2005.

Lindsay, D. M. *Faith in the Halls of Power: How Evangelicals Joined the American Elite.* New York: Oxford University Press, 2007.

Linn, J. *Big Christianity: What's Right with the Religious Left.* Louisville: Westminster John Knox, 2006.

Lippy, C., and R. Krapohl. *The Evangelicals: A Historical, Thematic, and Biographical Guide.* Westport, Conn.: Greenwood Press, 1999.

Locke, J. *The Political Writings of John Locke.* Edited by D. Wootton. New York: Mentor, 1993.

Loveland, A. *American Evangelicals and the US Military, 1942-1993.* Baton Rouge: Louisiana State University Press, 1996.

Lowe, B. *Green Revolution: Coming Together to Care for Creation.* Downers Grove, Ill.: InterVarsity, 2009.

Luckmann, T. *The Invisible Religion.* New York: Macmillan, 1967.

Luhmann, N. *Soziale Systeme: Grundriss einer allgemienen Theorie.* Frankfurt: Suhrkamp Verlag, 1987.

Madison, J. *Memorial and Remonstrance against Religious Assessments.* 1785. http://religiousfreedom.lib.virginia.edu/sacred/madison_m&r_1785.html.

Marin, A. *Love Is an Orientation.* Downers Grove, Ill.: InterVarsity, 2009.

Marsden, G. *Fundamentalism and American Culture: The Shaping of Twentieth-Century Evangelicalism, 1870-1925.* New York: Oxford University Press, 1980.

———. *Understanding Fundamentalism and Evangelicalism.* Grand Rapids: Eerdmans, 1991.

Marsh, C. *Wayward Christian Soldiers: Against the Political Captivity of the Gospel.* New York: Oxford University Press, 2007.

Marshall, C. *Crowned with Glory and Honor: Human Rights in the Biblical Tradition.* Studies in Peace and Scripture, vol. 6. Telford, Pa.: Cascadia Publishing House, 2002.

Martin, D. *A General Theory of Secularization.* Oxford: Blackwell, 1976.

Martin, W. *With God on Our Side: The Rise of the Religious Right in America.* New York: Broadway Books, 1996.

Marty, M. *Righteous Empire: The Protestant Experience in America.* New York: Harper Torchbooks, 1970/1977.

Marty, M., and R. S. Appleby. *Fundamentalisms Observed.* Chicago: University of Chicago Press, 1994.

McCreary County v. ACLU. 2005. http://www.oyez.org/cases/2000-2009/2004/2004_03_1693/.

McGraw, B., and J. Formicola, eds. *Taking Religious Pluralism Seriously: Spiritual Politics on America's Sacred Ground.* Waco, Tex.: Baylor University Press, 2005.

McKibben, B. "Taking the Gospels Seriously." *New York Review of Books* 55, no. 1 (January 17, 2008). http://www.nybooks.com/articles/20943.

McKinley, J., Jr. "In Texas, a Line in the Curriculum Revives Evolution Debate." *New York Times,* January 22, 2009. http://www.nytimes.com/2009/01/22/education/22texas.html?th&emc=th.

McLaren, B. *A Generous Orthodoxy.* Grand Rapids: Zondervan, 2004.

———. *Everything Must Change.* Nashville: Nelson, 2007.

McLaren, B., and T. Campolo. *Adventures in Missing the Point: How the Culture-Controlled Church Neutered the Gospel.* Grand Rapids: Zondervan/Youth Specialties, 2006.

Meacham, J. *American Gospel: God, the Founding Fathers, and the Making of a Nation.* New York: Random House, 2006.

Mead, W. "God's Country?" *Foreign Affairs,* September/October 2006. www.foreignaffairs.org/mead_reading.

Meckler, L. "Obama Walks Religious Tightrope Spanning Faithful, Nonbelievers." *Wall Street Journal,* March 24, 2009. http://online.wsj.com/article/SB123785559998620329.html?mod=googlenews_wsj.

Moore, D. "Public Favors Voluntary Prayer for Public Schools: But Strongly Supports Moment of Silence Rather Than Spoken Prayer." Gallup poll, August 26, 2005. http://www.gallup.com/poll/18136/Public-Favors-Voluntary-Prayer-Public-Schools.aspx.

Moorhead, J. "Prophecy, Millennialism, and Biblical Interpretation in Nineteenth-

Century America." In *Biblical Hermeneutics in Historical Perspective,* edited by M. Burrows and P. Rorem. Grand Rapids: Eerdmans, 1991.

Murphy, T. "Evangelicals, Catholics Applaud DNC's Abortion Language Change." Religion News Service, August 12, 2008. http://pewforum.org/news/display .php?NewsID=16249.

National Association of Evangelicals. *For the Health of the Nation: An Evangelical Call to Civic Responsibility.* Washington, D.C., 2004. http://www.nae.net/images/ civic_responsibility2.pdf.

———. *Homosexuality.* 2004. http://www.nae.net/resolutions/180-homosexuality -2004.

———. *An Evangelical Declaration against Torture: Protecting Human Rights in an Age of Terror.* 2007. http://www.esa-online.org/Images/mmDocument/Declarations %20&%20Letters/An%20Evangelical%20Declaration%20Against%20Torture .pdf.

———. "NAE Ad Urges Bipartisan Immigration Reform." Press release, May 13, 2010. http://www.nae.net/news-and-events/444-immigration-ad.

———. "NAE Urges Cancellation of Planned Qu'ran Burning." Press release, July 29, 2010. http://www.nae.net/news-and-events/469-press-release-nae-urges -cancellation-of-planned-quran-burning.

National Marriage Project and the Institute for American Values. *When Marriage Disappears: The New Middle America.* Marriage in America: The State of Our Unions, 2010. Institute for American Values, University of Virginia, December 2010. http://stateofourunions.org/2010/SOOU2010.pdf.

Nelson A. Rockefeller Institute of Government, The. "Taking Stock: The Bush Faith-Based Initiative and What Lies Ahead, the Final Report by the Roundtable on Religion and Social Welfare Policy." June 11, 2009. http:// religionandsocialpolicy.org/final_report/exec_sum_060809.pdf.

New Evangelical Partnership for the Common Good. N.d. http://www.newevangelical partnership.org/?q=node/1.

Niebuhr, R. *Moral Man and Immoral Society.* 1932. New York: Scribner's Sons; Louisville: Westminster John Knox Press, 1960.

Noll, M. *America's God: From Jonathan Edwards to Abraham Lincoln.* New York: Oxford University Press, 2002.

———. *The Rise of Evangelicalism: The Age of Edwards, Whitefield, and the Wesleys.* Downers Grove, Ill.: InterVarsity, 2003.

———. *God and Race in American Politics.* Princeton: Princeton University Press, 2008.

Novak, M., and J. Novak. *Washington's God.* New York: Basic Books, 2006.

Ott, B. "School Prayer: Teen Support Hinges on Type; Least Likely to Support Spoken Prayer That Mentions Jesus Christ." Gallup poll, August 25, 2006. http:// www.gallup.com/poll/17494/School-Prayer-Teen-Support-Hinges-Type.aspx.

Paley, W. *Evidences of Christianity.* 1794. http://www.gutenberg.org/etext/14780.

Pavlischek, K. "Just War Theory and Terrorism: Applying the Ancient Doctrine to the Current Conundrum." Family Research Council, Witherspoon Lectures, November 21, 2001. www.frc.org/get.cfm?i=WT01K2.

Pedreira v. Kentucky Baptist Homes for Children. 2008. http://www.aclu.org/pdfs/lgbt/ pedreira_finalsignedappealbrief_7_17_08(2).pdf.

Perry, D. *Breaking Down Barriers: A Black Evangelical Explains the Black Church.* Grand Rapids: Baker, 1998.

Pew Forum on Religion and Public Life. "Faith-Based Funding Backed, but Church-State Doubts Abound." April 10, 2001. http://pewforum.org/events/ 0410/report/execsum.php.

———. "Americans Struggle with Religion's Role at Home and Abroad." 2002. http://people-press.org/report/150/americans-struggle-with-religions-role -at-home-and-abroad.

———. *Lift Every Voice: A Report on Religion in American Public Life.* 2002. http:// pewforum.org/publications/reports/lifteveryvoice.pdf.

———. "Many Americans Uneasy with Mix of Religion and Politics." August 24, 2006. http://pewforum.org/docs/?DocID=153.

———. "Religious Displays and the Courts." June 2007. http://pewforum.org/ assets/files/religious-displays.pdf.

———. "U.S. Religious Landscape Survey." April 19, 2008. http://religions .pewforum.org/reports.

———. "Courts Not Silent on Moments of Silence." April 24, 2008. http:// pewforum.org/docs/?DocID=300.

———. "American Evangelicalism: New Leaders, New Faces, New Issues." May 6, 2008. http://pewforum.org/events/?EventID=186.

———. "Assessing a More Prominent 'Religious Left.'" June 5, 2008. http:// pewforum.org/events/?EventID=187.

———. "More Americans Question Religion's Role in Politics." August 21, 2008. http://pewforum.org/docs/?DocID=334.

———. "Analyzing the Fall Campaign: Religion and the Presidential Election." September 9, 2008. http://pewforum.org/events/?EventID=197.

———. "John DiIulio Previews How Faith-Based Initiatives Would Change If Barack Obama Is Elected President." September 23, 2008. http:// pewforum.org/events/?EventID=202.

———. "Americans Wary of Church Involvement in Partisan Politics." October 1, 2008. http://pewforum.org/docs/?DocID=358.

———. "A Post-election Look at Religious Voters in the 2008 Election." December 8, 2008. http://pewforum.org/events/?EventID=209.

———. "Faith-Based Aid Favored — with Reservations." January 30, 2009. http:// pewforum.org/docs/?DocID=340-33k.

———. "Overview: The Conflict between Religion and Evolution." February 4, 2009. http://pewforum.org/docs/?DocID=395.

———. "An Overview of Religion and Science in the United States." November 5, 2009. http://www.pewforum.org/docs/?DocID=471.

———. "Public Opinion on Religion and Science in the United States: Views on

Science and Scientists." November 5, 2009. http://www.pewforum.org/docs/
?DocID=472.

———. "The Future of Evangelicals: A Conversation with Pastor Rick Warren."
November 13, 2009. http://pewforum.org/events/?EventID=221.

———. "Faith-Based Programs Still Popular, Less Visible." November 16, 2009.
http://www.pewforum.org/docs/?DocID=483.

Pew Forum on Religion and Public Life and the Pew Hispanic Center. "Changing
Faiths: Latinos and the Transformation of American Religion." 2007. http://
pewforum.org/surveys/hispanic/.

Phillips, K. *America Theocracy: The Peril and Politics of Radical Religion, Oil, and Bor-
rowed Money in the 21st Century.* New York: Viking, 2006.

Quebedeaux, R. *The New Charismatics, II.* San Francisco: Harper and Row, 1983.

Rauschenbusch, W. *Christianity and the Social Crisis.* 1907. Edited by D. Ottati. Louisville: Westminster John Knox, 1992.

———. *Christianity and the Social Crisis in the 21st Century: The Classic That Woke Up the
Church.* 1907. New York: HarperOne, 2007.

Reed, R. *Active Faith: How Christians Are Changing the Soul of American Politics.* New
York: Free Press, 1996.

Religion & Ethics Newsweekly/United Nations Foundation. "Religion & Ethics
Newsweekly/UN Foundation Survey Explores Religion and America's Role in
the World." October 22, 2008. http://www.pbs.org/wnet/religionandethics/
episodes/by-topic/civil-society/religion-ethics-newsweekly-un-foundation
-survey-explores-religion-and-americas-role-in-the-world/1190/.

Report of the National Study Conference on the Church and Economic Life. New York: Religious Publicity Service of the Federal Council of the Churches of Christ in
America, 1947.

Rich, F. "The All-White Elephant in the Room." *New York Times,* May 4, 2008. http:/
/www.nytimes.com/2008/05/04/opinion/04rich.html?th&emc=th.

Robinson, M. "Illinois Moment of Silence Ruled Unconstitutional." Associated
Press, January 22, 2009. http://www.msnbc.msn.com/id/28788715/.

Rush, B. *Letters of Benjamin Rush.* Edited by L. H. Butterfield. 2 vols. Princeton:
Princeton University Press, 1951.

Rushdoony, R. J. *The Institutes of Biblical Law.* Phillipsburg, N.J.: P&R Publishing,
1973.

———. *Thy Kingdom Come: Studies in Daniel and Revelation.* Fairfax, Va.: Thoburn
Press, 1978.

Sandler, L. *Righteous Dispatches from the Evangelical Youth Movement.* New York: Viking,
2006.

Scarborough, R. *In Defense of Mixing Church and State.* Lufkin, Tex.: Vision America,
1999.

Schieder, R. *Sind Religionen gefumahrlich?* Cologne and Berlin: Berlin University
Press, 2008.

Schweiger, B., and D. Mathews, eds. *Religion in the American South: Protestants and*

Others in History and Culture. Chapel Hill: University of North Carolina Press, 2004.

Selman v. Cobb County School District. 2005. http://fl1.findlaw.com/news.findlaw .com/cnn/docs/religion/selmancobb11305ord.pdf.

"Sen. McCain's Agents of Intolerance." *New York Times,* May 24, 2008. Editorial. http://www.nytimes.com/2008/05/24/opinion/24sat2.html?_r=1&th&emc =th&oref=slogin.

"Separated Brothers: Latinos Are Changing the Nature of American Religion." *Economist,* July 16, 2009. http://www.economist.com/world/unitedstates/ PrinterFriendly.cfm?story_id=14034841.

Serjeant, J. "US Evangelicals Strive to Change Attitudes on AIDS." Reuters, November 28, 2007. http://www.reuters.com/article/latestCrisis/idUSN27516593.

Sheinin, A. "Reed to Refashion Coalition." *Atlanta Journal-Constitution,* July 12, 2009. http://www.ajc.com/metro/content/printedition/2009/07/12/reed0712.html ?cxntlid=inform_sr.

Sheldon, C. *In His Steps: What Would Jesus Do?* 1896. Reprint, Ada, Mich.: Revell/ Baker, 2004.

Sider, R. *Rich Christians in an Age of Hunger: Moving from Affluence to Generosity.* Nashville: Nelson, 1977.

———. *Just Generosity.* Grand Rapids: Baker, 1999.

———. *The Scandal of Evangelical Politics: Why Are Christians Missing the Chance to Really Change the World?* Grand Rapids: Baker, 2008.

Sider, R., and D. Knippers. *Toward an Evangelical Public Policy.* Grand Rapids: Baker, 2005.

Sider, R., P. Olson, and H. Unruh. *Churches That Make a Difference: Reaching Your Community with Good News and Good Works.* Grand Rapids: Baker, 2002.

Skillen, J. *Recharging the American Experiment.* Grand Rapids: Center for Public Justice, 1994.

Skillen, J., and K. Pavlischek. "Political Responsibility and the Use of Force." *Philosophia Christi* 3, no. 2 (2001).

Smith, G. S. *Faith and the Presidency: From George Washington to George W. Bush.* New York: Oxford University Press, 2006.

Smith, T. *Revivalism and Social Reform: American Protestantism on the Eve of the Civil War.* New York: Abingdon, 1957.

Stassen, G. *Just Peacemaking: Transforming Initiatives for Justice and Peace.* Louisville: Westminster John Knox, 1992.

Stassen, H., and D. Gushee. *Kingdom Ethics: Following Jesus in Contemporary Context.* Downers Grove, Ill.: InterVarsity, 2003.

State Historical Society of Wisconsin. *Collections of the State Historical Society of Wisconsin.* Vol. 6. Madison, 1920.

Stern, M. "Will Gay Rights Trample Religious Freedom?" *Los Angeles Times,* June 17, 2008. http://www.latimes.com/news/opinion/commentary/la-oe-stern17 -2008jun17,0,3683979.story.

Stockman, F. "Christian Lobbying Finds Successes: Evangelicals Help to Steer Bush

Efforts." *Boston Globe,* October 14, 2004. http://www.boston.com/news/nation/articles/2004/10/14/christian_lobbying_finds_success/?page=2.

Stone, D. "One Nation under God?" *Newsweek,* April 7, 2009. http://www.newsweek.com/id/192915.

Stone v. Graham. 1980. http://www.oyez.org/cases/1980-1989/1980/1980_80_321/.

Stutz, T. "Texas Rejects Effort to Require Teaching of Evolution 'Weaknesses.'" *Dallas Morning News,* March 27, 2009. http://www.dallasnews.com/shared content/dws/news/texassouthwest/stories/DN-evolution_27tex.ARТо.State.Edition1.4a7acaf.html.

Surdin, A. "Calif. Court Considers Medical Rights: Justices Weigh Whether Doctors, Citing Religion, Can Refuse to Treat Some Patients." *Washington Post,* June 19, 2008. http://www.washingtonpost.com/wp-dyn/content/article/2008/06/18/AR2008061802913_pf.html.

Sweeney, D. *The American Evangelical Story.* Grand Rapids: Baker Academic, 2005.

Tomma, S. "Influence of Christian Right in the GOP Wanes." McClatchy Washington Bureau, September 30, 2007. http://www.sacbee.com/111/v-print/story/406777.html.

Toulouse, M. *God in Politics: Four Ways American Christianity and Politics Relate.* Louisville: Westminster John Knox, 2007.

"Treaty of Peace and Friendship, Signed at Tripoli November 4, 1796." Yale Law School, Lillian Goldman Law Library. http://avalon.law.yale.edu/18th _century/bar1796t.asp.

Troeltsch, E. *The Social Teaching of the Christian Churches.* 1912. Louisville: Westminster John Knox Press, 1992.

Tuveson, E. *Redeemer Nation.* Chicago: University of Chicago Press, 1968.

Van Orden v. Perry. 2005. http://www.oyez.org/cases/2000-2009/2004/2004_03 _1500/.

Vu, M. "Evangelicals Make Case for Welcoming Immigrants." *Christian Post Reporter,* April 1, 2009.

Wacker, G. *The Christian Right: The Twentieth Century; Religion and the National Culture.* Durham, N.C.: Duke University Divinity School, National Humanities Center, 2000. http://nationalhumanitiescenter.org/tserve/twenty/tkeyinfo/ chr_rght.htm.

————. *Heaven Below: Early Pentecostals and American Culture.* Cambridge: Harvard University Press, 2001.

Wallace v. Jaffree. 1985. http://www.oyez.org/cases/1980-1989/1984/1984_83_812/.

Wallis, J. *The Soul of Politics: Beyond "Religious Right" and "Secular Left."* Eugene, Oreg.: Harvest Books, 1995.

————. *God's Politics: Why the Right Gets It Wrong and the Left Doesn't Get It.* San Francisco: HarperOne, 2005.

————. *The Great Awakening: Reviving Faith and Politics in a Post–Religious Right America.* New York: HarperOne, 2008.

————. "A New Conversation on Abortion." *God's Politics* (blog). October 16, 2008. http://blog.sojo.net/2008/10/16/a-new-conversation-on-abortion/.

Wallis, J., and B. Moyers. *Faith Works: How to Live Your Beliefs and Ignite Positive Social Change.* New York: Random House, 2005.

Wallis, J., and G. Schlabach. *Just Policing, Not War: An Alternative Response to World Violence.* Collegeville, Minn.: Liturgical Press, 2007.

Whitcomb, J., and H. Morris. *The Genesis Flood.* Phillipsburg, N.J.: Presbyterian and Reformed Publishing, 1961.

Will, G. "A Debate That Does Not End." *Newsweek,* July 4, 2005. http://www.newsweek.com/id/50448.

Williams, R. *The Bloudy Tenent of Persecution for Cause of Conscience.* 1644. In *The Complete Writings of Roger Williams.* New York: Russell and Russell, 1963.

————. *The Bloudy Tenent of Persecution for Cause of Conscience.* Edited by R. Groves. Macon, Ga.: Mercer University Press, 2001.

Wills, G. *Democratic Religion: Freedom, Authority, and Church Discipline in the Baptist South, 1785-1900.* New York: Oxford University Press, 1997.

————. *Head and Heart: American Christianities.* New York: Penguin, 2007.

Wilson, J., and D. Drakeman, eds. *Church and State in American History: Key Documents, Decisions, and Commentary from the Past Three Centuries.* 3rd ed. Boulder, Colo.: Westview Press, 2003.

Women Donors Network and Communication Consortium Media Center. "Moving Forward: On Reproductive Health and a Broader Agenda" (2008). http://www.importantlifedecisions.org/decisions/overview.pdf.

Wood, G. "American Religion: The Great Retreat." *New York Review of Books* 53, no. 10 (June 8, 2006).

Wuthnow, R. *The Restructuring of American Religion: Society and Faith Since World War II.* Princeton: Princeton University Press, 1988.

Yale Center for Faith and Culture. "A Christian Response to 'A Common Word between Us and You.'" 2007. http://www.yale.edu/faith/abou-commonword.htm.

Yoder, J. *The Politics of Jesus.* Grand Rapids and Cambridge, U.K.: Eerdmans, 1972.

Zelman v. Simmons-Harris. 2002. http://www.oyez.org/cases/2000-2009/2001/2001_00_1751.

Index